INTERNAL COACHING

The Professional Coaching Series

Series Editor: David Lane

Other titles in the series

INTERNAL COACHING
The Inside Story

Katharine St John-Brooks

Routledge
Taylor & Francis Group

LONDON AND NEW YORK

First published 2014 by
Karnac Books Ltd.

Published 2018 by Routledge
2 Park Square, Milton Park, Abingdon, Oxon OX14 4RN
711 Third Avenue, New York, NY 10017, USA

Routledge is an imprint of the Taylor & Francis Group, an informa business

British Library Cataloguing in Publication Data

A C.I.P. for this book is available from the British Library

ISBN-13: 9781780491721 (pbk)

Typeset by V Publishing Solutions Pvt Ltd., Chennai, India

*I dedicate this book to my mother, Diana
St John-Brooks, for her inspiration*

CONTENTS

ACKNOWLEDGEMENTS AND PERMISSIONS

I would like to start by thanking Ingrid and Tom Beazley for lending me their Covent Garden flat to write in. Without that, there would be no book. Thank you too to Elizabeth Crosse, Sue Bradbury, and Philip Whiteley for helping me out with the text in the final stages when I got too close to it and to Professor David Lane for asking me to write the book in the first place. The whole roller coaster experience started with that seminal conversation. Thank you too to everyone at Karnac Books for their endless patience in helping me through the process.

Many of the stories and quotations in this book stem from the material provided by the 123 internal coaches who took part in my original 2009 research into the ethical dilemmas that arise for internal coaches. You know who you are! So many people since then have been so generous with their time in talking to me about their experiences. Thank you all. I am particularly grateful to the following:

Eunice Aquilina, Kathy Ashton, Tim Bright, Louise Buckle, Kate Buller, Alison Carter, Janice Clare, Claire Davey, Julia Duncan, Trevor Elkin, Karen Gallagher, Jenny Garrett, Dee Gibson-Wain, Alison Hodge, Sara Hope, Caroline Horner, Gill How, Zoe Hudson, Sam Humphrey, James Hutton, Coral Ingleton, Ian Jenner, Dena Jones, Linda Linehan, Katherine Long, Liz Macann, Clive Mann, Alison Maxwell, Jenny

Mitchell, Sue Mortlock, Edna Murdoch, Dawn Nisbet, James Pritchard, Jane Saunders, Louise Sheppard, Sarah Snape, Deborah Southon, Ken Smith, Laura Taylor, Helen Tiffany, Eve Turner, Joanna Valentine, Trayton Vance, Barbara Wallis, Matt Watson, Carol Whitaker, Matthew Wilkinson, and Ildeniz Yagcioglu Watt.

Finally, thank you to my husband, Vivian Bazalgette, for his endless support and to my children: Victoria, Louise, and Joseph Bazalgette for their encouragement.

Permissions

I would like to thank the publishers, organisations, and individuals who granted permission to reference, adapt, or reprint the following cited material:

Alison Carter and Coaching at Work (www.coaching-at-work.com) for permission to reproduce the table on "Top tips for better business focus".

Jessica Kingsley Publishers for permission to quote extracts from Carroll & Shaw's *Ethical Maturity in the Helping Professions* (2013).

Svetlana Yedreshteyn for permission to quote extracts from her doctoral thesis "A qualitative investigation of the implementation of an internal executive coaching program in a global corporation, grounded in organizational psychology theory" (2008).

Kogan Page for permission to reproduce Declan Woods' extract from a learning diary in J. Passmore (Ed.), *Supervision in Coaching: Supervision, Ethics and Continuous Professional Development* (pp. 265–284), 2011.

Paul Stokes for permission to reproduce his table on the personal skills and attributes desirable in a "skilled coachee" taken from his paper delivered at the 14th EMCC Conference in Stockholm, 2007.

Ken Smith for permission to quote an extract from The Listener (www.kensmithcoaching.co.uk).

Professional Coaching Publications, Inc. for two abridged case studies taken from Carter, A., Wolfe, H., & Kerrin, M. (2005).

PEANUTS © 1972 Peanuts Worldwide LLC. Dist. By UNIVERSAL UCLICK. Reprinted with permission. All rights reserved. (For Charlie Brown quotation).

The Chartered Institute of Personnel and Development (www.cipd. co.uk) for permission to quote extracts from *Coaching Supervision: Maximising the Potential of Coaching* (2006) by Hawkins and Schwenk.

The case studies that I use in this book are genuine and are drawn from the stories of people whom I know personally, or with whom I have worked professionally. On occasion, to protect confidentiality, I have changed names, and certain stories are a blend of several people's experiences.

ABOUT THE AUTHOR

Katharine St John-Brooks is an executive coach and consultant specialising in the strategic use of internal coaches within organisations. She has an MSc in organisational behaviour and an MA in professional development (coaching), is a fellow of the Institute of Consulting, and runs her own business, Working Solutions. In her coaching work she focuses on board-level executives. Katharine has extensive experience of working in private, public, and not-for-profit sectors, and regularly speaks at conferences and workshops about coaching. She chairs the EMCC's (European Mentoring and Coaching Council) public sector coaching and mentoring forum, co-chairs their internal coaching and mentoring special interest group, and chairs a charity that offers friendly volunteer support to isolated older people in Southwark. Katharine sings, has three grown-up children, and lives in London with her husband, Vivian Bazalgette.

SERIES EDITOR'S FOREWORD

The Professional Coaching Series aims to provide core reading on issues important to the field of coaching. It also uniquely creates opportunities for specialist areas of practice such as education and family business to receive due attention. It is based on a core belief that we need practical resources that are fully underpinned by research.

One of the most important areas of practice, which have so far received limited attention, has been the field of internal coaching. This book is long overdue, given the prevalence of internal coaching and the huge interest in it. Around eighty per cent of organisations use internal coaching in some form and this is expected to increase again. This expectation of increasing use has appeared consistently in the literature since the year 2000, so this is a trend set to continue.

However, organisations, when setting out on the path to create internal coaching, can sometimes start in the wrong place. They decide that training an internal coaching resource is a "good thing", without necessarily thinking through what organisational problem the coaching is seeking to solve. The book explains in straightforward terms the value of working out what the coaching strategy should be from the outset.

As is our practice when commissioning books for the Professional Coaching Series, we look for someone who is close to practice yet thoroughly informed by the literature and original research. Katharine St John-Brooks is ideally placed for this task. She is an experienced coach who has researched the field and run numerous workshops for practitioners. She has stayed closely connected to developments within professional bodies. This is clear in the relevance of the examples she presents. The book's strength is that it draws directly on the testimony of many internal coaches at the sharp end.

St John-Brooks takes her reader carefully through the thinking process for setting up an internal coaching resource. She identifies what it is that internal coaches need to know, their role, the forms of coaching undertaken, and what it feels like to be an internal coach. She addresses the rewards and challenges of the role. The internal coach faces very particular ethical issues and rather than giving limited space to this she takes on board the very serious implications for client, coach, and organisation of the issues that arise. She both identifies the concerns and provides practical ways to address them. This is the most comprehensive coverage of this central concern for internal coaches that I have seen in the literature. She is to be commended for tackling this in such detail. Internal coaches will welcome her attention to the details of those concerns.

The question of what organisations need to know is then addressed. She asks why organisations need to have internal coaches and provides clear answers. She considers the advantages that the resource brings, the potential challenges and the relationship with external coaching.

While explaining the benefits of internal coaching, the book does not duck the difficult issues that come with the territory. As such, this is an intensely practical book. It raises the concerns but addresses them within the realities that most organisations face. For example, while the author believes strongly in the value of supervision, she recognises the reality of constrained budgets and suggests all sorts of alternatives for offering coaches support and opportunities to reflect on their practice. Similarly, while recognising that too few organisations evaluate their internal coaching schemes, she shows that it need not be a very time-consuming exercise. Simple evaluation mechanisms can be built from the outset of any programme.

I am happy to recommend this latest edition of our Professional Coaching Series. It absolutely fits with our core belief that the series provides practical approaches underpinned by research. Internal coaches and organisations that provide or are thinking of creating internal coaching resources will find in Katharine St John-Brooks' work a resource of immense value.

Professor David A. Lane
Professional Development Foundation

FOREWORD

This book is written out of admiration for the unsung heroes and heroines working as internal coaches in organisations up and down the land. As an external coach myself, I was unaware of the terrific work that they do until I undertook some research in 2009, as part of my coaching Masters, to explore the whole phenomenon of what it was really like to be an internal coach. I focused, in particular, on the dilemmas that internal coaches encounter and the kind of support they receive from the organisations for which they work. I knew little then about the challenges peculiar to internal coaching that internal coaches face—there had been very little research—but I was eager to find out. What I encountered was a committed bunch of passionate coaches (123 of them took part in my research) who cared deeply about their coaching, gained a huge amount of satisfaction from it but, in too many cases, felt unsupported by their organisational sponsors. I had not expected to become an advocate but that, in effect, is what I have become. I felt cross then about the lack of support for some but also impressed by the gold standard support for others.

Since then I have presented my findings at a variety of workshops (including to the alumni of Coaching Masters programmes at Ashridge Business School, the School of Coaching, and the Academy of Executive

Coaching) and coaching conferences—including those organised by the NHS, EMCC, and OCM (formerly the Oxford School of Coaching & Mentoring)—and have also conducted many, many interviews with internal coaches, lead coaches, supervisors of internal coaches, and internal coach trainers. This has confirmed my impression of the fervour and dedication of internal coaches. After all, if you are going to coach on top of your "day job"—which the vast majority do—you really have to care about it.

My mission is to make a difference through feeding a description of their unique experiences back to an interconnected audience of internal coaches, employers, researchers, and coach training organisations with a view to:

- shedding light on what it is actually like being an internal coach—to provide insights both for people thinking of being trained for the role and for coaching sponsors;
- identifying what internal coaches and their sponsors can do differently or better; and
- sharing practice so that organisations using internal coaches—and those who are thinking of setting up an internal resource—can think about what the best way of going about it is for their organisation.

You will hear a lot of internal coaches' voices: the book is overflowing with their own words. I have also peppered their experiences with research from writers who are academics as well as consultants working in organisations, with the aim of making their material easily accessible to hard-pressed practitioners who may not have the time to read it at source.

My rule of thumb has been: if this piece of experience or the findings of that piece of research could be useful to someone, keep it in. My dream is that, every few pages, a reader somewhere will think: "Now *that's* a good idea. It could work here. We might think about introducing that." What I am not aiming to do is be prescriptive or claim that any particular approach or strategy is "best practice" (only time will tell if any particular practice is, after all). Not only are there plenty of ways to skin a cat but something that works well in one organisation might not fit the culture of another. What I am seeking to do, though, is a) to pose a series of questions for coaches and organisations to think about and b) to give plenty of examples of how some organisations are addressing particular issues so as to stimulate further thought.

As a coach myself, I am very aware of the power of questions for developing people's understanding and helping them to think about what they might do differently. If you are asked if you have a mechanism for harvesting the learning from the coaching conversations taking place in your organisation—and you do not—then you are going to start thinking about whether you might. Even if you decide not to, the possibility has become part of your consciousness. Each chapter ends with a series of questions on which to reflect. I should say here that the focus of this book is one-to-one coaching. Team coaching is becoming an increasingly popular topic but is not my subject.

My longest chapter is given over to supervision and other forms of support for internal coaches. In my view there are still too few internal coaches with access to supervision. I don't live in cloud cuckoo land. I know the financial pressures that many organisations are living with (particularly in the public sector) and that a gold-plated support system of monthly supervision and continuing professional development (CPD) sessions to keep internal coaches at the top of their game is unrealistic for many. What I have aimed to do is to provide examples of alternative ways, too, for continually developing and enhancing the skills of the coaches.

It is perhaps worth mentioning that where an external coach gets to know an organisation, and the people in it, very well then many of the ethical dilemmas that arise for internal coaches are just as relevant to them. They may find Chapters Three and Four, in particular, of value. However, external coaches are often in a stronger position than internal coaches to resist, say, pressure from senior people in the organisation who may try to exercise their position power. They can always walk away.

In the book I use the following terms interchangeably: organisation/ business/employer. I describe the person being coached as the "client" though the term "coachee" is used in many of the quotations included. Finally, when talking about an individual—whether coach, manager, or client—I have referred to that person as "they". I know that grammatically this will be anathema to many but it does get around the endless him/her, he/she, and I am afraid I cannot quite stomach using the word "him" to encompass both "him" and "her".

I hope you enjoy the book.

Katharine St John-Brooks

CHAPTER ONE

Introduction

There is a multitude of coaching books on the market, but none focusing exclusively on internal executive coaching. You might think that the dearth of attention is because, to all intents and purposes, there are few differences between internal and external executive coaching but this is not so—neither from the point of view of the coaches nor of the organisations that deploy them. The fact that internal coaches coach within the organisation that employs them has a variety of consequences for the coaches, some beneficial, some less so, that need exploring. Also, from the point of view of an organisation wanting to provide coaching for its managers, the processes involved in selecting, training, and supporting a cadre of internal coaches are vastly different from those required for procuring the services of external coaches. The costs, benefits, and challenges presented by the two options for providing coaching are sufficiently different for internal coaching to deserve special attention.

What do we mean by internal coaching?

Over the past fifteen to twenty years, most managers have become aware of the terms "executive" or "business" coaching as a service procured from an external provider, often reserved for senior managers and those recognised as having high potential. The idea of in-house or "internal" coaches is a newer concept but one that is being embraced by organisations in the UK and is currently experiencing a surge in popularity. So what has led to this development?

In the 1990s, a trend for making cuts in human resource (HR) departments and passing responsibility for a number of personnel functions, including staff development, to line managers, gathered speed. It was driven partly by cost considerations and partly by the recognition that managers were best placed to deliver those functions (staff development, in particular). In many organisations, the transition was bumpy. Managers often received little guidance in how to carry out their development role, found it uncongenial, or had little aptitude for it. However, since then the use of coaching to develop managers has risen dramatically (Feldman & Lankau, 2005) and management development programmes have gradually encouraged a switch in style from a directive management style to a more facilitating, coaching approach to developing their staff (Tamkin, Hirsh, & Tyers, 2003). Two further developments have also taken place:

- employees themselves are now generally expected to take a measure of responsibility for their own development and
- some organisations are developing a cadre of specialist "internal coaches" to enrich the development activities available to staff.

It is important to distinguish between "managers as coaches", that is, managers using a coaching style with their staff, who are not the focus of this book, and "internal coaches", who are. Frisch (2001) described internal executive coaching as:

> a one-on-one developmental intervention supported by the organisation and provided by a colleague of those coached who is trusted to shape and deliver a programme yielding individual professional growth. (p. 242)

He stressed that internal coaches should not be in the chain of command of those they coach. This sharply differentiates internal coaches from managers as coaches. I would add that ideally internal coaches should not even work in the same part of the organisation as their clients for a number of reasons that will become clear.

Carter (2005) clarified the nature of their role when she wrote:

> The internal coach is comparable in every sense to the external coach, with the exception that the internal coach is an employee of the same organisation as their coachees. (p. 7)

Hunt and Weintraub's (2006) definition adds a further dimension: the fact that the coaching is for the benefit of both the individual and their organisation, defining "developmental coaching" as:

> individualised, relationship-based dialogues that promote learning from on-the-job experiences and have as their goal improving the short-term and/or long-term effectiveness of the coachee and, as such, his or her organisation. (p. 1)

So the key features of internal coaching are:

- that it is a learning and development activity delivered by one employee of an organisation to another (working in different chains of command)
- that it aims to deliver professional growth to the employee and improve their effectiveness
- that it is analogous to external coaching (with all that that implies in terms of training, ethical behaviour and professionalism) and
- that it involves two clients—the coaching client and the organisation.

Why a book on internal coaching now?

Frisch described internal coaching as having been "flying under the radar" of mainstream coaching (Frisch, 2001) but that is the case no longer. A series of reports from the Chartered Institute of Personnel & Development (CIPD, 2008; CIPD, 2009) and the Ridler Reports (Ridler & Co, 2008; Ridler & Co, 2013) have charted the increase in the prevalence of internal coaching, and the following is just a small selection of other references to its rise:

> … the most rapid area of growth in distribution of developmental coaching services may be those provided by well-trained internal coaches. (Hunt & Weintraub, 2006, p. 1)

> More organisations are developing a cadre of internally accredited coaches ... to work below top team level. (Lambert, 2008, p. 8)
>
> Large organisations are now employing fewer external coaches as they develop their internal coaching capability. (Hawkins, 2012, p. 6)
>
> 79% of organisations expect to see a small (40%) or large (39%) increase in internal coaching over the next three years. (Ridler & Co, 2013, p. 8)

In addition, the coaching professional bodies are waking up to the fact that many of their members are now internal coaches. In 2011, the European Mentoring & Coaching Council, UK (EMCC UK) set up an internal coaching special interest group and, in February 2013, devoted a specific area of its website to internal coaching. Sessions at coaching conferences focusing on internal coaching—usually led by a lead coach practitioner—have also made an appearance. And finally, coach training providers have witnessed the trend: where ten years ago participants on coach training programmes were almost entirely independents setting up external coaching practices, now there are many more internal coaches joining open programmes, plus a rise in organisations buying in coach training for a cohort of employees who will coach internally.

It is no accident that the trend towards building an internal coaching capability coincided with a world recession. When the economic downturn bit, and economies were sought in many organisations, some finance directors were startled to discover how much was being spent on external coaches and looked to learning and development (L&D) departments for options to reduce the bill. Even before that, organisations were looking at ways to meet demand for coaching from their employees:

> Where demand for coaching has exceeded supply, the favoured response has been to encourage the use of more internal coaching— nearly 50% of those whose coaching budget was under pressure have responded in this fashion. (Ridler & Co, 2008, p. 1)

However, while cost savings may often be the catalyst for the development of cadres of internal coaches, organisations are finding many other benefits too, which I shall describe.

In the UK, internal coaching is becoming particularly well established in the public sector, largely in response to deep cuts in L&D budgets and, in many cases, very close scrutiny of the use of external consultants and coaches. But as Hawkins has noted as a possible future scenario:

> The public sector will continue to cut all external coaching and put further pressure on internal coaches to make their services spread further, in a shorter time, without the requisite support infrastructure. (Hawkins, 2012, p. 179)

This lack of the "requisite support infrastructure" is a theme that will be explored further. It is not only a risk in the public sector.

How does the book work?

The inspiration for this book, and the "**Facts and figures**" in each chapter, come from research I carried out (St John-Brooks, 2010) with 123 internal coaches in over thirty organisations based in the UK, supplemented by around fifty interviews with coaches, coach supervisors, coach trainers, and lead coaches. Its purpose is to provide insights into the world of internal coaching. I have included case studies and questions to help you to think about "how is this relevant to me?" It is not designed to be a textbook prescribing best practice to setting up and running an internal coaching scheme, but a way of sharing the experiences of the many organisations that have already done so. The aim is to provide readers with choices.

In Part I (Chapters Two to Four), I focus on the experience of being an internal coach. It is designed primarily for internal coaches or managers who are deciding whether to volunteer to become an internal coach. It will also be of value to those of you who are thinking of setting up a coaching cohort—providing a taste of what it is actually like.

In most ways the internal coaches in my research operated no differently from their external coach colleagues in terms of what approaches they used, or the skills and techniques they deployed. Some had postgraduate qualifications and many had years of experience. However, it was also clear that they encountered a myriad of ethical issues, most of which arose solely because they coached internally.

The idea that internal coaches are likely to have to deal with more ethical dilemmas than external coaches equates to the notion that the role of external coach is "cleaner" than that of the internal coach: that is, the management of confidentiality, boundaries, and conflicts of interest is likely to be more challenging for internal coaches than for most external coaches. When I first published my research findings, they came as no surprise to experienced internal coaches but were an eye-opener to some coaching sponsors who had not previously appreciated the complexity of the world that internal coaches inhabit.

A key issue peculiar to internal coaching is the intricate network of relationships that the coaches have to manage and the pressures that come from being part of the same "system" as their clients. The interviews that I carried out with around fifty practitioners suggest that while this by no means hamstrings internal coaches' activities, it does mean that they need to be alive to the challenges, contract with their clients very tightly, and be more alert to the possibility of ethical dilemmas than would be the case for an external coach.

Part II (Chapters Five to Ten) is aimed principally at people, often in human resources (HR) or learning and development (L&D) functions, who already have or are seriously thinking of setting up an internal coaching cohort within their organisation—of becoming, in fact, the "lead coach" in their organisation. Part II also embraces coaching champions, coaching supervisors, and coach trainers. It draws on and shares the experiences of numerous organisations, many of whom have now employed internal coaches for a number of years, to offer ideas on the whole process, from the selection, training, and matching of coaches to clients, through the marketing of the coaches to the organisation, the support provided to the coaches, and the options for evaluating the effectiveness of the internal coaching service. I make no apology for devoting a lot of space to the ways in which organisations can support their coaches. My main concern, flowing from my research, was the sense I received that many internal coaches were operating in a vacuum. Even if money is tight, there are many options for offering them support, and I outline a number of them.

The fact that the practice of internal coaching has unique characteristics when compared with other kinds of coaching and development activities would in itself merit special attention. However, there is also a need for guidance on the process of setting up an internal coaching resource. Are you clear about the purpose for which your coaching pool is being set up? Is there buy-in from the board? Has the strategy been properly worked through? Will the coaches get the support they need—in particular, continuous professional development and supervision? Are there fully thought through policies and guidance on such issues as how to deal with coaching relationships that are not working, how session records are kept, or what happens if a client keeps cancelling sessions? Is there a code of ethics? There is some evidence to suggest that some organisations have regarded internal coaching as a quick, cheap fix. Where this is the case, internal coaches have been left without support, isolated and at risk. This book makes the case for changing that state of affairs.

Summary

If you are an internal coach or coach lead, I hope that this book will leave you feeling fully affirmed in all that you do and inspired to do even more. I hope you will feel more able to identify ethical dilemmas and the implications for your practice and how to resolve them, and also more knowledgeable about what the options are for your further development. If you are thinking about becoming an internal coach, I hope you will have a clearer idea about what it involves, both the challenges and the huge rewards.

If you are running an internal coaching pool, I hope the book will provide you with a benchmark of how other organisations are approaching this in terms of: working to a clear coaching strategy, having robust policies, providing a good training and development programme for the coaches, and evaluating success. And if you are thinking about setting up a pool, I hope you will gain a strong sense of what your choices are.

PART I

WHAT INTERNAL COACHES
NEED TO KNOW

Part I is designed for those of you who a) are deciding whether to volunteer to become an internal coach; b) are already working as an internal coach; or c) are thinking of setting up a cohort of internal coaches. It aims to provide a feel for what it is actually like as well as a means for benchmarking your practice.

CHAPTER TWO

The role of the internal coach

It's hugely rewarding to feel that you have fundamentally improved someone's take on, approach to, or enjoyment of their professional life

—*Internal coach*

What this chapter is about

Internal coaching, like any other professional activity, can be delivered in many ways. It is clear that organisations are adopting a variety of different models for organising and managing their internal coaching according to their needs, resources, and culture. If you are thinking of becoming an internal coach you may be interested in what sorts of people it appeals to, what the role involves, and what it is like.

This chapter explores:

- Who internal coaches are
- What internal coaches do
- What internal coaches do not do

- What internal coaching is like:
  - how much coaching coaches do
  - what support is available
  - whom they coach
- The rewards and challenges of internal coaching.

Who are internal coaches?

Where do they work?

Not surprisingly, organisations look to HR, organisation development (OD), and L&D practitioners when seeking volunteers to train as internal coaches. The rationale is that they will often have relevant skills and there is a high likelihood that they will use the enhanced skills that they acquire during the coach training in their day jobs. They may already be involved in, say, giving feedback to managers about their performance and may already be trained in relevant instruments such as a 360-degree feedback tool or MBTI (Myers Briggs Type Indicator) which can be helpfully used also in their formal coaching. Indeed, many internal coaches are qualified to use a psychometric or profiling tool with MBTI, 16PF, Hogan, OPQ and FIRO-B the most common (some of which are commonly used in recruitment and assessment rather than development).

Other organisations positively avoid selecting HR specialists for coach training, partly because of their concern about the enhanced scope for role conflict. As one lead coach said: "I have been involved in coaching individuals around their performance and then subsequently been asked to provide HR support to a disciplinary process or grievance involving the same individual." Certainly the high proportion of HR coaches in my research was likely to have contributed to the fact that role conflict was way up the list of ethical dilemmas encountered by internal coaches.

Facts and figures 2.1: Functional roles held by coaches

- Over half the coaches worked in HR or L&D, either at the corporate centre or in an HR business partner capacity.
- Around a third worked in an operational department or business function.

How old are they?

Managers thinking of training to become internal coaches are sometimes concerned that they might appear too young to have credibility with clients. Part of this is probably a hangover from the idea of the mentor—someone who has "been there, done that" with the grey hairs to prove it. Coaching and mentoring are not the same thing, even though coaches and mentors use many of the same skills. Much more important than age or seniority are the relevant skills and experience that a coach can bring, the reputation they have within the business for what they do in their "day job", and the degree to which they project confidence in their role as a coach.

My research showed that employees of all ages are practising as coaches.

Facts and figures 2.2: Age range of internal coaches	
Age range	*Rounded %*
25–34	11
35–44	39
45–54	39
55–64	11
	100

What are internal coaches there to do?

Varieties of coaching undertaken

Internal coaches may specialise in a particular variety of coaching, for example, career development coaching or maternity coaching because a) it is of particular interest to them; b) it is what their training has equipped them to do, or; c) it is what the coaching pool was set up to deliver. Most internal coaches, however, coach on a whole range of issues (see table on the next page for the coaching that internal coaches who took part in my research were delivering). These categories are not mutually exclusive. For example, as part of coaching someone who has recently been promoted into a managerial position, it may be necessary also to undertake some skills development work in areas such as chairing meetings, public speaking, or delegation.

Facts and figures 2.3: Types of coaching undertaken by internal coaches	
Types of coaching	%
Performance coaching	83
Personal development	79
Career development	70
Leadership development	65
Behaviour change	57
Transitions	56
Skills development	50

In practical terms, internal coaches can play a wide variety of roles, depending on the purpose for which the pool was set up. For example:

- to embed an initiative with sales people to improve their ability to build relationships with customers
- to support a talent management programme by helping participants to translate what they have learned into how they actually function in the workplace
- to champion a change programme around shared values as a result of a merger by demonstrating the values through their own behaviours, or
- to support an organisational restructure by means of career and transition coaching.

What is the coach not there to do?

Chapter Three explores the issue of boundaries from the perspective of the coach. For example, does your organisation expect you to mentor your clients too or is the coaching model you use a very "pure" one? What if you held a similar role, some years ago, to the one that your client now occupies? Do you feel that you should help them out if you can see that they are struggling with something that you could explain to them in no time? An experienced coach might tell you that you would be doing more good in terms of building their capability and resource-fulness if you persevered with getting them to think through where they could get the advice they need or find out the data or answer for themselves. But is that always the case?

Another interesting boundary issue is "Who is the client?" Should internal coaches' loyalties be mainly to the organisation or to the client in front of them? Are they there simply to respond to client needs? Can they coach the client on anything that they bring to the table? Hawkins (2012) writes about the dangers of coaching "becoming too focused on the individual client and under-serving the organisational client". He was talking about external coaches but it is likely to be no less true for internal coaches. He points out that:

> At worst this can deteriorate into a "drama triangle" (Kaupman, 1968) where the coach sees the coachee as victim, the organisa-tion as a persecutor and themselves as the rescuer. Good executive coaching always maintains focus on all three clients: the individual, the organisation and the relationship between the two. (p. 56)

Facts and figures 2.4: "Who is the client?"

Internal coaches came up with very different responses:
- "My main loyalty is to the organisation; however self-awareness kicks in when the collusion bells start to ring!"
- "My instinctive answer was to say my coachee, but then the organisa-tion should be the primary responsibility."
- "I have no difficulty encouraging the client to take action that is to their benefit but perhaps not to the 'employer'".
- "The whole concept of the employers' interest is fraught with diffi-culty: indeed so difficult is it to determine that it is not even worth considering."

One of the most difficult things for a coach can be managing the boundary between work and personal issues. This may not necessarily be clear-cut. If your client is depressed about his weight, says that the way he looks is undermining his confidence at work, and asks if weight loss could be one of his coaching goals as he feels that this will motivate him to stick with the weight loss programme he has signed up to, how would you answer? Is he your principal client or is your employer? Would your employer be content to be financing supporting someone to lose weight, if they knew? The answer may be yes but how confident are you about that? Do you need to find out or discuss it with someone? The next chapter looks at these issues in more depth.

What is internal coaching like?

How much coaching do internal coaches do?

Most internal coaches coach on top of their "day job". The fact that they hold two roles within the organisation—their functional role and their coaching role—is at the root of many of the challenges with which they are faced. Equally, it is the source of many benefits for both the individuals and for the organisations in which they work. Sometimes their coaching role is an acknowledged component of their formal job, forms part of their annual objectives, and is included in appraisal processes. More usually, coaching is an add-on activity that has been formally approved by the coach's line manager, in the sense that they have given permission for the individual to spend a specified amount of time on coaching, but the coach receives no formal recognition for the coaching they do through the line management chain. The deal is that as long as they deliver on their day job commitments, they can coach too. This is an arrangement that most internal coaches are content with.

In my research nearly sixty per cent of the coaches described themselves as coaching "on top of their formal role", and thirty-five per cent as coaching being a "recognised part of their role". There was a suggestion that some were gradually moving from the first category into the second, for example: "It wasn't a part of my formal role until my job description was re-written more recently. It is now formally something that I am appraised on."

The other five per cent worked for the small number of organisations—only two in my sample—that have taken the path of recruiting full time internal coaches. These coaches are usually well qualified and already experienced before they arrive in the organisation and will carry a full coaching load. The fact that they have no role other than a coaching role removes the potential for problems that can arise from role conflict, but because they are part of the same system as their clients, many other causes of ethical dilemmas remain.

Internal coaches' line managers will not necessarily even know how many clients they have and will not feel that it is their concern as long as the day job gets done. Often, however, there will be a maximum commitment agreed, for example one day a month, and it is the coach's responsibility to manage that.

Facts and figures 2.5: Time commitment

What proportion of your time, on average, do you spend coaching?

	%
Under 5 hours a month	41
5–10 hours a month	35
10–20 hours a month	9
20–30 hours a month	6
30–40 hours a month	2
More than 40 hours a month	2
Full time	5

Data extracted on 18 June 2013, by mye-coach (a coaching management system run by Coaching Focus Ltd) especially for this book, showed that the 594 internal coaches, from around sixty organisations, who use the system were coaching the following number of clients:

	%
No clients	10
1 client	32
2 clients	23
3 clients	21
4 clients	5
5 clients	5
More than 5 clients	3

The largest number of clients being coached by one person was twelve. Data from the same source showed that the average length of a coaching session was around one hour and that the average number of sessions was four, though the range was from three to twelve sessions.

What support do they get?

A very mixed picture emerged of the support provided by organisations to their cohort of internal coaches (and interviews conducted more recently suggest that the picture is still mixed). Some organisations provided an impressive array of supervision and CPD opportunities. For example, one coach said: "They have funded my attendance at Academy of Executive Coaching Masterclasses, NLP diploma, Gestalt workshops." Other organisations offered little, if any, support. Indeed, one tenth indicated that they had access to no support at all: "There is no provision for internal coaches but I have my own supervision arrangements and my own CPD, which I fund myself as it is a disgrace that none is provided."

Support for coaches is usually the responsibility of the lead coach to organise. However, where the spirit of a real community of coaches has been engendered, there will often also be a degree of self-help with coaches making opportunities to meet up and "co-coach", that is, take it in turns to coach each other. The table below outlines the sorts

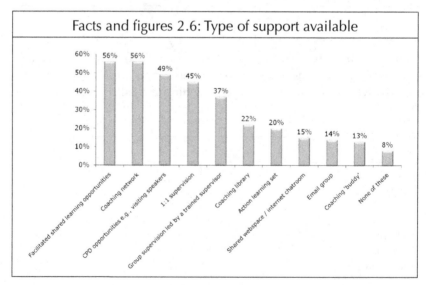

Facts and figures 2.6: Type of support available

of provision being offered in different organisations. Chapter Nine discusses this issue in more depth, including exploring the pros and cons of different approaches to coach supervision.

Whom do they coach?

Some internal coaches in my research coached the top team—which gives the lie to the view that only external coaches do so—but certainly the majority of the coaches did tend to coach middle and senior managers and "high potentials". The most senior staff do often opt for external coaches for reasons of perceived additional confidentiality, status, reputation, or a view that they would benefit from a level of challenge or range of experience that internal coaches might not be able to provide. The Ridler Report (Ridler & Co, 2013) showed that eighty-five per cent of participating organisations agreed that their most senior executives prefer an external coach to an internal coach. Choices made will reflect how the scheme is set up; the seniority of the coaches being trained; the reputation and depth of the training they receive (e.g., is it externally accredited?); how the internal coaching is promoted and positioned within the organisation, and so forth.

There are examples of very senior internal coaches who can coach at the highest level in the organisation. Mukherjee (2012) describes an internal coaching programme in an engineering company in the USA where the coaches were recruited from the very senior ranks and, in the National Health Service (NHS), the first cohort of internal coaches to be trained included a number of chief executives who could and did coach at all levels. Similarly, in the British Broadcasting Corporation (BBC), several of the internal coaches involved in launching the initial scheme were highly experienced and coached at very senior levels.

One consultant, who has been a party to many organisations' discussions of how internal coaches' profiles should be presented to potential clients, commented to me that a sensitive and hotly argued issue can be whether to identify coaches' levels in the organisational hierarchy. The concern can be that a manager might reject an excellent coach on the grounds that they are junior to them. One lead coach in an organisation in which internal coaching is very well established—and where coach and client are matched centrally rather than the coach selecting from a register of coaches—said that they were very determined about keeping grade out of the picture. When they trained a new cohort of internal

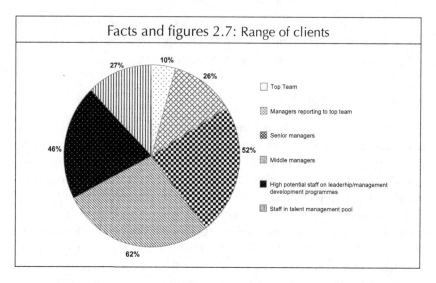

Facts and figures 2.7: Range of clients

- Top Team
- Managers reporting to top team
- Senior managers
- Middle managers
- High potential staff on leaderhip/management development programmes
- Staff in talent management pool

coaches they even instituted a rule of "first names only" to establish a level playing field and ensure that trainees did not arrive with a sense of who was senior to whom.

Sometimes it can be the coach, rather than the potential client, who sees difference in seniority as a difficulty:

> "I have learnt that coaching someone more senior (in the hierarchy) than me in the organisation is no different to someone below me. It took a little time to get over this, but now it is not an issue. And when asked for feedback, the more senior people never saw this as an issue."

What are the rewards and challenges of being an internal coach?

The experience of being an internal coach will differ from organisation to organisation depending on a wide variety of factors: what are the challenges for the organisation as a whole? What's morale like? What's the reputation of coaching within the organisation? How many other coaches are there? What support do you get? How many clients do you have? How comprehensive was your training? How experienced a coach are you? What's your background? How heavily loaded is your day job? All these factors and many others can make a significant difference to how it feels.

Your experience of coaching may even feel quite different from that of other internal coaches working alongside you because you will be bringing diverse knowledge, capabilities, and approaches with you to your coaching.

In Spring 2012 I was running a workshop about ethical dilemmas in a large public sector organisation where one internal coach spoke about a client who wanted to talk about her marriage breakup and how she could better manage her feelings so that she was less erratic and emotional at work. The coach felt that if they made progress on this then the client's performance and productivity at work could be significantly improved. While not a particularly experienced coach, she was a former long time volunteer with Samaritans and felt comfortable listening to personal issues. However, she was concerned about whether this was a boundary she should not cross and an interesting discussion ensued. One of her fellow internal coaches listened in surprise and said that under no circumstances would he ever go anywhere near such issues with a client and no clients had ever raised such personal issues with him. Their experiences of being an internal coach will have been very different.

Even though the nature of the role can vary considerably from person to person, however, internal coaches agree about many of the rewards and challenges associated with doing the job.

The rewards

The rewards fall into four main categories: making a contribution, being part of something bigger, personal growth/learning, and increased organisational awareness.

Making a contribution

Coaches gain considerable fulfilment from seeing the results that they help clients achieve.

- *Feeling that you are making a difference*: There are few things that match the buzz of a client's having a big "aha!" moment. But even something as small as asking a client who has been wrestling with some issue: "Do you have to do this by yourself? Is there a colleague who could help you to think X through?" and the client pausing then saying

"Well, I've just realised that Y has relevant experience. I wonder why I didn't think of her before …" provides satisfaction. Ask any coach—it is immaterial whether they are internal or external.

- *Seeing clients grow*: Many internal coaches talk about finding coaching a "privilege". To be invited into a colleague's life, to share their hopes and fears and play a role in helping them to become more effective at what they do (or happier in their work or more comfortable in their relationship with a colleague) is a special experience. As one internal coach working in a media company said, "It's hugely rewarding to feel that you have fundamentally improved someone's take on, approach to, or enjoyment of their professional life".

- *Giving something back*: Managers who decide to train as coaches fairly late in their careers are often motivated by wanting to give something back. In a large Indian production company, senior general managers were trained as coaches. When they were asked why they should be included in the programme, they said that one of the reasons was that they wanted "to give back something to the organisation before they retire" (Mukherjee, 2012, p. 80).

Being part of something bigger

If your organisation develops a coaching network of all its coaches and keeps you all in touch with one another through events and group emails then there can be a real sense of a joint endeavour for the benefit of the whole organisation—not just a benefit to the individual client.

- *Being part of a community of coaches*: Internal coaches tend to greatly enjoy getting to know their fellow coaches in other parts of the firm and forming new relationships. One said: "Several have become friends and we lean on each other a lot when the going gets tough! As well as supporting each other in our coaching work … it has spilled over into supporting each other more generally at work too."

- *Feeling valued by the organisation*: Coaches appreciate the fact that their potential has been recognised and that their employer has invested in them: "Knowing that the business has input into my training and development to become a coach—that's the personal reward I take from the coaching programme."

- *Expanding internal network*: By becoming part of a coaching community, coaches meet other coaches and other clients from new areas of the business that extends their personal network: "You get to meet people from other disciplines you wouldn't normally."

- *Knowing you are delivering something important*: Where the coaches are kept informed about the strategic purpose of the coaching and any changes in the corporate or business strategy that they can be keeping in mind when coaching, there can be a strong flavour of "we're all in this together to make the organisation work more effectively".

Personal growth/learning

One of the many benefits of training as a coach is the difference that using a coaching approach can make to your effectiveness as a manager/ leader in your day job. In addition to that, however, coaches learn a lot from their clients.

- *Becoming a better leader/manager*: Many coaches feel they have enhanced their leadership skills in their day job by deploying a coaching approach with staff and peers: for example, listening more effectively and focusing more on developing their staff. One said: "I could get frustrated with not knowing how to get the best out of someone and I think coaching enables me to."
- *Expanding your horizons*: Some coaches say that they have also learned a lot about strategy, project management, and dealing with complex issues through coaching leaders who were grappling with issues that they had not yet encountered themselves.
- *Gaining confidence in your abilities*: Hearing about how other managers in the business see their role and cope with the challenges can also help coaches to benchmark their own capabilities: "Coaching my peers and sometimes my seniors has boosted my own confidence as I now realise that they struggle with difficulties and doubts just as much as I do."

Increased organisational awareness

An unexpected benefit can be the degree to which coaches, through coaching people with different skillsets from theirs and working in other functions within the organisation, can learn more about how their organisation works.

- *Understanding the organisation better*: Several coaches mentioned that there were large parts of the organisation where they had previously known no-one and did not really understand what those departments did. Working with clients (and meeting their line managers) from those areas had assisted in breaking down silos, helped them to identify some common interests, and contributed to their doing their job better: "I find it rewarding to meet different people from around the business and learn more about what they do and how their department works. This has helped me to learn about my company."

- *Understanding the internal politics better*: Hearing about others' approaches to issues can be an eye-opener to the coach and reframe how they think about an issue. One said: "I have always felt that 'internal politics' were not for me but I have learned a lot from my clients about the importance of convincing the movers and shakers if things are to get done. Formal channels are only one way of influencing an outcome."

The challenges

The challenges fall into five main categories: handling ethical dilemmas, balancing the roles, being part of the same system, practical issues, and coping with emotions.

Handling ethical dilemmas

Part and parcel of being an internal coach is resolving actual or potential dilemmas—whether it is coping with a powerful figure who is pressurising you to break confidentiality; dealing with role conflicts ("I have become more sensitive to conflicts of interest and thinking where do they work, would we ever work together, who do I know in their management chain?"); or deciding how to handle a client situation involving disciplinary issues. These can be made easier to manage by tight contracting with the client from the outset, experience, and using supervision or peer support, but can still represent a challenge particularly for:

- inexperienced coaches and
- coaches who sit at the centre of the organisation (e.g., HR, OD, or L&D).

This is such an important issue for internal coaches that the following two chapters are devoted to addressing it in much more depth.

Balancing the roles

Discharging your responsibilities both in your day job and in your role as coach can be demanding.

- *Time pressures*: This can be a real issue. You may decide to train as a coach at a time when your day job is easily containable within normal working hours and then hit a busy spell or take on additional responsibilities that put you under a lot of pressure. At such times your line manager may have second thoughts about the desirability of your being a coach so you may have that to handle too.
- *Guilt*: Internal coaches often report feeling guilty and talk about the difficulty in getting the balance right, reminiscent in tone to working parents' guilt when trying to combine work and childcare. Even if the actual sessions can be accommodated, internal coaches may feel that they should not take time for preparation, reflection after a session, CPD, or supervision—without which the coach's performance (and therefore the experience for the client) is likely to suffer.
- *Switching your "head space"*: Most internal coaches are also managers and spend the time when they are not coaching making decisions, organising work, delivering projects. As a manager you are a multitasking doer whereas as a coach you listen, avoid being directive, and give your undivided attention to the client. One said: "It's difficult trying not to tell them what to do and how to do it!" This switch can be hard to achieve—even for experienced, trained coaches—when you have just torn yourself away from a demanding work environment and know that there will be countless pressing issues competing for your attention when the client session is over. Another said: "It is hard to switch off before going into a coaching session. In an ideal world you'd have a bit of time out to calm the mind ahead but that's not always feasible. The client, too, may have the office on their mind when they are talking to you."

Being part of the same system

Internal coaches often talk about the difficulties thrown up by being part of the same system as the client.

- *Maintaining objectivity*: You may sometimes find it hard to stay objective. The following are both quotations from internal coaches: "It can be hard to disassociate your own experiences and your own feelings towards the business situation or structure that a client is describing, as you help them work through their challenges and remain neutral", and: "The issues that affect all staff also affect us. It can be more difficult to step back and take an independent view about an issue that causes concern for you, too, as an employee."

- *Knowing the same people*: While care will usually be taken to ensure that the coach and client work in different parts of the organisation, you may still find that you know some of your client's colleagues: "When coaching someone who is talking about someone you know, it's hard to not let your own views get in the way."
- *Providing an appropriate level of challenge*: Coaches need to strike a balance when it comes to supporting the client while still holding them to account. On the one hand, you may well say to your clients in the contracting phase that you expect them to take responsibility for their own learning and actions and that while you are in charge of the process, the client is in charge of the agenda and how they use the learning. On the other hand, clients do value being challenged—there may be no-one else prepared to do that. Yedreshteyn (2008) points out that "… clients want coaches to follow up, challenge them, and hold them accountable for meeting their goals. Coaches suspected this when they said they wished they had challenged their clients more, as that is exactly what their clients wanted" (p. 86). This can feel uncomfortable for coaches, particularly less experienced ones, but following up and holding the client accountable could be crucial in helping them to achieve sustainable change.

Practical issues

It can be useful to understand that some of the following practical issues can arise.

- *Dealing with cancellations*: Internal coaches can find themselves with clients who keep cancelling or postponing sessions. In some organisations this can be quite prevalent. By and large, external coaches charge for cancelled sessions and this discourages cancellations but the same leverage is not available to internal coaches, unless there is some system of cross-charging. With clear contracting and organisational support for the coach's taking a robust attitude, this problem can usually be overcome.

- *Not having enough clients*: Coach supervisors report that internal coaches often refer to a lack of clients. There can be many reasons for this: for example, the scheme may not be marketed well enough within the organisation; a highly pressurised period could mean that fewer people feel that they have time to be coached; or a particular coach may have specialist skills that are temporarily not called for by clients. This can be a challenging time for a coach who may feel deskilled and demotivated as a result.

- *Finding an appropriate venue*: Conventional wisdom holds that clients get more out of coaching sessions that take place away from the office, not least because their thoughts are more freed up. As one coach noted: "The office environment is not necessarily conducive to a coaching session." Most offices are open plan, so meetings have to be held in meeting rooms that can have an institutional feel not favourable to rich coaching. Another said: "More often than not it's a challenge to find somewhere discreet in proximity to the office." Few organisations would be prepared to pay for an off-site venue for internal coaching sessions. They may also be unenthusiastic about time being taken up by the coach and client travelling to and from the foyer of a local hotel (which in any case might be an unsuitable venue if the client were to become distressed during a session). Equally, lead coaches may feel that commercial confidentiality could be compromised if their managers discussed organisational issues in the local coffee shop. Finding suitable venues can be a challenge.

- *Geography*: When people think of internal coaching they often imagine that the coach will work on the same site as the client but this may by no means be the case. They may work in different parts of the country or another part of the world. Some internal coaches have to learn to work with video conferencing facilities, which sometimes involve a time lag, or do most of the coaching by telephone: "I have had to overcome this by developing my skills by coaching on the phone which isn't ideal sometimes." In such multinational companies another issue can be that coach and client may be in different time zones and finding a time when both are in the office can be complicated.

Coping with emotions

In a well-managed scheme, the internal coaches will have access to plenty of support in the shape of the lead coach, other internal coaches, and, ideally, a dedicated supervisor, "buddy", or mentor. Some schemes, however, are poorly resourced or may still be in their infancy so the coaches may have to cope alone with feelings such as isolation or not feeling valued.

- *Feelings of isolation*: While they are training, internal coaches have considerable support: they will be part of a cohort with other trainee coaches and will have coaching or supervisory support from the training provider throughout the programme. The lucky ones will then be introduced into their organisation's coaching community that meets regularly to provide mutual support; participates in regular supervision; shares experiences; and receives CPD. However, this is not a universal experience and some coaches find that once they finish their training they are on their own. The system for recruiting clients may be via an intranet—so, little contact with the lead coach—and supervision or CPD may not be available. In such circumstances, a coach would do well to be proactive, find out who the other coaches are, and indulge in a little self-help (while putting pressure on their employer to, at the least, facilitate regular gatherings of the internal coaches where they can exchange experiences and offer each other support).
- *Feeling under-valued*: Internal coaches can have a sense of not being valued as highly as external coaches even though they feel that the service delivered is as good. One said: "The organisation does not recognise internal excellence, but appears to see external coaches as more professional." If they coach on top of the day job, their line manager will probably know little, if anything, about the coaching work that they are doing (unless they work in the department that runs the coaching scheme) and may not even understand what coaching is about. If the coaching scheme involves formal feedback from the client at the end of the assignment, that can meet the need for feeling valued, or if the coaching scheme is run actively by the lead coach then they might provide the "strokes" to the internal coaches that most people find helpful and motivating. Many internal coaches, though, will need to be content with the direct feedback that they get from their clients during sessions.

Summary

The role of the internal coach is a rich and varied one, which can look and feel very different depending on an organisation's requirements.

This chapter has taken you through a number of factors that have an impact on what the "job" of an internal coach will look like. It invites you to consider these in relation to what you know about your own organisation's approach. Having a clear understanding of what your organisation's expectations are and the support that is available to you will help you decide if you want to make the commitment to become an internal coach.

QUESTIONS TO REFLECT ON

Factor to consider	What are the implications for me?
Who are the internal coaches? What areas of the business do they come from? For example: • Central functions/HR • Operational areas/Business functions	• What added skills and experience do I bring to coaching by the nature of my job role? • Would there be areas of the business that I would not want to coach in?
What is the coach there to do? What variety of coaching will I be expected to undertake? For example: • Performance coaching • Career development • Leadership development • Transitions to a new role	• What type of coaching am I most interested in delivering? • What type of coaching would I not want to be involved in?
How much coaching will the internal coach do? How many coaching hours per month will I be expected to deliver on top of my "day job"?	• How will I ensure the support of my line manager? • How will I balance the twin demands on my time? • How will I manage client expectations? • What long-term career aspirations may I want to take into account when considering working as an internal coach?

(Continued)

QUESTIONS TO REFLECT ON   (*Continued*)

Factor to consider	What are the implications for me?

What support will be provided?
What are the options for support in my organisation? For example:
- Facilitated shared learning activities
- Coaching network
- CPD opportunities
- Coaching library
- 1:1/Group supervision

- What type of support works best for me?
- What type of support is a "must have"? What is "nice to have"?
- What may I want to initiate in my organisation?
- What am I prepared to invest in my own development?

Whom will they coach?
What levels in the organisation will I work with? For example:
- Top team
- Senior managers
- Middle managers
- High potential staff

- At what level in the organisation am I most comfortable coaching?
- Where may I need to challenge myself?

What are the benefits for internal coaches?
The benefits can include:
- Making a contribution
- Seeing clients grow
- Being part of a community of coaches
- Feeling valued by the organisation
- Understanding the organisation better

- What is my motivation for being an internal coach?
- What personal benefits will I get?
- What will I be giving up to allow me to coach?

What are the challenges for internal coaches?
The challenges can include:
- Handling ethical dilemmas
- Maintaining objectivity
- Time pressures
- Balancing coaching with the "day job"
- Dealing with cancellations
- Not having enough clients

- What challenges am I most likely to experience?
- What challenges most concern me?
- What do I need to have in place to help address these challenges?

CHAPTER THREE

Recognising ethical dilemmas

Life was much simpler when my biggest dilemma in life was
deciding what Pop-Tart to eat for breakfast

—Unknown

What this chapter is about

What would you do if you smelt alcohol on your client's breath at
ten o'clock in the morning? Or your client wants to discuss a difficult
relationship with a colleague who happens to be a close friend of yours?
An understanding of coaching ethics and the ability to apply them
appropriately is fundamental to being a coach. This chapter explores:

- What are ethical dilemmas and how to recognise them
- The three most common areas for ethical dilemmas:
  - boundaries: the different varieties of boundary; raising your
    awareness of them and how to avoid crossing them
  - confidentiality: the challenges of confidentiality, what are the limits
    and where are the strains?
  - dealing with power differentials: the impact of power inside and
    outside the coaching relationship.

31

What are "ethical dilemmas"?

Perhaps it is first worth examining the term ethical dilemmas. I am aware that there is something about the word ethical that can make people switch off. If you were to say to a roomful of coaches: "Let's talk about ethics in coaching" you would get a very different response than if you were to say: "Let's discuss what you might do if your coaching client let drop that they had resumed recreational use of cocaine." As Judit Varkonyi-Sepp put it in her report on the eighth annual conference of the British Psychological Society's special group in coaching psychology (Varkonyi-Sepp, 2013): "The word 'ethics' might send shivers down one's spine thinking about this as an abstract, boring, legislation-filled dry topic, but it is not ... Ethics is everywhere in what we do and it was a light bulb moment to recognise how very practical it is" (p. 108).

Kitchener (2000) defines an ethical dilemma as:

> ... a problem for which no choice seems completely satisfactory, since there are good but contradictory reasons to take conflicting and incompatible courses of action. (p. 2)

The "client taking cocaine" example mentioned above would be a prime instance. Does it actually create a dilemma for you? You may feel that how clients choose to spend their spare time is up to them. But what if the client's drug use was affecting their performance or they had charge of vulnerable people or heavy machinery? Do you know if Class A drug use is a criminal activity? Is there anything in your organisation's disciplinary policies around drug use off the premises? Would your own reputation as a coach be at risk if the client's drug use became known for some reason and it later emerged that you had been privy to the information and did nothing with it? Also, is there any chance that the client has let this drop into the conversation because they actually want you to challenge them on it? Or, that they, at some level, want you to blow the whistle because they need help with facing up to it? The answers to those questions might present you with a dilemma as to what you should do next.

Some of the more common varieties of dilemma are in the table on the next page.

Facts and figures 3.1: Common types of ethical dilemma

Potential dilemma	*Occurrence* (%)
• Your client wants you to coach them to prepare for an interview outside the organisation that they haven't told their line manager/sponsor about	37
• You have information about the client that is relevant to their performance but they don't know that and are not putting it on the table so you feel that you cannot raise it either	36
• You are under pressure from line manager or sponsor to provide a view on how coaching client is "getting on" or whether they are "making progress"	32
• You learn from your client that they are being bullied (or subject to some other unacceptable behaviour) but your client does not want you to tell anyone	26
• You find yourself coaching two people who are involved in different sides of a dispute that they want to discuss	15
• A conflict of interest between your managerial/functional role and your role as a coach only becomes apparent after you have taken a particular client on	11
• HR is instituting disciplinary proceedings with your client and wants some input from you	10
• Your client is planning on a course of action that would be unacceptable to the organisation if they knew	9

Specific dilemmas do not necessarily fit into neat categories—the cocaine example above could be regarded as mainly about confidentiality but it is also relevant to a discussion of boundaries too—but I am going to group the discussion around three key areas that can often throw dilemmas up:

- Boundaries
- Confidentiality
- Dealing with power differentials.

A final word before we plunge into the swirling waters of ethical dilemmas: it is important to keep things in proportion. The issue is about being aware. There is no need for us to throw up our hands and say: "If these are the sorts of things that internal coaches have to contend with then it is all too difficult". Dilemmas can be managed.

Boundaries

Maintaining boundaries in coaching is about being alert to where the limits to your role as a coach are and not going beyond them. Some boundaries will be the same for internal and external coaches but, given the interlocking relationships that internal coaches have to contend with in their organisations, recognising and holding the boundaries can be more complicated for you. You may find yourself under more pressure to blur the boundaries than is the case for your external counterparts. The result is that more thought and care will need to be given to managing them.

Professional competence

The EMCC's code of ethics says that coaches will "ensure that their level of knowledge is sufficient to meet the needs of the client". We need to be clear with ourselves and our coaching clients about what we are competent to coach them on and what we are not. At the "contracting" stage—the initial conversation that the coach and client have to agree what the coaching relationship is to be about, why they are there, and what expectations they can have of each other—a coach will remind the client of what they are not there to do. This may include, for example, acting as a consultant, or therapist, or mentor. An inexperienced coach may feel uncomfortable saying they do not have the expertise to deal with a client's issue, perhaps fearing that their credibility could suffer or perhaps simply because they want to be able to help the client. I tend to use the formulation with clients that "if the conversation moves into territory where I feel that I am not competent to coach you: for example, difficulties with your marriage, or with your finances, or with your mental health, or with alcohol, then I will tell you and we can discuss alternative sources of support".

Competence may be about knowledge or experience limitations but it could equally well concern emotional limits. I know of coaches who say that they cannot coach well if the client wants to discuss issues around shame. Bullying at work is another subject that some coaches choose not to coach people on, often because they have experienced it themselves (either at work or in childhood) and therefore find it hard to stay dispassionate. The key is for us to be honest with the client if an issue is broached where we feel we cannot add value for whatever reason and to make alternative arrangements for them.

Referrals: The boundary between coaching support and therapeutic support can be a fuzzy one. When does a highly stressed executive who has been carrying a heavy workload for too long become someone with clinical depression who needs professional medical help? When does worry become debilitating anxiety? Does a client have to be experiencing panic attacks for anxiety to become a mental health issue? Coaches are not expected to "diagnose" the client but simply to notice our responses to their levels of stress and ask them the question whether they might need to consult their doctor or access other professional help.

The Association for Coaching's code of ethics and good practice says:

> Your experience should be appropriate to the needs of your client. If you do not have the necessary or relevant skills, you should refer your client to those who have, such as more experienced coaches, counsellors, psychotherapists or others offering specialist services.

I asked a number of internal coaches what they would do if they suspected that a very busy and stressed client might be tipping into depression/serious anxiety/the mental health arena. The boundaries were clearer to some than others and some were more interventionist than others. However, there was a definite awareness that a boundary would be crossed if coaches attempted to deal with this simply as part of the coaching. The majority would advise the client to seek professional help, with a number specifically suggesting that the client might make an early appointment with their GP. A number said that their first thought would be to seek advice from their supervisor/supervision group or their lead coach. Others would consult their organisation's employee assistance scheme about their client's options without identifying the client. Some were much more interventionist and took the lead in directly referring the client to professional help.

Some responses discussed the desirability of suspending the coaching until the client was on a more even keel, specifically pointing out that dealing with such issues was outside the terms of the coaching contract. Others felt that keeping some continuity of support from the coach, alongside any other arrangements, was important.

So why might this issue turn into a dilemma? First, an inexperienced coach might feel wary of broaching the subject at all, so that might feel like a dilemma in itself. The problem could become bigger if the coach had genuine concerns that the client might do something "of harm to themselves or others" and if the client brushed off the suggestion that they might seek professional help. If the client is senior and responsible for many staff then their condition could be having a significant impact on others. One internal coach in the NHS referred to a complicated dilemma they had in relation to a severely depressed client:

> "I had a problem referring a client to another health professional
> and hearing that they did not attend the appointment—particularly
> as they led me to believe that they had."

There are, of course, other types of issues that may require the coach to suggest to the client that they seek help from another professional. The most commonly cited were problems with drugs or alcohol, personal finances, bereavement, and marital or other family relationships.

Deciding where to refer a client was more straightforward for some coaches than others. Two comments were: "I lack information on who to refer clients to with needs greater than coaching", and "I need to build up a more comprehensive list of support organisations."

Some coaches work in companies where employees can access a free BUPA counselling service—which makes referral straightforward. Other organisations have an employee assistance scheme, a wellbeing service, or a similar welfare service. However, sometimes the services of these departments can be "hard charged" to business units. Although the content of such sessions would be confidential, the client's line manager might know that they had accessed those services and this might discourage the client from taking that route. An additional problem can be that the confidential service provided is either not trusted or not very good. You could find yourself being asked for guidance on where to go for help outside the organisation. If a client tells you that they have accessed an external source of mental health provision, it is good practice to make a note in your records to that effect.

Role conflicts

Conflict of interest: Managing the boundary between an internal coach's coaching role and their "day job" is one of the most common challenges encountered by internal coaches. Yedreshteyn (2008) points out that "boundary maintenance may be less of a concern if the coach does not interact with the same group of people his or her client does". If the internal coaching scheme involves a managed matching process between coach and client, then the matcher will normally try to avoid the possibility of the coach's and clients' networks overlapping too much. Where the process involves the client selecting potential coaches from a register, then it is your responsibility as the coach to check out, in the so-called "chemistry meeting" (an initial meeting in which the coach and potential client decide if they can work well together), whether the two of you work in sufficiently different areas to minimise the risk of role conflict and whom you might know in common. This is more difficult to achieve if the coach and client are very senior, as the pyramid in most organisations narrows significantly towards the top.

If a coach works in the centre of the organisation, for example, HR, OD, or L&D, the potential for role conflict rises exponentially.

Facts and figures 3.2: Role conflict issues

These comments from internal coaches working in HR illustrate the types of role conflict issues that can occur:

- "Some conflict of interest when I have been involved in coaching internal clients through to partnership, as I am also (one of many people) involved in the sign-off process for them becoming a partner."
- "I have had to declare that as a result of potential confidentiality issues I was unable to take part in a personnel selection process."
- "I have been involved in coaching individuals around their performance and then subsequently been asked to provide HR support to a disciplinary process or grievance involving the same individual."
- "Where a line manager wanted to get advice about one of her members of staff that she was having problems with, and did not know that I was that individual's coach (as the person had self-referred)."

One HR director, who did not want to be quoted, described a vivid example of the difficulties that internal coaches working in HR can encounter. He found himself in a conversation with his coaching client's line manager that shifted into a discussion about the client's potential. He was surprised into being asked for a view that was then repeated back by the line manager to the client.

Insider knowledge: An additional challenge of being an internal coach working in HR is that you may find yourself privy to information about a client or relevant to them that the client does not know. This can happen to internal coaches who are not in HR too—though less frequently—as sometimes line managers tell coaches things about their clients that it would be easier for them not to know.

Facts and figures 3.3: Insider knowledge

- "A sponsor informs me that a client is not going to be promoted but has not yet told the client."
- "Where the client has shared they are going for a promotion or intending to leave the organisation and I have knowledge regarding the situation which could influence their decision."
- "Knowing that an individual I was coaching was going to be made redundant further to organisational review."
- "I have been told about a coachee's lack of suitability for a senior position, but the coachee has not been told and I am then unable to tell them."

This kind of situation can provide a real dilemma for a coach in deciding what to share and what not to share. I have myself had the experience of coaching someone specifically to be well prepared for a promotion process and then being told privately a month before the assessment board that I "should know" that there was no chance that my client would gain promotion as the panel was being chaired by someone who held the fixed view that it was essential that the post-holder should be a graduate (and my client was not). Whatever action you decide to take, there might still be an interim phase during which you could not be fully authentic in the coaching relationship and that is an uncomfortable position for any coach.

Wanting to fix a problem: Another aspect of the coaching role and day job conflicting is the temptation that the coach may have to "fix" a problem for the client. As one internal coach working in OD put it:

> "You want to rescue the individual and have to keep checking with yourself: 'Are you sure you're not on your White Charger?' There's a tendency to want to save the individual as there *are* levers that OD could pull."

The temptation to rescue in this way is an issue that coach supervisors confirm comes up in supervision from internal coaches who work in HR and OD. The other side of this coin was identified in some research by Wrynne (2011) where he noticed that the client of an internal coach perceived his coach as "an extension of the organisation that should be supporting him" (p. 33). He had an expectation that he would not have had of an external coach that, by virtue of her day job, the coach would make something happen for him. Wrynne describes the client as "expecting his coach to use her proximity to organisational power and pull on an organisational 'lever' to actively support him" (p. 58). The internal coach had to disabuse the client of this notion and empower him to shift for himself.

Poaching: Finally, a very specific phenomenon that can arise is the temptation to poach a member of staff. I have come across examples in a number of organisations where either the coach has been so impressed by the client that they have wanted to poach them to work in their own division or vice versa. This can cause a dilemma and bad feeling if the line manager of the person being poached does not want to lose them, and can give coaching a bad name.

Maintaining objectivity and independence

The potential for unconscious collusion with a client is considered to be generally greater for the internal coach because they are swimming in the same cultural pond as their client. Clearly this is an ever present danger that internal coaches need to be vigilant about. When exploring the benefits of using external coaches, organisations often cite the value of fresh perspectives and a different way of looking at issues.

A very specific issue that can make it hard for coaches to maintain objectivity arises from the simple fact that you will know many people in the organisation.

Facts and figures 3.4: Knowing people in the organisation

- "It's almost impossible not to have your own views on people in the organisation. It's an ongoing challenge not to let that get in the way of the coaching: for example, if your client has a problem relationship with someone whom you have a problem with too—or who is a friend—you mustn't let it get in the way but it can be a huge effort. Sometimes getting in the right headspace is hard, particularly if you're coaching in the office or if you're tired."
- "Having knowledge or personal friendships with individuals that the coachee is talking about or having difficulty with, which was unknown when the coaching contract was agreed."
- "Client discussing the negative impact a colleague's behaviour is having on them—the colleague is a personal friend of mine."
- "I knew the manager of one coachee very well through work: although he is a charming character, I consider him to be a very poor manager. This caused me some problems, in that I had to try to remain neutral during coaching sessions, and to challenge the coachee's equally low opinion of her manager."

Dealing with this issue is a fact of life for internal coaches. How you manage it, though, says something about the way you operate. Will you and your client decide at the outset how you will treat such situations? Or will you first wait to see if a problem arises and then discuss in the moment whether to proceed with the conversation or not? Or do you find it sufficiently easy to compartmentalise for this not to be a real problem for you? Many coaches would say that it would be impossible to maintain the requisite level of impartiality if a client wanted to discuss a difficult relationship with someone you know really well, or that it would produce unhelpful "noise" in your head, making it hard to give your full attention to the client. But others think these arguments can be overdone. The really important thing is to be aware of it as an issue and consciously decide in the moment how you are going to handle it.

Work life vs. *personal life*

In the last chapter I raised the topic of "what is the internal coach *not* there to do?", including where the boundary lies between coaching the client on work issues and personal issues. I suggested that this boundary may not necessarily be a clear one.

Facts and figures 3.5: Conversations dealing with non-work issues

Ninety-one per cent of internal coaches answered yes to the question: "Are you content for a coaching conversation to go beyond work issues?" The sorts of topics outside current work issues that coaches had let clients bring to the sessions included:
- Family situation/relationship issues
- Work–life balance
- Bereavement/illness/fertility treatment
- Dealing with anxiety/building confidence/raising self-esteem
- Giving up smoking/losing weight.

When I fed the findings in **Facts and figures 3.5** back to a meeting of around half a dozen HR directors of large companies, in 2009, several of them were surprised, and one of the views expressed was "that is not what we invested in training up internal coaches for". Some of the coaches had shared the following rationales for going beyond purely work issues:

- Because personal issues were directly affecting the client's performance at work ("Home life and other factors often have a bearing on performance, so are legitimate topics if the client wishes to discuss them")
- Because it was important to be holistic ("Life cannot be compartmentalised")
- Because people's pasts shape their present ("People's background, culture and upbringing have significantly shaped their current behaviour. This can come up when discussing values and limiting beliefs and can be helpful to talk through").

Some of the HR Directors were convinced by these reasons but others were not.

A senior lead coach who runs an internal coaching cohort in a public sector organisation in the North West takes a view that was clearly shared by most of the internal coaches in my research: if it seems to make sense to move into personal territory in order to resolve an issue for a client, then do so. She made the point to me that in these times of austerity, many senior leaders are having issues around resilience and she could not think of a better way for such leaders to spend coaching sessions than exploring their personal coping strategies. In Chapter Six I cover the issue of work *vs.* personal from the point of view of the employer.

So where are the boundaries in relation to what issues clients in your organisation can or cannot bring to the coaching relationship? Coaches know how a session labelled, say, "career coaching" can swiftly become a highly emotional exploration of a client's fears about possible redundancy and the impact it could have on their family. But does your employer understand that? Is there any guidance that your client will have seen and that you can reinforce in your initial "contracting" meeting? Or is this left to your discretion as a professional with responsibilities to both the individual and the organisation?

This boundary between work and the personal is reflected at a more strategic level in the debate about "who is the client?" Providing internal coaching support to employees is not costless to the employer and Hawkins (2012), Hunt and Weintraub (2006), and others have drawn attention to the importance of the coach recognising that they have responsibilities to the organisation as well as to the client:

> In order to be an effective developmental coach, the coach must be able to deal with the needs of two clients: the coachee and the organisation. (Hunt & Weintraub, 2006, p. 3)

It is part of the role of a coach to take a position of unconditional regard for the client and to try to see the world and the workplace through their eyes. What, though, if you have begun to feel that your client is taking the organisation for a ride? What if the discussion is all about how your client can get their work–life balance into sync and work nine-to-five when you know that everyone else is under huge pressure and giving considerable "discretionary effort" well above that to the organisation? What if you suspect that the client may even be lazy and there seems a surprising dearth of discussion of how they might become more effective at what they do but a lot about how to get their boss off their back? At what point do the needs of the organisation kick in for you?

Case study 3.1: Who is the client?

Paul has been coaching Angela for three sessions and there are another three to go. Initially she had seemed to be engaging in the process but he is having doubts about her commitment to change—she tends to promise much but does not carry through. They have talked about procrastination and what might be stopping her but she continues to show little energy around her agreed actions. However, she does have energy around the idea of training to become an internal coach herself and repeatedly returns to the issue. In her first session she referred to the fact that her job is under-loaded and her fears that her role might become redundant and Paul recognises that she thinks a second role as a coach might make her position less vulnerable. Having a coaching qualification and coaching experience could also put her in a better position to find freelance work outside if the redundancy goes ahead. In the guise of "career development" she would like to put her other issues on hold and for Paul to coach her through the rigorous application process for the next round of internal coach selection. This is not what they originally contracted to address and Paul has doubts about her suitability. Paul perceives this as an ethical dilemma. He told her at the outset that the agenda was hers but their original brief was around helping her to become a more effective manager and leader. If she trained as a coach he has no doubt that this would be of benefit to her in her job but it would not directly address the issues agreed in the initial three-way meeting with her line manager. On the other hand, there is an organisational policy around managers using a coaching style so switching the coaching in that direction could be argued as aligning with it. He is confused about to whom his primary loyalty should be—to his client or to the organisation.

Question: What would you do in Paul's position?

Coaching vs. *mentoring*

Some boundaries are important to some coaches and not at all to others. The boundary between coaching and mentoring is one of these. First of all, what is the difference? When I trained as a coach over ten years ago there was a big debate about this with leaders in the field in the UK sometimes using the opposite definitions from one another. However, the debate seems to have settled down and it is commonly accepted that while coaches are there to use listening and questioning to develop an individual's capability and focus on their personal and professional growth, mentors are: "people who impart their own experience, learning and advice to those who have less experience in a particular field" (Wilson & McMahon, 2006, p. 55). Mentors often focus on helping the mentee's career advancement, drawing on the mentor's experience, knowledge of the organisation and networks.

Why might this boundary be problematic? Well, most coaches are trained in the "pure art" of coaching: that is, to be non-directive, to act as a mirror, to ask "clean" questions and to provide accurate feedback with the aim of providing an environment in which to help to build the client's capacity to think things through for themselves and develop their resourcefulness. It can come as a shock if their client's perception of a coach is of an advisor who can tell them—based on their own experience—how to be a more effective manager or leader. A number of factors can make this perception more likely:

- If the organisation provides little or no information or guidance to clients before the coaching relationship begins, they will simply rely on their general knowledge of what coaching is, which may be inaccurate;
- If the coach is senior to the client, the client may feel that they should have the benefit of that person's experience; and
- If the coach is a lot older than the client, the client may unconsciously move into "pupil" mode and want to be told what to do.

However, it is for the organisation to take a view on what kind of coaching they want. Evidence that some organisations regard the roles as different is that they offer their high potentials both a coach and a mentor. Many of the skills of coaching and mentoring do overlap—particularly the ability to build a quality one-on-one relationship with the interests of the client very much at heart—and many coaches, if they have experience that could be of value to their clients, are relaxed with the idea of moving between coaching and mentoring as appropriate.

There is no doubt that some clients do want some mentoring from their coach. One lead coach whom I interviewed referred to a manager who pressured the coach into being a mentor and "showing him the ropes", as he had recently been promoted into the grade that the coach held. If that happened to you, would you comply with their wishes? Or should a coach who has a background in, say, OD and has relevant knowledge and experience to offer be allowed to make this available to a client who is struggling with managing a change programme? Perhaps a better approach would be to offer a meeting with that as the agenda rather than as part of the coaching session. Macann (2012a) noted that requests for external coaches with experience of the appropriate business area were increasing. There is thus a question mark as to whether clients today are actually looking for pure coaching or whether increasingly they are looking for an element of mentoring too.

Yedreshteyn (2008) noticed that some participants on a leadership development programme, when assigned their coaches, were:

> disappointed not to have a more senior leader from their function, someone who could serve the role of mentor and help them grow in the corporation … [They were] confused as to why they were not assigned a mentor as part of the Leadership Development program and "checked out" of the relationship after learning they had not been partnered with a mentor. (pp. 86–87)

This is not to say that internal coaches "should" have permeable boundaries when it comes to coaching *vs.* mentoring—indeed most clients really are looking to work with a coach not a mentor. However, some do; some clients welcome it and there are some benefits. The key message is that employers should think about the issue and coaches should be clear about it.

The role boundary between a coach and the client's line manager

Yedreshteyn (2008) points out that where clients are disappointed that their coach does not play a mentor type role "this could suggest they just want their manager to be more involved in their development and to help them to grow in their position" (p. 87).

This raises the whole issue of the boundary between the responsibilities of the coach and those of the client's line manager. This is rarely talked about but supervisors report that it often comes up in supervision sessions with internal coaches though rarely with external coaches. As one internal coach said:

> "A lot of people want to be coached on a specific short term problem, something to do with their current work load, and I think you have

to remind them that sometimes this is more appropriate for their
line manager, not a coach."

In many coaching schemes, the coach, coaching client, and line manager
will have a three-way meeting at the outset of the coaching programme.
The coach and line manager can often forge a sense of being in an alliance to help the client to make progress on agreed goals. The line manager may see the client day-to-day (if they work on the same site) and
be in a position to provide feedback in the moment on behaviour or
changes that they have observed. The coach can additionally offer the
client that space where they can feel free to be honest about fragilities,
insecurities, and vulnerabilities that they would prefer not to share with
their line managers. However, coaches can sometimes feel that they are
simply carrying out the role that a line manager should be doing if they
had the time to, interest in, or aptitude for. Where would you draw the
line? And what if the client says that their line manager is never there?
Or is not prepared to take the time? Or is off sick long term? Is it in the
client's and organisation's best interests for you to step in or would it
be considered that you are inappropriately usurping the line manager's
role?

Facts and figures 3.6: Blurring of coach's and line manager's roles

- "Being asked to coach someone by a line manager who has an ulterior
  motive of wanting to 'ease' the individual out of the organisation."
- "Being asked to coach an individual to a position where they decide they
  don't want to become a director: that is, the line manager did not want to
  have an honest conversation but wanted me to push them to a position
  where they came to that conclusion for themselves."
- "As an internal coach, I don't want to be linked with the performance
  management process. Sometimes I have to make it clear to the line manager that that's not my role ..."
- "I have had an instance where a sponsoring line manager wanted a report
  on the client's response to coaching. The client had not fully engaged in
  the coaching relationship, which I suspected was being used as a substi-
  tute for performance management."

In such situations, experienced coaches would put the ball back into
the line manager's court but issues of power (see page 59 for more on
this) can sometimes play a role in making this hard for the coach.

Confidentiality

The notion of confidentiality lies at the heart of coaching relationships. Without the client believing that what they say in a coaching session will go no further, the much-valued "safe environment" would disappear, as would the basis of the whole enterprise. The concept of maintaining confidentiality appears very early on in most coach training programmes and is an essential ingredient in the codes of ethics of all the coaching professional bodies. But what does it mean in practice and how easy is it to maintain, particularly for an internal coach?

Invitations to internal coaches by third parties to breach confidentiality tend to be the most common variety of dilemma cited by them. Frisch (2001) observed that, for internal coaches, confidentiality will be "tested more" (p. 246). Other commentators in the research literature also highlight confidentiality as a potential issue for internal coaches: for example, Wasylyshyn's (2003) outcome study about, *inter alia*, the factors influencing clients' choice of coach found that four fifths said they would not want an internal coach "due to coaches' potential conflict of interest, trust and ability to maintain confidentiality" (p. 99). Hunt and Weintraub (2006) talk of the need for internal coaches to manage "limited confidentiality", and Rock and Donde (2008) suggest that issues to be managed by internal coaches include credibility, trust and confidentiality, conflict of interest, and boundaries. The point, as noted by Carter (2005), is that confidentiality is particularly salient for internal coaches, as opposed to external coaches, precisely for the reason that:

> the internal coach has much more interaction (both formally and informally) with other organisational members than the external coach does. In relation to this, internal coaches need to develop a diplomatic way of responding to questions regarding how certain coachees are doing ... This can put the coach in a difficult situation, as they may feel pressurised by senior management into divulging certain sensitive information about one of their coachees. (p. 12)

She points out that:

> The internal coach must always be on their guard, innocent questions answered around the water-cooler, for example, can lead to serious breaches of confidentiality. (p. 13)

Mackintosh (2003), reflecting on six years' experience as an internal coach, describes how uncomfortable it can sometimes be to maintain strict confidentiality:

> I remember, on a number of occasions, incurring the wrath of my manager when I refused to answer questions about a particular employee. This was extremely difficult for me to do, as I had always been brought up to respect authority and when your boss said jump ... you jumped! It was painful but I stuck to my guns. (p. 1)

In most situations, however, internal coaches find that maintaining confidentiality is one of the more straightforward issues to deal with. Managers normally understand, once reminded, why it must be observed. One experienced internal coach told me:

> "I take the approach that if it is confidential then any perceived breaches (whether they have happened or not) are a reflection on my personal professional status. In the past when this has happened I have challenged and stood my ground as it is about the client's information and my reputation. Once a reputation is lost in terms of confidentiality it is lost forever".

Facts and figures 3.7: Maintaining confidentiality

- "I can be put under pressure to share some of the client's progress with his/her line manager. Never have, and when explained why, the line manager accepts that."
- "Being asked by the line manager how someone is doing. I said 'great' in response and encouraged him to have the discussion with their direct report (my coachee); reminding him of the contract discussion and expectation laid out re progress updates they had agreed between the two of them. He accepted this and was very keen to do just that in order to demonstrate his continued interest and support of the individual."
- "Regularly asked by the sponsor to provide information on how the coaching is going to a level of detail that we cannot provide but we do have clear boundaries around this."
- "Having been an internal coach for nearly eight years, I am now very rarely asked to comment on my clients and there is a trust and respect built up within the organisation whereby the leaders know the sessions are completely confidential."

Limits to confidentiality

Do you consider the fact that you are coaching a particular individual to be confidential information in itself? Most coaches do, and if this is your view you might give some thought to where you hold your coaching sessions (see section on venues later in the chapter).

Second, what limits do you put upon confidentiality? It is essential that at the beginning of the coaching relationship it is made clear exactly what is confidential and what is not. Some organisations provide a written contract for coach and client that includes what the client can expect by way of confidentiality. Others expect this ground to be covered orally in the first session. One formulation that can work well is for the coach to say that they will not talk to anyone about the content of client sessions unless the client is present.

Facts and figures 3.8: Limits to confidentiality

- Approximately ten per cent said they promised the client "complete confidentiality"—a risky stance;
- Most offered the more usual "session content would be kept confidential unless they believed their client might harm themselves or others or was breaking the law";
- Over fifty per cent had the further limit that they could not guarantee confidentiality if they believed their client was breaching the organisation's own disciplinary code.

Violating the organisation's disciplinary code: Unless instructed otherwise, most coaches stick with the variety of confidentiality taught to them when they trained, usually based on one of the professional bodies' code of conduct. This would not normally make any reference to breaching an organisation's own disciplinary code.

Bullying was the most common example given by coaches of a violation of the organisation's policies that could put confidentiality at risk. This issue can place the coach in an uncomfortable situation because victims of or witnesses to bullying are often reluctant to take action for fear of making the situation worse or finding themselves sucked into an unwelcome formal process. At the same time, the coach is now in possession of information that goes beyond the confidentiality agreement. Three examples:

> "Client told me that she knew a colleague was being bullied, and she had known for two years. Colleague did not want to tell

anyone. Client was breaching bullying and harassment policy by not taking any action."

"A junior client being bullied and feeling intimidated but not wanting to take it any further or talk to HR. Also here I had a concern around what is the duty of care as an internal coach and did the person, by telling me about their situation, feel they had told someone in 'authority'?"

"Where a client was referred and it turned out she had been bullied and was clearly suffering emotionally and confidence wise. I encouraged her to speak to her boss about it and took it to supervision. I kept asking the question about whether I could get involved in blowing the whistle on the bully but in the end had to accept the person's choice not to take it further. I did also encourage her to get some external counselling."

The flipside to promising confidentiality is "whistle blowing". Coaches would normally regard this as an absolute last resort. While this would be an extreme form of confidentiality breaking, coaches need to be clear that when they specify limits to confidentiality then they are saying that if the client reveals something beyond those boundaries then they may feel bound to do something with that information, whether with or without the client's permission. One internal coach interviewee was quite clear that coaches must abide by that and said if a client told her about something that she felt could not be kept confidential, she offered them three choices:

1. Tell a manager themselves and provide evidence to her that they had
2. Go with her to tell a manager
3. Understand that she would have to go and tell a manager.

Another interviewee, working as a coach and coach supervisor within the NHS, said:

"Anything around child protection or harm to self or others and it leaves the room instantly".

She had done that in the past and had gone directly to the CEO to explain what she knew.

Strains in keeping confidentiality

Clients sometimes tell coaches about things that are clearly within the boundaries of confidentiality but still result in soul searching for the coach. The coach may feel frustrated that they have information that could benefit the client, the team, or the organisation if they shared it but they are unable to do so. The issue for the coach is how to process their feelings about this so that their frustration does not damage their relationship with the client or their delivering effective coaching to them. Two common categories are:

- Client's personal issues having an impact on their performance (but the client not wanting anyone to know)
- Being unable to use information that could benefit the team/ organisation.

Personal issues: Clients sometimes have family problems that impact negatively on their performance: for example, the long term illness of a parent or child or a mental health issue for the client themselves that they do not want people, including their line manager, to know about. This can be exasperating for the coach who may feel that they would be better able to access support if they shared the information. However, some people tightly guard their privacy.

Case study 3.2: Managing confidentiality

In their third session Sam, Ayesha's client, had revealed to her that she had been diagnosed with depression. In addition, her partner was having problems with anxiety that made it even more of a challenge to cope with her three young children. She was receiving counselling to address the non-work issues. After a discussion they decided that Sam would continue with the coaching as this was focused on her work performance. They agreed that if either Ayesha or Sam felt that her personal issues were impacting on her ability to get the most out of coaching they would take a break until Sam was in a better position to continue. Sam also said that no one at work was aware of her personal problems or that she was receiving counselling and she wanted it to remain that way. A few days later Ayesha received an email from Sam's line manager asking why Sam was underperforming at work as she wanted to know how she could help.

Question: What would you do in Ayesha's position?

Information that could benefit the team/organisation: Coaches will become aware of emerging organisational themes, such as very low morale in a particular part of the business because of the leadership style of one or more senior managers, and not necessarily know what to do with that information. Some organisations have set up mechanisms for garnering such systemic data but by no means all. See Chapter Five for more about this.

Coaches can also experience frustrations such as knowing that high performers whom senior managers consider to be heading for the top have no knowledge that they are regarded in this way and are planning to leave. The coach is not in a position to tell anyone of the client's intentions. They may, however, find a way of ensuring that the client at least receives the positive feedback from someone, without breaching their confidence.

Line managers' needs for information

Many coaches reported approaches from clients' line managers asking how the clients were getting on but acknowledged that the reason the managers were asking was usually less about curiosity and more about wanting to support the client.

Most coaches considered that it was the responsibility of the client to do any sharing of information with their line manager except where the accepted process involved a three-way meeting with the coach, client, and line manager at the beginning and end of the coaching programme.

A coach and the client's line manager can form a powerful alliance to support the client and as long as the client's confidentiality is protected, this can have great benefits. Amplification of some coaches' views on whom to share information with included:

> "It depends on the contracting. Most of my coaching is on a two-way contract, in which case the client manages what and how information from sessions is disclosed to others. Occasionally there is three-way with the line manager, where I give them both the choice as to how they want to agree and share goals."

> "Depends on the reason for the coaching and whether they have been referred by someone (e.g., line manager) or self-referred."

"Client's sponsor and anyone else my clients choose to share them with".

A number of coaches also made the point that some goals may be shared with the line manager while other, more personal, goals are not.

None of the coaches shared the content of sessions with the line manager but, where they had a supervisor or were a member of a supervision group, they explained to the client that they shared information with that person or group on a non-attributable basis.

Keeping records of coaching conversations/using work email

Record keeping: It is good practice to keep client records of practical details, contact information, the signed contract and a log of the coaching undertaken. In addition, many coaches keep brief notes of coaching sessions. You should always be mindful that whatever you put in writing may be seen by others. The Data Protection Act is relevant to the security and retention of client records, and the legal requirements in it are discussed in Chapter Seven.

Facts and figures 3.9: Keeping records

- Ninety-three per cent of the internal coaches kept records of coaching conversations.
- In seventy-five per cent of those cases, only the coach had access to the notes (although the client has the right to see them under the Data Protection Act).
- In twenty per cent of them, the notes were sometimes shared with the clients.

A number of the coaches made the distinction between the notes they took about content and their personal reflections for their own development as coaches. One said:

"I'm happy to share these notes with my coachees. These would be notes made in the coaching session, but I would choose not to share my learning log with the coachee."

Most of them were unaware of any policy around how long client records should be retained.

A very small number of the coaches had a PA who could access the cabinet where the coaching notes were stored. If you are in this position, give some thought to how you can ensure that your client's privacy is not compromised.

Case study 3.3: Safeguarding clients' notes

Mary is head of strategy in a multinational company. She is an enthusiastic champion of the internal coaching effort, having originally trained many years ago, and is an active internal coach herself. She has been coaching in her current organisation for five years and has had around fifteen senior manager clients over that period. She has her own large office and keeps her coaching notes in a locked four-drawer filing cabinet next to her desk. She generally works from home on Fridays. One Friday she comes into work unexpectedly and finds her PA in her office, sitting at her meeting table, avidly reading the coaching notes that she has taken from the cabinet. After roundly reprimanding her PA she is faced with the dilemma of whether she should tell her clients that the confidentiality of their relationship has been breached.

Question: What would you do in Mary's position?

Using email: Another angle that coaches need to be aware of is the potential dangers of using company email for sensitive exchanges with clients. Using internal email for confidential correspondence does have its risks. Many senior managers' emails are seen by their PAs and even if the client is the only one who can normally access their in-box, they may give access to a colleague when they are out of the office for any significant length of time. A salutary case study on this issue appears in Chapter Seven.

The physical environment

Chapter Two mentions the difficulty of finding a coaching space that is conducive to good coaching: that is, one that avoids the formal, corporate feel of most meeting rooms but provides more tranquillity for reflection than is provided by a coffee shop and more privacy than is offered by a hotel lounge or café style area in an office building.

Linehan (2011) undertook some first stage research with fellow coaches into the impact of the venue on coaching relationships and noted the importance of discussing the client's preferences with them at the outset. Reflecting on the findings, she observed that the coaching environment—just like everything else in the coaching relationship—is co-created and is therefore also worth reflecting on with the client, and certainly worth revisiting periodically.

One important aspect to the physical environment highlighted by Linehan as needing attention is the confidentiality afforded by the venue and space used for the client session. There are three aspects to consider:

- Keeping the fact of the coaching relationship confidential
- Keeping the content of the sessions confidential
- Keeping any emotional component of the sessions confidential.

Keeping the fact of the coaching relationship confidential

In my research, eighty-nine per cent of the coaches considered the fact that they were coaching a particular individual to be confidential information in itself; six per cent did not; and four per cent were not sure. What is your view? Does your organisation have a policy on this? Is the fact that they have a coach something that your client has shared with their colleagues? Does it matter to them if you coach them in their part of the building where people who know them, and perhaps members of their team, will see them? If you are known to be an internal coach and you and your client are seen going into a meeting room together or leaving the building together, people may draw their own conclusions. Does this matter? It might be worth establishing this.

Keeping the content of the sessions confidential

Linehan noted that it is often the coach, rather than the client, who is conscious of being overheard in a public venue. The client can sometimes be blissfully unaware and happy to speak loudly about coaching issues. She commented that membership clubs or the foyer or lounge of a large hotel may seem ideal coaching locations but asks what happens if someone sits down near you and is reading a newspaper or working at a laptop and can therefore overhear? What if your client wants to discuss their relationship with senior people in the organisation whom the unwitting eavesdropper may coincidentally know?

Keeping any emotional component of the sessions confidential

Linehan's work also noted the possibility that a client might well become very emotional during a coaching session. If it is taking place in a public space, this could at worst cause them discomfort and acute embarrassment and at best leave them feeling exposed which could impact negatively on the effectiveness of the coaching conversation and potentially cause a rupture in the relationship. Meeting rooms with glass walls present similar risks of being seen at one's most vulnerable and may hinder the establishment of a safe coaching environment. Even a session that is billed to be about something cerebral can become emotional unexpectedly.

The impact of power in internal coaching

Issues involving organisational and position power can throw up dilemmas for internal coaches. This can come up in different guises.

Power within the coaching relationship: Ideally coaches want a coaching relationship to be collaborative, with the coach offering knowledge and expertise about the coaching process and the client offering knowledge and expertise on themselves and their area of work. The client is in charge of the agenda—though the coach may challenge them if they stray from what has been contracted for—and responsible for their own learning.

However, Wrynne (2011) noted that the clients in his study coached by internal coaches tended to look on their coaches as being "the embodiment of [the] organisation as if attributed with this power" (p. 59). This resulted in their casting their coaches in the role of mentors and founts of wisdom, as well as assuming that they could pull on levers to make things happen for them. Wrynne speculates:

> it might be suggested that there could be a perceived power imbalance more generally, whereby the internal context might frame the internal coach as distributing organisationally accepted knowledge or truth as an expert consultant rather than a collaborative partner. (p. 59)

The idea of the coach embodying the organisation can also result in the client looking to exert influence over the coach for their own ends.

Facts and figures 3.10: Client trying to influence the coach

The following are examples cited by internal coaches of the client having an agenda:

- "Coachee divulges information about close colleagues inviting me as his coach to collude."
- "Clients sharing views regarding colleagues and expecting me to share my own view."
- "One instance where I was asked to coach someone who had received feedback that he had been behaving inappropriately—negative comments about colleagues and excessive criticism about their organisation. He tried to use the coaching relationship to build a case for his defence."
- "Client 'used' coaching to complain about his experience of his line manager."

Sometimes the client, by telling the coach about their situation, feels they have told someone "in authority". This can be particularly pertinent when clients talk about bullying. You may need to be aware that the client could, consciously or unconsciously, be vesting you with this organisational authority.

Impact of power outside the coaching relationship: Hunt and Weintraub (2006) make the general point that the internal coach has to be careful about tangling with powerful figures in the organisation:

> The coach is dependent on the organisation for his/her salary ...
> [and] ... has to have the courage to speak truth unto power and the
> skill to know when and how to do so. (p. 3)

Some of my interviewees provided examples of where a power differential had thrown up a dilemma:

- It became clear fairly early on in a coaching assignment that a client was seriously under-performing, was unlikely ever to perform satisfactorily, and that the line manager was attempting to duck his responsibilities by handing the problem over to the coach rather than addressing it himself. The coach knew that he should tackle the line manager about this but he also knew that this manager, a dominant and somewhat abrasive character, was a rising star who was likely to be increasingly influential in the future and could one day be his boss.

- A gifted coach with a busy day job was asked by her client, a senior leader in another part of the business, if she would work with his entire team. While it was a massive compliment and would be an exciting assignment, she was already stretched by fitting just one coaching client in with her existing workload, never mind four. However, she felt hesitant about refusing the client as he was a powerful leader in the organisation who had a reputation for categorising people as "for him" or "against him".
- A very experienced coach found that she was hearing stories from different clients about the same senior person using bullying behaviour. She knew that she should "speak truth unto power" but she also knew that the person to whom she should take the issue, the HR director, was a close friend of the alleged bully and had bullying tendencies herself.

Deciding how to handle issues that throw up ethical dilemmas is the subject of the next chapter.

Summary

The purpose of this chapter was to raise your awareness of the practical nature of ethical dilemmas rather than seeing them as abstract concepts. Being able to recognise situations that require a decision or action to prevent your professional integrity as a coach being compromised is key. This will help you to put in place the processes and support mechanisms that minimise the risk of making poor decisions or taking no action when action is needed.

Case studies unpacked

Case study 3.1 [page 45]

Paul discussed this with his supervisor. He realised that there were three issues for him:

- His judgement around Angela's suitability for being a coach
- His feeling of being manipulated: when Angela said she wanted to be "coached through the application process" his sense was that she really wanted some insider information on the types of questions

and so forth since Paul had been through the process successfully seven months earlier, and

- The purpose of the coaching in the original contract, that the organisation was supporting, was to increase her effectiveness as a leader in some specific ways.

Having explored the issues with his supervisor, Paul decided to front up the issue around the purpose of the coaching and the original three-way contract. In his next coaching session with Angela he explained his position and suggested that they explore some options. They discussed Angela's talking with her line manager, and agreed that the next session would focus on helping her prepare for this meeting. Angela said she would think about it and get back to Paul. She did not schedule another meeting.

Case study 3.2 [page 53]

Ayesha had a discussion with the HR business partner to check the relevant policies around disclosure and confirmed that there was no duty on her as a coach to disclose information relating to health or well-being. However, she was concerned that Sam's determination not to tell her boss was actually sabotaging her ability to access help. Over a number of sessions Sam came to her own conclusion that it would be a good idea to share the situation with her line manager, on condition that Ayesha accompanied her to the meeting. At the meeting, it was agreed that her workload would be reduced for a short period.

Note: Often the client is not prepared to co-operate in this kind of approach and the coach may find themselves listening to the line manager or other colleagues talking about their puzzlement as to why the client's performance has taken a dive but being unable to shed any light on the matter.

Case study 3.3 [page 56]

After a quick telephone conversation with her supervisor, Mary decided to get her PA to sign a short agreement that she would not divulge any of what she had read to anyone; and to take the matter no further. However, she made it very clear to her PA that it was never to happen again.

QUESTIONS TO REFLECT ON

Factor to consider	What are the implications for me?
What are ethical dilemmas? What are the potential ethical dilemmas for an internal coach, in a role like mine, in my organisation?	• Does my role make me particularly susceptible to any particular variety of ethical dilemma?

Areas that can throw up dilemmas **Boundaries** The following issues relate to boundaries for what is in and out of scope for my coaching:
• Professional competence
• Role conflicts
• Maintaining objectivity and independence
• Work life *vs.* personal life
• Coaching *vs.* mentoring
• The role boundary between a coach and the client's line manager
	• What type of issues may be "out of scope" for me as I do not have the experience to deal with them?
	• Where may it be a challenge for me to stay dispassionate? What type of issues are difficult for me?
	• What options are available in my organisation for me to refer clients to who may need counselling or other types of professional support?
	• Where may my functional role have the potential to raise a conflict of interest in relation to the clients I choose to work with because:
	  – our professional networks overlap
	  – "insider knowledge" may mean I may have relevant information pertaining to my client that I cannot share
	  – I have the ability to "fix" a problem for my client
	• If my client appears to need a more "mentoring approach" or asks me for advice, what will my response be?

(Continued)

QUESTIONS TO REFLECT ON   (*Continued*)

Factor to consider	*What are the implications for me?*
	• How do I feel about three-way meetings with my client and their line manager? Is this something I want to initiate if it is not a requirement in my organisation?
	• How will I deal with a client's line manager who wishes me to do his job as a manager for him?
Areas that can throw up dilemmas **Confidentiality** Areas I need to consider dealing with:	
• Limits to confidentiality	• Where could maintaining client confidentiality contravene organisational policies?
• Strains in keeping confidentiality:	• How familiar am I with organisational policies? How will I deal with these issues?
– Client raising personal issues	
– Having information that may benefit the team or organisation	• Who has access to my filing cabinet, computer, calendar, emails? What are the implications for:
– Line manager wants information	– storing my coaching records?
– Keeping records of coaching conversations/using work email	– recording coaching sessions in my calendar?
– The physical environment	– using work emails to correspond with my clients?
	• Where will the best places be to hold coaching sessions so that I can ensure:
	– the coaching relationship is kept confidential (if applicable)
	– no one can overhear us
	– no one can see the client if they become emotional

(*Continued*)

QUESTIONS TO REFLECT ON   (*Continued*)

Factor to consider	What are the implications for me?
Areas that can throw up dilemmas **Power Differentials** I need to consider power differentials, including: • Clients attributing me with the ability to "make things happen" because of my position in the organisation • Senior members of the organisation having their own agenda	• How will I identify clients who have an "agenda" for coaching unrelated to their development needs? If I recognise this is happening how will I deal with it? • What can I do to ensure I do not get caught in the middle of a "power play"?

CHAPTER FOUR

Addressing ethical dilemmas

In the Book of Life, the answers aren't in the back

—*Charlie Brown*

What this chapter is about

I hope that I have whetted your appetite for thinking about the ethics of coaching and have removed any mystique there may have been around the word ethical in the context of coaching. This chapter aims to demonstrate the importance of ethics in an internal coach's practice and offer some ideas for those occasions when a dilemma is that bit trickier to resolve. In the last chapter, I made reference to a variety of dilemmas of varying difficulty but was careful to avoid suggesting that there was a "right" answer for any particular situation. This is because the defining feature of a dilemma is that there is probably no one right answer—it will come down to context, culture, and the ethical stance of the individual. Basically we will not all necessarily make the same decision when faced with the same situation.

This chapter explores:

- Contracting: reducing the scope for ethical dilemmas
- The importance of behaving ethically: three main theoretical stances
- What unethical behaviour looks like and the three levels of factors—personal, situational, and organisational—that can make it more likely to occur
- Where our own personal ethical codes come from
- Ethical maturity and ethical sensitivity
- Making and implementing ethical decisions
- How we live and learn from our decisions
- A framework for ethical decision making.

Some of you may not yet have encountered an ethical dilemma or, if you have, it may have been fairly easily addressed. But it would be a very unusual coach who never had to resolve an ethical dilemma in the course of their coaching. The importance of being able to recognise and handle dilemmas ethically is recognised by the coach selectors in an international bank referenced by Hawkins (2012). They said that one of the questions that helped them to separate the external coaches that they accepted from those they turned down was: "Please describe an ethical dilemma you have faced in your coaching and how you dealt with it" (p. 53). The thinking underlying my original research with internal coaches was that they were likely to be exposed to more dilemmas than external coaches are and that is why how to recognise and resolve ethical dilemmas holds a special place in this book.

A number of writers have written thoughtfully on this subject. Drawing on their work, I will describe a practical process for ethical decision-making that can help you to work your way through to a resolution of an issue or, if not a resolution, then at least an accommodation.

First, however, let us address how to minimise the likelihood of dilemmas arising in the first place, through the use of tight contracting.

Contracting

At the beginning of every coaching relationship is a conversation about each party's expectations of the other and what the ground rules are. Chapter Seven covers in more detail what such an oral or written contract might cover. Sometimes it is only when a difficult situation arises that a new coach appreciates the crucial importance of the contracting phase. When your client cancels a session at very short notice for the third time, at considerable inconvenience to you, then you might wish that you had remembered to discuss the arrangements around cancellations at the outset. Or if you have inadvertently implied that you are offering your client complete confidentiality, with no exclusions, then you will be in a very difficult place if she owns up to something fraudulent and refuses to do anything to redress the situation. Or if you have said nothing about boundaries and the client wants to discuss his marriage problems with you in session three and becomes irate when you explain that it is beyond your brief because "you said that the agenda was mine to decide and now you're changing the rules", you might think ruefully of how you could have expressed yourself better.

Tight contracting will not wholly ensure that ethical dilemmas no longer arise. However, by being very clear with the client from the start what the ground rules are around the sharing of information and boundary management, you can reduce the scope for dilemmas further down the track. In my 2009 research, I asked a question at the end of the survey questionnaire about what aspects of their role as an internal coach the questionnaire had helped them to reflect on. A number of them volunteered that it had either reminded them of the importance of clear contracting or made them realise that they needed to pay more attention to it.

If you have a written contract with the client, you are less dependent on remembering to contract for everything important in the first coaching session (as long as you draw the client's attention to what is in the contract and make sure that they have read it).

The importance of behaving ethically

Ethics—the three main theoretical stances

Many of us, if asked what moral framework we espouse or what our moral philosophy is, would stumble giving an answer. If asked specifically in the context of our work as a coach, some of us might refer to the code of ethics espoused by our particular professional body (if we belong to one) or perhaps a code that we were introduced to while training. But how recently would we have read it? How much does this matter? All the coaching professional bodies require their members to abide by their ethical codes and the International Coach Federation (ICF) requires members to sign a statement of agreement and compliance with the pledge of ethics and standards of ethical conduct as part of their application for accreditation and whenever they renew their credentials. We shall come to codes of ethics a little later. For now, let us look at the dominant theories about ethics.

The Oxford English Dictionary defines ethics as "the moral principles that govern a person's behaviour". These moral principles have, of course, been the subject of debate for thousands of years. The next few paragraphs offer a very simplified account of the three dominant theories. For more about them, particularly how they play out in relation to coaching and counselling, see Carroll and Shaw (2013) and Williams and Anderson (2006). Steare (2009) has written about how to behave ethically and I am using the labels he proposed for the three theories as they are somewhat more accessible than the labels used by philosophers. I am also drawing on some of Steare's explanations.

Principled conscience

Known as "virtue ethics", this school of thought originated with Aristotle (384–322 BC). In this approach our decisions are driven by the values we live by, such as: courage, trust, truth, respect, humility, fairness, loyalty, kindness. So we make decisions as much with our hearts as with our heads and they come from somewhere deep within us. If we successfully live by our values we can be said to have integrity. However, problems can occur if a situation forces us to choose between two (or more) competing values: for example, truth and kindness. Say you have interviewed half a dozen of a client's colleagues as part of a qualitative 360-degree feedback exercise (i.e., getting feedback from the client's boss, peers, and staff) and are now typing up a non-attributable report based on the interviews. Usually you quote interviewees' views *verbatim*, and have always done so when writing such reports in the past, but three of your client's colleagues have suggested that he is incompetent, using phrases like: "Does this guy ever do any work? I've yet to see the evidence" and "You ask about his strengths but I simply can't think of one". You had suspected that your client might be underperforming and you know that he is currently anxious and severely lacking in confidence but you were not expecting the 360 to be so brutal. Do you include all the remarks, however expressed (truth), or modify them to avoid undermining him still further (kindness)?

Social conscience

Known to philosophers as "utilitarianism", this moral theory was pioneered by Jeremy Bentham (1748–1832). His doctrine holds that an action is "right" if it is useful or for the benefit of the majority. People sometimes talk about this theory in terms of "maximising happiness and minimising suffering". If our natural stance is utilitarian, we are likely to take decisions with our heads rather than our hearts, in the sense that it involves a careful weighing up of the pros and cons of any course of action and the likely consequences of what we decide to do. If you take this view, what impact might it have on a decision, say, as to whether to report a colleague who uses bullying behaviour? A problem with the utilitarian approach is: if your action reflects the interests of the majority, how should you protect the interests of the minority?

Rule compliance

This approach, known as "deontology" (derived from the Greek word for "obligation") was first developed by Immanuel Kant (1724–1804). It describes an ethical stance that springs from our perception of our rights and duties. We would aim to take the "right" decision according to our legal and moral obligations. Laws emerge from a collective agreement (mandated to our members of parliament) as to our rights and responsibilities as citizens or employers. In the workplace, rights and responsibilities are agreed by the employer, often in consultation with representatives of employees, enshrined in an employee handbook, and enforced by HR.

Steare (2009) notes that rule compliance "tells us what's right" and "helps when we can't always agree on what's right". However, he also points out that "too many rules tend to make us lazy in taking responsibility for our own actions and we can never write enough rules to cover every situation" (p. 31). If we have a strong sense of the importance of obeying rules, where might it take us in a situation where our client is something of a free spirit and, say, displays what we regard as a rather cavalier approach to the claiming of expenses?

An example of these three approaches in action: your boss unnecessarily and, in your view, brutally dresses down a colleague in front of the whole team. The colleague abruptly leaves the room, visibly upset. You are shocked and after careful thought decide to go and see your boss to say that you regard his behaviour as unacceptable ("speaking truth unto power"). Your grounds for deciding to take this action could be:

- You would rather temporarily damage your relationship with your boss than witness this kind of disrespectful behaviour without speaking out (principled conscience—your boss has violated your values in relation to showing respect for others and kindness);
- Others might suffer from the same behaviour if you do not take action and bring your boss up short (social conscience—your relationship with your boss might be harmed in the short term but a number of your colleagues will benefit if your boss's behaviour changes); or
- There is an anti-bullying policy in your organisation and one of the organisational values that senior managers have all signed up to is "showing respect" (rule compliance—your boss has broken the rules).

On the other hand, you might judge that your boss's response to an intervention from you would result in making your life very difficult while failing to benefit your colleagues. This could still be interpreted as a utilitarian (social conscience) stance, but is very different from the one cited above. What then? My purpose in outlining these theories here is that they can act as a catalyst for reflecting on what our own moral drivers might be, and what that reflection might mean for a) how we usually take ethical decisions and b) whether we might consciously adapt our approach in future.

What does unethical behaviour look like?

When thinking about ethical behaviour in the context of coaching, it can be instructive to start with what unethical behaviour looks like. Allan, Passmore, and Mortimer (2011) provide some examples of behaviour that most of us would immediately recognise as unethical:

- Telling your friends and family interesting details about clients
- Using the names of "impressive" clients to drum up more business
- Claiming to have experience you don't have
- Reading a book about suicide because you have no idea what to say in the next session to a coachee who said she wanted to kill herself

- Agreeing to coach someone on the basis that "we just need you to deliver three sessions here because we can say we tried, but they are getting the push anyway". (p. 163)

Additional examples of obviously unethical behaviour based on some of the situations raised in the last chapter could be:

- Encouraging a client to talk about their negative experiences of working with a colleague whom you know well, without revealing that you know them, because of your curiosity about what they might say
- Omitting to declare that you are coaching one of the candidates in a promotion process where you are one of the selectors
- Colluding with the client to develop a strategy for undermining a colleague whom the client is having trouble with and whom you don't like either.

It is the huge grey areas, however, that are more of an issue. Take the situation where your client wants to discuss their relationship with a colleague whom you know very well. Have you contracted with the client about what you will do in a situation like this? Do you decide to keep your counsel? Do you tell them that your relationship with the other person precludes your coaching them on this topic? Do you declare your interest but then carry on? Do you refer them to another coach for this particular topic? Do you discuss with the client the possibility that you may have more than this person in common and whether they should permanently switch to another coach?

Carroll and Shaw (2013) draw attention to factors at three levels that can make unethical behaviour more likely, such as:

Personal factors: A major personal factor is a lack of self-awareness. Others could be self-interest, laziness, or a lack of courage. Sometimes we may put our own interests ahead of those of our clients or the greater good—or we may take the easier path of doing nothing out of indolence or faint-heartedness.

Situational factors: We all feel the need to be accepted and could find ourselves acting unethically if the alternative is to be out of step with the group. We have to keep working with the other people involved. Many of us also feel some deference to authority and would find it difficult to stand out against the views of a senior colleague. Both these factors can undermine our good intentions (and underline the importance of the lead coach setting a good example and reminding all the internal coaches regularly of the importance of behaving in an ethical way).

Organisational factors: Organisations can develop a tolerance of unethical behaviour such as turning a blind eye to fiddling expenses, using the internet recreationally during working hours, or knowingly selling to a customer products that do not meet their needs. An organisational culture that tolerates such behaviour can influence an individual coach's reaction to situations that require an ethical response. For example, if HR practices are known to be lax in an organisation, it could be considerably more difficult for a coach to speak up if a client were to let slip that they were having an affair with someone in their team whom they were going to promote.

Why do ethics matter?

Highly ethical behaviour is particularly important in coaching because of the intimate nature of many coaching relationships. Clients are putting themselves in a vulnerable position by sharing their feelings, anxieties, and innermost thoughts and we must respect the trust that the client puts in us. There are a variety of reasons why it is important that, as an internal coach, you behave—and can be seen to behave—ethically. The following are a few of them:

- At work, as in life in general, it is important to do what is "right";
- As a coach you are setting an example to your client, whether that is how you see your role or not;
- As a coach you are setting an example within your organisation, whether that is how you see your role or not;
- If you collude with your client or fail to take appropriate action on something that you become privy to through your coaching relationship with them, and it comes out, it could severely damage your personal reputation, your reputation as a coach, and the reputation of coaching within your organisation;
- As a coach, you are subject to your profession's code of ethics (whether you are formally a member of a professional coaching body or not) so are under an obligation to behave ethically.

The potential for damage, if an internal coach makes an unethical decision or fails to take a decision at all, can be greater than if the same situation arose for an external coach because you represent the values of the internal coaching service. Some of the reasons above clearly reflect one of the dominant moral philosophies. Which of them speaks to you most strongly will reflect your own natural ethical stance.

Where do our personal ethics come from?

We get our sense of what is right and wrong from our parents, extended families, friends, neighbourhood, and national culture. When I grew up, the process for making telephone calls from public phone boxes involved putting in the coins, dialling the number, pressing Button A if you got through (and you would hear the coins dropping inside the machine) or pressing Button B if you did not (and your coins would be returned to you). Occasionally an absent-minded caller who had failed to get through might forget to press Button B to retrieve the coins so would leave them behind. School friends alerted me to this situation and every time I passed a phone box I would nip in and press Button B, just in case. One day I returned from school in triumph: I'd pressed Button B and some coins came out! But my father was horrified. In his mind it was tantamount to stealing. My mother disagreed with him. I was only eight but I still remember it. Whose side would you be on?

Developing ethical maturity

Carroll and Shaw (2013) in their terrific book *Ethical Maturity in the Helping Professions: Making Difficult Life and Work Decisions* write about how we can train ourselves to develop ethical maturity. They define it as: "Having the reflective, rational and intuitive capacity to decide actions are right and wrong or good and better, having the resilience and courage to implement those decisions, being accountable for ethical decisions made (publicly or privately), being able to live with the decisions made and integrating the learning into our moral character and future actions" (p. 137).

In this short chapter I obviously cannot do full justice to the entirety of the book but I highly recommend it to any coach wanting to develop their ethical instincts. It caused me to reflect on a number of past decisions and learn from them in a way that I would not otherwise have done. The next sections draw heavily on their work.

Carroll and Shaw suggest six component parts to ethical maturity:

1. To foster ethical sensitivity and watchfulness: the creation of ethical antennae that keep us alert to when ethical issues/dilemmas are present

2. The ability to make a moral decision aligned to our ethical principles and values
3. To implement ethical decisions made
4. The ability to articulate and justify to stakeholders the reasons why ethical decisions were made and implemented
5. To achieve closure on the event, even when other possible decisions or "better" decisions could have been made.
6. To learn from what has happened and "test" the decision through reflection. The integration of what we have learned into our lives develops our moral character and extends our ethical wisdom and capacity.

Ethical sensitivity

As mentioned earlier, I see ethical decision-making in a coaching context as an intensely practical subject. We are not conducting an esoteric discussion about how many angels can dance on the head of a pin. But rather, recognising and resolving real life issues such as: whether we should tell a client to stop wasting their own and our time agonising about whether to go for a potential promotion because we know, wearing another hat, that it's already sewn up; whether we should accept a client because we suspect it could be useful to our career in the organisation to build that relationship, even though we know that another coach has more relevant skills and experience; whether to tell someone that our very stressed client has mentioned, lightly, that sometimes they fantasise about "ending it all". How good are we at spotting when something *is* an ethical issue?

Depending on your personal ethical stance—irrespective of whether it is instinctive or articulated—a decision on one or more of the three examples in the last paragraph might be completely obvious to you or might involve a great deal of thought. Carroll and Shaw's thesis is that while we have inherited a particular moral template from our families, peers, and communities, by examining and articulating our values and ethical stance we are in a better position to evaluate them and, if necessary, change them. Do our inherited values reflect what we now, as an adult, believe? This line of thought may also highlight for us that there are some perspectives that do not come naturally to us.

Carroll and Shaw (2013) float some ideas as to how we might foster our ethical sensitivity. Some of these are:

- Knowing ourselves
- Raising our levels of awareness
- Being aware of our values
- Empathising with others' perspectives
- Active listening to ourselves and others
- Reflecting on our actions. (pp. 150–151)

These activities are all pretty familiar territory for coaches. The processes of giving and receiving feedback, raising our levels of self-awareness, reflecting on our core values, beliefs, biases, and actions, and empathising with others, are central to our training and continuous learning. One could argue that coaches should, in that respect, be ahead of the game. Developing our ethical maturity is partly about consciously taking into that ethical arena our ability to reflect on our practice and to challenge ourselves. Are we confident that our instincts accurately let us know when an issue needs our mindful attention?

One way of developing our ethical antennae is to think about how we would respond in certain scenarios. I hope that the examples in Chapter Three will have provided some practice. One very helpful source of scenarios is "The Ethics Column", written by Dr. Julie Allan in *The Coaching Psychologist*: a journal published by the British Psychological Society's special group in coaching psychology (SGCP). The column often includes a hypothetical situation entitled "What would you do if …?" and provides points for reflection.

Facts and figures 4.1: The value of reflection

The questionnaire I used in my research asked the internal coaches what aspects of their role the questionnaire had helped them to reflect upon. Some of their responses were:
- "Very helpful in reflecting on my own ethical practice."
- "I realise I need to think more deeply about my ethics and ensure they are clear. I need to write them down."
- "Recognising ethical dilemmas. There are times when I have not fully addressed these and preferred to continue in the hope that they will resolve themselves."
- "My preparedness to deal with difficult ethical issues—I think I would manage, but haven't had much preparation."

The point here is that the simple process of completing a questionnaire had been the catalyst for some helpful thinking. We all need some kind of trigger to ensure that we make the time for conscious reflection. Supervision is, of course, an example of protected time for such thinking.

I am not aware of any research looking at the relationship between experience as a coach and incidence of ethical issues arising. One could argue that experienced coaches are more likely to contract strictly and clearly and therefore encounter fewer dilemmas. Anecdotal evidence from my interviews with internal coaches over the past few years, however, suggests that experienced coaches are much more likely to identify an issue as having an ethical aspect, which probably reflects a more developed ethical sensitivity.

Making ethical decisions

A dilemma is not a dilemma if there is an obvious line to take. It would be an unusual coach who did not recognise that it was completely out of order to:

- Sexually harass the client
- Encourage them in illegal activities, or
- Ignore clear evidence that they were physically harming themselves or colleagues.

Many ethical issues that arise, however, are less clear-cut and each one is unique. Even if the issue is a common one, the culture of the organisation, the context, the client, the interested parties (and what their various interests are), and your own beliefs, values, age, experience, education, and so forth, will differ from another coach's. You may subscribe to the view that there are objective truths to be discerned, or that you create your own truths based on your own moral values, but either way your challenge is to find a way forward that will be aligned with those truths.

Fans of the developmental tool MBTI (Myers Briggs, 2000), based on the theories of Carl Jung, will be familiar with the concept that people tend towards taking decisions either with their heads or with their hearts. It is common for the former to examine carefully the pros and cons of doing something, stepping back, and trying to consider the issue objectively, and for the latter to come to a decision intuitively, often driven by their values and by the importance to them of their relationships with the people likely to be affected by the decision.

Some would argue that one can never be truly impartial and that the "thinkers" underestimate the actual influence of their emotions on the decision (and how their emotions may be skewing the readiness with which various pros or cons come to them) and that the "feelers" will unconsciously be bringing to bear what they have cognitively learned from past experiences when they get their hunches about what the "right" decision is.

Carroll and Shaw make the case for consciously using a multi-perspective approach to decision-making. So:

- Reflecting on the issue in a mindful way
- Being aware of our biases, drivers, and motives
- Getting in touch with what our feelings are telling us, and
- Using our thinking selves to articulate the arguments for different potential ways forward.

The emphasis is on the importance of taking care to examine any ethical dilemma from a number of perspectives in a deliberate and conscious way rather than simply automatically taking our usual preferred approach to decision-making.

One of the benefits of a deliberative process, in addition to ensuring that we take a step back and challenge our automatic responses, is that we articulate our rationale, and this allows us to critique it. If we then discuss that rationale with someone we trust, such as another coach or our supervisor, and it stands up, we can begin to have some confidence that it is the right approach—or at least an ethically defensible one.

The final stage before moving to implement the decision might be to ask yourself the following sorts of questions:

- If the client were to take out a grievance against me, how would I explain my decision?
- What did the person I discussed it with think of it?
- How would my professional body (if any) view it?
- If another coach came up against a similar issue, would I suggest they made a similar response?
- If it became public that this was what I had done, would I feel in any way ashamed of it?

Then there is the killer question: If I am reluctant to talk about this or share it with others then do I need to review the decision I am thinking of making or the action I am planning to take?

Resources, skills, and self-awareness necessary to make mature ethical decisions

Resources

- Knowledge of ethical theories and codes
- Clear problem-solving model using supervision and others, e.g., peers, to help make clear decision
- Discussions with others (particularly those with a different viewpoint)

Skills

- Systemic approach (needs of individuals, community, society, and professions)
- Able to integrate emotion, intuition, reason, and decision-making
- Able to reflect deeply
- Able to be open, stand back from, and keep bigger pictures in view
- Notice external pressures to make a decision one way or another

Self-awareness

- Access feelings, hunches, and intuition
- Aware of own ethical stance
- Alert to assumptions brought to ethical discernment
- Knowing own vulnerabilities and biases
- Awareness of usual approach to decision-making (alive to strengths and limitations)

(Adapted from Carroll & Shaw (2013, p. 206) with permission from Jessica Kingsley Publishers)

Looking at the components of resources, skills, and self-awareness needed to make mature ethical decisions, how would you self-assess against each of the requirements using a scale one to ten, where ten is "fully met"? Where you scored yourself nine or lower, what would you need to do to get yourself to a ten?

Implementing ethical decisions

I suspect that many coaches have had the experience of discussing an ethical issue with their supervisor or another coach, deciding to take a particular action, and then not doing so. By the time we next see the client, the situation may have changed or moved on, or the issue no longer seems so important to them. There might be countless good reasons why we tell ourselves that it was no longer appropriate to pursue it. Equally, it may be that we lacked the courage to follow through so, in effect, took the "do nothing" option. Where was the value in the agonising and the deciding if we did not follow through? It may have sharpened our ethical sensitivities but surely that is not enough in itself?

The subtitle of Steare's (2009) book about ethics is: *How to Decide What's Right and Find the Courage to Do It.* The word courage also appears in Carroll and Shaw's definition of ethical maturity. Sometimes taking a particular decision to act, particularly if a senior or powerful player within the organisation is involved, can require the coach to dig deep. Clarkson (1997) talks about how we can find ourselves taking the "bystander stance" and letting things happen. Do you feel that you hold your clients to account? What about a client who makes, say, a racist or a sexist joke in a session or in your presence in front of other people. Would you collude and say nothing or speak up?

I have been fortunate in speaking to many internal coaches who have acted on their ethical instincts. One very experienced coach, with an HR background, told me that she had had to take a variety of issues outside the coaching room in her ten years as a coach. They included bullying, sexual harassment, mental health, assault, and alcohol abuse. She had never had to blow the whistle, as such, but found other ways of resolving the situations.

There can be all sorts of reasons why we fail to implement an ethical decision. Lack of courage may well be one, particularly if the client is resisting all attempts to resolve the issue and whistle blowing begins to look like the only option left. But we may also fall prey to convincing ourselves that the issue is not so important after all or simply find ourselves procrastinating. As coaches, many of us will have approaches that we use with clients to help them to conquer procrastination. These are the times when we need to draw on those strategies ourselves. A classic one is to tell someone what we plan to do, to give us that extra little piece of motivation actually to do it.

Carroll and Shaw (2013) suggest some questions that you could ask yourself if you know you are not implementing a decision that you should:

- What steps do I need to take to implement my ethical decisions?
- What people are involved and need to be told?

- What restraints are there on me *not* to implement this ethical decision (politics, protection of someone or some organisation, rationalisation, my image, etc.)?
- What support is needed by me (or others) to implement this decision?
- What risks am I taking in implementing my ethical decision?
- What other ethical issues arise as a result of implementing this decision? (pp. 234–235)

There is also, of course, the classic coaching question to ask yourself honestly: "What's stopping me?"

Articulating the rationale/ethical accountability

Carroll and Shaw talk about justifying to stakeholders the reasons why ethical decisions were made and implemented and being accountable for them. Of course, the vast majority of ethical decisions that we make as coaches will not be occasions for major whistle blowing, pose a risk to our jobs, or appear in newspapers. They are more likely to be decisions taken and implemented with only ourselves and our client knowing about them—or even just ourselves. But Rawls' test: "*Every moral action must meet the test of publicity*" (Rawls, 1971, p. 175) is still a helpful one.

If we have thought through our decision from multiple perspectives; discussed it with our supervisor or another experienced coach; articulated a defensible ethical rationale (including, if relevant, what rules, policies, or ethical codes we have consulted); and then implemented it, then we should be in the best possible position to explain why we have done what we have done if the issue were ever to come into the public domain. Carroll and Shaw, in including this element in their steps to ethical maturity, are concerned that we also continue to tell the "truth" about why we took the action we did and that we should be alert to our natural propensity to present our intentions and actions in the best possible light by massaging the story retrospectively. That is why it is so important to put into words—written down—our reasons for taking the action we have and to double check with a peer or supervisor (or anyone prepared to give attention to our story and challenge us, if necessary) our real motivations and whether we have enacted the values that we claim to espouse.

The following story illustrates a situation where a different decision would have been taken if the coach had articulated her rationale and tested it out with someone.

Case study 4.1: Managing personal boundaries

A coach at a conference told me about an incident that, retrospectively, she recognised as having been a poor decision. Her client had become very anxious and had been prescribed medication, which had helped but had made her feel sluggish. She had lost all motivation at work and kept referring to what a mess her house was in and how, after a house move some months before, she still had not unpacked. A particular room full of unpacked boxes seemed to have become a physical metaphor for her lack of motivation on all fronts. After several unproductive sessions the coach, who happened to live not far from the client, asked if she would like her to visit one weekend and help to unpack that room of boxes. Her rationale was around seeing if removing the physical block had a positive impact on the mental block and that it might allow the client to access her energy again, plus a desire to signal her support for the client. She knew that she was doing something unconventional. The outcome for the client's motivation seemed positive and the client was also grateful that the coach had gone the extra mile. However, over the following months the coach realised that by crossing that boundary into the client's private life she had created a different kind of relationship, involving an element of dependency, which proved hard to break. When she eventually disentangled herself, it was at a permanent cost to the relationship. The coach told me that if she had had to articulate the rationale for her decision, given it some real, deliberative thought, and had tested it (she did not have a supervisor at the time), she would have known that it was a false step, as it would not have stood up to that level of scrutiny. She also recognised, in retrospect, that the driver had actually partly been her own intense frustration at the client's lack of progress. The room of boxes had actually become a symbol of her own inability as a coach to help the client to move forward. She had been seduced into inappropriately crossing a boundary in trying to rescue the client rather than building the client's capacity to progress by herself.

Nash (2002) suggests that when we review our decision, we ask ourselves the following sorts of questions (which we could just as well use when we are in the midst of taking the decision):

- If my decision were to receive heavy media coverage, would I blush in shame or beam with pride?
- Could I explain my ethical decision with clarity and honour to those I love (my partner, my children, and my closest friends)?
- Would my professional community support my decision with enthusiasm and without reservation?
- Would my personal integrity remain intact if my decision became known? If not, am I willing to compromise it for the sake of doing the expedient thing, or merely pleasing others?
- Could I defend my decision before the ethics committee of my professional organisation?
- Would I make the same decision again in similar circumstances? (Cited in Carroll & Shaw, 2013, p. 248)

At the end of the day, as professional coaches we are both responsible for what we do and accountable to others for doing it ethically. Being able to articulate the reasons for our actions is an important element in the process of being held to account.

Living with the decision

Nobody's perfect. We will not always make the best decision or we might make an excellent decision but then bungle the implementation or fail to implement it fully. But for good or ill, once it's done, it's done. Carroll and Shaw make a bid for our not being too hard on ourselves. We have to live with our limitations as well as the consequences of our decisions. Supervision can help a great deal here. If we fear that we have stood by when we should have made a stand, but the time for doing so has passed, then we need to forgive ourselves.

Reflection is good but there is a difference between healthy, generative reflection that builds our ethical awareness and allowing past mistakes to prey upon our minds. However, if our reflection leads us to realise that there is some ameliorative action or apology that we could make, then that is all to the good and will, once done, leave us in a more serene place.

Learning from the decision

An important aspect of developing ethical maturity is learning from experience. Carroll and Shaw refer to creating new habits of excellence through reflecting on ethical decisions we have taken and integrating those reflections into our learning. Reflection can be done in many ways: in a solitary state or in a dialogue with one or more other people. Some people swear by learning journals, others find discussions much more fruitful. Chapter Nine outlines a variety of ways in which coaches might be supported in their reflection (such as one-to-one or group supervision, guided critical reflection, action learning, continuous professional development, peer coaching, and others). The supervision space is not just for helping to make a decision in the first place, or for talking about client issues, but is also an opportunity to reflect at intervals on our own practice including how we can integrate the learning from past decisions into our ethical approach for the future. Sometimes we need some time to elapse after the event to make sense of it—and also to know what the longer-term consequences of it may have been for the people involved.

An ethical decision-making model

I believe that we all either have or could benefit from having a model to help us to think through how we resolve specific dilemmas that we encounter in our practice. The following draws on both Carroll and Shaw's work on ethical maturity and Duff and Passmore's (2010) ACTION model. Obviously the process will not always, in practice, be as linear as it looks.

1. *Awareness*: This involves being aware of a) our own ethical stance, values, and beliefs and b) our professional body's code of ethics (or the code of ethics to which our own organisation subscribes). In Chapter Seven I discuss the need for organisations to adopt a code of ethics for the guidance of their internal coaches.
2. *Identification*: Is the issue an ethical dilemma? What makes it a dilemma? From where does the sense of conflict or competing interests arise? Is there a sensitive power dimension? Who are the interested parties? What would the consequences be if we did nothing? How much would that matter? On a scale of nought to

ten how important does it feel that we should do something? What feelings does it raise for us?

3. *Reflection*: Taking a multi-perspective view-point, rather than playing simply to our own preferences, helps us to avoid missing something important:

- Reflecting on the issue in a mindful way
- Being aware of our biases, drivers, and motives
- Getting in touch with what our feelings are telling us, and
- Using our thinking selves to articulate the arguments for different potential ways forward.

The aim of our reflections will be to identify our options for action.

4. *Consultation*: This is the point at which we check out our emerging conclusions with others, whether a supervisor, a fellow coach, or simply someone whose judgement we respect and trust. In some cases we may need to consider consulting a lawyer. If one of the potential ways forward is "do nothing" (as will often be the case) then it should be subjected to intense scrutiny, with the aid of the colleague, in case we have been seduced into Clarkson's (1997) bystander stance and are allowing ourselves the excuse that "It's really nothing to do with me" or "I don't have all the relevant information". At the end of the day, if we omit to take appropriate action and it comes out, our reputation is as much on the line as if we took some inappropriate action.

5. *Evaluation*: The options need to be considered in the light of our ethical code and any relevant contracting document, such as between coach and client or coach and employer. This is the stage at which the consequences of different courses of action for everyone involved, including ourselves, should be evaluated—in particular, how each of those courses of action would affect the welfare of each party.

6. *Decision*: Having arrived at a decision as to the best way forward, this is the moment to be making the final check against the sorts of questions outlined earlier in this chapter: for example, "Would my professional community support this decision without reservation?" and "If it became public that this was what I had done, would I find it easy to defend?" and so forth. Then we should articulate our rationale as honestly as we can and make a record of how we arrived at our conclusion.

7. *Implementation*: As described earlier in this chapter, this may require courage, energy, or, at the least, one or more difficult conversations,

so support from a supervisor or colleague can be invaluable in deciding exactly how and what we are going to say and to whom.

8. *Learning*: We may not be able to get the full learning until some time later when we have seen what the consequences of our decision were for all the parties involved. A combination of our own reflection and guided reflection with someone else may be the best strategy to get the maximum learning from what happened and to help us to integrate it into our ethical capacity for the future. It is a lifelong journey.

Summary

Acting ethically requires self-awareness and courage. As coaches, it is important that we can define our own values and articulate our personal code of conduct as well as being "signed up" to our professional body's standards of ethical conduct.

This chapter has provided information to help you think about and reflect honestly on how you make and implement ethical decisions. Understanding the personal, situational, and organisational influences in a situation and the impact of them on how we behave is an important aspect of developing our ethical maturity. As we become more self-aware it is easier to find the resolution to take the action required to resolve ethical dilemmas, which, by their nature, are rarely easy.

QUESTIONS TO REFLECT ON

Factor to consider	What are the implications for me?

Contracting
How can I use contracting to reduce the likelihood or incidence of ethical dilemmas?
	• How will I "contract" with my client:
	  – what does my contracting process need to include?
	  – do I need a written contract?
	  – what will I cover in the chemistry meeting or first session to ensure my client has a clear understanding of how confidentiality works and the necessary boundaries of the relationship?

(Continued)

QUESTIONS TO REFLECT ON   (*Continued*)

Factor to consider	What are the implications for me?
The importance of behaving ethically Do I have a sense of which of the three main theoretical stances I share? • Principled conscience • Social conscience • Rule compliance	• Looking back at a situation when I found myself with a dilemma, which of the three stances was I drawing on to decide what was "right"?
What does unethical behaviour look like? What type of factors: personal, situational, or organisational could make unethical behaviour more likely for me?	• How easily influenced am I by others? • Where may I be in danger of putting my own interests ahead of the client, or take the easier path of doing nothing? • What situational factors could undermine my good intentions? • How ethical is my organisation's culture? Will my compliance with an ethical code of conduct require me to stand out against it? Where might I find support?
Why do ethics matter? I need to protect my clients' interests As a coach I am a role model for others in the organisation	• What are my personal motivations for behaving ethically? • When am I most likely to be in danger of justifying what I know to be unethical behaviour?

(Continued)

QUESTIONS TO REFLECT ON   (*Continued*)

Factor to consider	*What are the implications for me?*
Where do our personal ethics come from? How has my upbringing shaped my behaviour?	• What "rules" have I inherited from my parents? • When I think about my values now, do those rules still reflect who I have become? • How do I hold myself accountable to my own standards of behaviour?
Ethical maturity How shall I nurture my ethical maturity in the following respects? • Ethical sensitivity • Making ethical decisions • Implementing ethical decisions • Articulating the rationale • Living with the decision • Learning from the decision	• How can I get a better understanding of my "blind spots"? • How clear am I about my own values and how I act if they are challenged? • Where may I be at risk of doing nothing once I have decided I need to take action to resolve an ethical dilemma? • How do I hold myself accountable once I have recognised the need to take the action required to implement an ethical decision? • What do I have in place which supports any difficult decisions I may have to make in relation to my coaching practice? • If I need to be able to justify my actions what are the implications for my record-keeping?

(*Continued*)

QUESTIONS TO REFLECT ON   (*Continued*)

Factor to consider	*What are the implications for me?*
	• Do I have trouble "letting go" when I have made a difficult decision? What can I do about that?
	• If things do not go as well as I planned how do I move forward?
	• What have I put in place to reflect on my own practice? What opportunities do I create for doing this?
	• How do I reflect and learn from decisions I have made? Do I need to make this process more robust?
Using a decision-making model Could this model be useful to me? • Awareness • Identification • Reflection • Consultation • Evaluation • Decision • Implementation • Learning	• Could I use the model for making ethical decisions in future? • Thinking back to a recent situation (coaching or general) that presented an ethical dilemma for me, if I had applied the model: – are there some additional steps that I would have taken? – would I have come to a different conclusion? – are there any implications for how I take decisions in future?

PART II

WHAT ORGANISATIONS NEED TO KNOW

Part II is designed principally for those of you who are responsible for learning and development in your organisation. It aims to distil some of the learning from the decade or so of experience that there now is of actually running internal coaching schemes, with two main purposes in mind:

a. to make it easier for you to decide if internal coaching is a way forward for your organisation (if you do not yet have internal coaches); and

b. to describe many of the approaches that organisations are adopting to setting up and running their internal coaching pools so as to share the learning (both for organisations that already have internal coaches and those of you who are thinking about it).

CHAPTER FIVE

Why have internal coaches?

The leader of the past was a person who knew how to tell. The leader of the future will be a person who knows how to ask

—*Peter Drucker*

What this chapter is about

An internal coaching resource can bring a huge number of benefits to an organisation. It is, however, not without its challenges. This chapter discusses the advantages and highlights some of the drawbacks, with the aim of improving your awareness of the issues and enabling you to decide whether internal coaching would be a good fit for your organisation.

The chapter explores:

- The advantages of internal *vs.* external coaches, examining a number of factors to take into account when assessing the costs and benefits to your organisation
- Potential challenges of using internal coaches:
  - Status/credibility issues for internal coaches
  - The increased scope for ethical dilemmas

- Issues associated with being part of the same culture
- How reciprocal arrangements with other organisations can work.

Every organisation that wishes to use coaches has to weigh up the pros and cons of bringing in external coaches as against developing their own internal coaching service. Many organisations deploy a combination of internal and external coaches to deliver their coaching needs. There are distinct advantages and disadvantages to each.

The factors in the following table are drawn from work by Carter (2005), Hall, Otazo, and Hollenbeck (1999), and Mukherjee (2012). They are corroborated by many practitioners, though the importance of some factors will depend on context. This chapter expands upon them.

Table 5.1 Advantages of using external and internal coaches.

External	*Internal*
Experience in a variety of organisations gives credibility, particularly with senior managers	Knowledge of organisational culture, politics, and internal dynamics
More objective and balanced view; more independent	Increased availability and easy to contact
More flexible resource	Less expensive
Clear role definition, no additional responsibilities	Can gather feedback more easily
Will not already know the coachee	Model for other managers
May generate more commitment from coachee	Responsiveness to organisation's needs
Can offer more challenging perspectives; wider range of ideas	Can coach further down the hierarchy
Experience in political nuances	Can have well resourced office on hand
Can say the "unspeakable"	Can use assessment tools and techniques (e.g., 360 tool) specific to the organisation
Safer space to discuss sensitive issues	Awareness of the coachee's specific context

(Continued)

Table 5.1 (*Continued*)

External	Internal
	If already successful managers, easier to gain the respect of the coachees and build rapport
	Easier to gather organisational learning
	Do not have a financial imperative for maintaining or prolonging a coaching relationship
	The organisation gets the benefit of development that the coach receives, as well as the client
	Strengthening internal networks across the organisation

Advantages that internal coaches have over externals

Lower cost

There are many good reasons for training internal coaches that are not about cost savings. However, most commentators would say that cost is an important factor in the increasing popularity of internal coaching. The Ridler Report (Ridler & Co, 2013), in which 145 organisations participated, reported that cost efficiency continued to be a significant driver. Economic pressures mean that organisations have been tightening their belts in recent years but there is little evidence that external coaches are lowering their fees in response (ICF, 2012). Many businesses are therefore seeking ways of providing coaching at lower cost.

While there is little doubt that cost savings will be driving some organisations' decision to develop a cohort of internal coaches, it should not be seen merely as a cheap alternative to using external coaches. As Hawkins (2012) puts it: "The journey towards creating, building and maintaining a quality community of internal coaches requires investment, long-term commitment and support, and careful planning. It should not be undertaken lightly" (p. 61). So if cost is your main driver, bear that in mind.

Familiarity with the organisation and culture

For many years, surveys of the preferences of clients procuring external coaching services showed that familiarity with the sector was at or near the top of the list. However much external coaches gnashed their teeth and expostulated that knowledge of a particular sector was neither here nor there in an effective coaching relationship, this has represented a comfort factor for coaching purchasers. By extension, you can see the benefits for clients of having an internal coach because the client has the confidence that the coach knows what is going on within the organisation and the types of issues with which executives in it struggle. As Yedreshteyn (2008) puts it: "This level of familiarity can help create a trusted relationship more quickly and give internal executive coaches more credibility than when working with an external executive coach who is new to an organisation and its idiosyncrasies" (p. 29).

And as one internal coach noted:

> "Being an internal coach can mean that you can quickly become effective in helping people as you know the organisation and culture and can quickly build credibility and rapport because of that, so although occasionally ethical issues arise, in general there are quite a few advantages."

There is something about having a shared knowledge of the environment, history, people, culture, and internal politics that can help internal coaches to build a trusting relationship quickly. And the fact that they are familiar with the prevailing management styles and organisational structures means that they are very well placed.

Hunt and Weintraub (2006) also note that an internal coach, by being part of the same organisation, should be in a good position to understand the business strategy within which the client operates. I would argue that you cannot necessarily assume that all internal coaches will be familiar with the business strategy, however. If it is important that they do, then make sure that they have regular briefings (although some of your internal coaches may well work in positions where this knowledge is part of the day job). Much will depend on the purpose for which the coaching scheme was set up and the seniority of the client. If the purpose is to help a middle manager work out what their personal development plan might include after a 360 feedback exercise, or how they might improve a difficult relationship with a colleague, or how they may enhance their ability to delegate, then knowledge of organisational strategy may not be imperative.

The multiplier effect

The principal aim of most coach-client relationships, irrespective of whether the coach is an internal or external coach, is for the client to get to where they want to go and make the changes that will be beneficial to them. However, there is an additional benefit to your organisation in using a trained internal coach because the client will not be the only one learning in the coaching relationship: the coach will be learning a great deal too. Internal coaches have reported numerous benefits ranging from learning more about how the organisation worked and how to tackle internal politics to being more effective in their own day jobs (Hall, Otazo, & Hollenbeck, 1999).

Mukherjee (2012), too, showed that internal coaches derived benefits from their coaching relationships. His research, carried out in a large state-owned oil and gas exploration company in India with more than 15,000 regular employees, found that working as internal coaches helped the managers to improve their interpersonal skills, listening capability, work–life balance, and self-confidence. The benefits cited by forty internal coaches (all senior managers themselves) involved in delivering a specific coaching initiative were significant and varied. This data came from asking the coaches: "What do you think you have gained personally and how will it benefit you in your professional and personal life?" Responses were:

- *Improved personal skills*: Sixty per cent felt that they had become more effective at dealing with their subordinates, peers and seniors.
- *Better listener*: Thirty-nine per cent reported that they had become better listeners, and calmer. One said he was able to concentrate more and comprehend better.
- *Increased confidence*: Almost twenty-five per cent experienced this even though they were already senior managers. Leedham (2005) mentions that confidence is the widely recognised "inner personal benefit" of coaching.
- *Better work–life balance*: Thirty-three per cent reported that their work–life balance had improved. When they used the "Wheel of Life" with

clients they realised their own low levels of satisfaction on family and personal fronts and started to give more attention to their personal and social lives.

- *Sense of achievement*: Thirteen per cent felt "immense joy in contributing to bringing various changes in the personal and professional areas of the coachees".
- *Broader vision*: Fifteen per cent reported that their overall vision had broadened and they could understand better their role as a manager in building organisational capabilities.

Mukherjee notes: "From these findings it can be argued that when an organisation develops high-quality internal coaches from successful leaders or managers within the organisation, besides addressing cost containment pressure, the organisation develops their leadership competences and confidence" (p. 85).

There is a strong case for saying your organisation would achieve even more of a multiplier effect from investing in internal coaches since the beneficiaries can be the client, the coach, the coach's team, the client's team, and the organisation more widely.

Benefits of being "on hand" and flexible

Some researchers (Carter, 2005; Hunt & Weintraub, 2006; Yedreshteyn, 2008) have commented that one of the advantages that internals have over externals is that they are more easily contactable and more available. They may also be in a position to observe the client in their day-to-day activities, such as attending a meeting or presentation involving the client, and then provide feedback in real time or at a later date. Or just the fact that they are "around the place" can act as a prompt to the client to remember any new behaviours they may be experimenting with. However, others have pointed out that this argument can be overplayed: if care has been taken (on the grounds of reducing the potential for role conflict) to ensure that the coach and client work in different parts of the business, this benefit is less likely to be realised. Also, if your organisation is large, then the coach and client may not work on the same site or even in the same country. However, for some internal coaching relationships there is the potential for real added value from being on the spot. The idea of internals being more available, however, is very much a moot point. An internal coach with a busy day job might be no easier or more difficult to reach than an external coach.

A further potential advantage mentioned is flexibility, in that if a client has to cancel at short notice then the internal coach can simply get on with their day job whereas an external coach would probably charge a cancellation fee. However, I am a little wary of mentioning this as a benefit because internal coaches can be rightly sensitive to any suggestion that their time is any less precious than that of an external coach. Most of them are juggling very busy jobs, and changes at short notice can be wearisome. On the other hand, having an hour or two freed up in one's diary unexpectedly can also be a boon.

Networking/breaking down barriers

Internal coaching provides the opportunity for the coach to deepen connections across the organisation and strengthen internal networks. In Chapter Two I refer to this as being one of the personal benefits that internal coaches say they get from coaching people in other parts of the business. There are clearly also organisational benefits from this.

Most large organisations have a concern about internal communications. They refer to the "silos" or "baronies" that can be created in different functions. These silos often have to compete with each other for resources and may fail to communicate to each other very well what their priorities and activities are going forward. This can result in organisations where employees do not fully understand how the different parts fit together, resulting in poor consultation or joint working—simply because of that failure to comprehend who else might usefully be involved. Organisations try a multitude of ways to get around this problem, whether it is full matrix working or a series of one-off project groups involving people from across the business. Having internal coaches with a day job in one part of the business working with clients in other parts of the business can play a very positive part in breaking down these structural barriers.

Developing a coaching community

The benefits just described, of coaches working across departmental boundaries, can be greatly amplified if care is taken to build a coaching community of all the coaches working in your organisation.

The principal benefits of investing time and energy in building this community are the support that the coaches can offer each other, the additional development that they get from training together, being supervised together and undertaking CPD together, and the contribution they can jointly make to developing a coaching approach within the organisation. However, a further benefit is learning from each other what is going on in other parts of the organisational forest. That bit of time spent on bringing the coaches together at intervals, say for a "brown bag" lunch, to update them on organisational strategy, discuss a new coaching book, or other informal development activity, can be time very well spent. So the networking benefits of training a pool of internal coaches will then include not just the relationships between coaches and clients but also between coaches and other coaches.

This idea of a coaching community is important. I have interviewed a lead coach in a government agency who did not actually know how many active coaches they had or who they were. The coaches operated independently and informally and were never brought together. It felt like a big missed trick to me—so many potential benefits not being realised. I would also lay odds that some of those coaches will have been feeling pretty isolated on occasion.

Many organisations actively foster their coaching community and bring the coaches together at regular intervals. Some organisations have gone further by involving their external coaches too and arranging annual or biannual events such as a one-day conference or workshop when all the coaches can learn from each other and share their experiences. Some external coaches might seek to charge for their time attending such an event but many would view it as a development opportunity and make no charge.

Contribution to organisational learning

One of the benefits of an internal coaching resource is the opportunity that it offers for feeding back into your organisation generic themes that emerge in coaching sessions to contribute to organisational learning. Hawkins (2012) writes about how he asks CEOs and HR directors of companies that have many coaching conversations going on in them the excellent question: "How does your organisation learn from these thousands of coaching conversations?" (p. 3). The learning does not happen by itself. Failure to set up a mechanism for extracting systemic information from the coaching conversations is a missed opportunity.

My survey suggested that fifty per cent of organisations had a mechanism for feeding back organisational learning. Arrangements included:

- Co-ordinated by the lead coach
- Picked up via supervision sessions or facilitated action learning sets
- *Ad hoc* or described as "informal routes".

There was also a variety of destinations for the information, once gathered. These included: the OD team; the L&D team; the HR Director; the organisational sponsor for the coaching; or the CEO. In Chapter Six I devote more space to how organisational learning can be harvested.

An integral part of developing a coaching culture

Much attention has been given in recent years to the idea of building a "coaching culture" in organisations and to the benefits of develop-ing leaders' and managers' coaching skills. Hawkins (2012) defined a coaching culture as follows:

> A coaching culture exists in an organisation when a coaching approach is a key aspect of how the leaders, managers, and staff engage and develop all their people and engage their stakeholders, in ways that create increased individual, team and organisational performance and shared value for all stakeholders. (p. 21)

However many external coaches you introduce into an organisation to work with staff at all levels, they cannot make as big an impact on an organisation's culture as can people working within it. The ideal might be a virtuous circle that involves the coach being trained to coach; the client experiencing the coaching so learning how to coach too; then the coach and client both role modelling the coaching approach back in their day jobs. If you add into that mix external coaches being brought in to coach specific people or for specific types of assignment and an active programme of training managers in a coaching style of manage-ment too, you can see how a "coaching culture" could become a reality.

Some would claim that even internal coaches alone can have quite an impact on the system:

> Teaching managers to coach is not only cost-effective for sustainable long term organisational benefits, but there are deep benefits in terms of their personal and professional gains. Focusing managers on their coaching skills and making them deliver formal coaching ... has a broad systemic impact across the board. (Mukherjee, 2012, p. 85)

The opposite view, however, is voiced in Snape's (2012) research where she quotes a company that has decided against introducing internal coaching: "We are building a coaching culture using a coaching style in conversations, rather than going to see someone for a session (during which people would not be working—is that productive during a recession?)". The company talks about their aim of building a coaching culture "that can benefit everyone rather than limiting the availability of coaching to a targeted few" (p. 34). In my interviews with coach trainers, I too have encountered the strongly held view that the best way forward to build a true coaching culture is to train all the managers at every level in how to use a coaching style. As ever, different approaches will suit different organisations—no one size fits all. So if your primary objective is to build a coaching culture within your organisation, as opposed to providing a high quality internal executive coaching resource, then you will need to think carefully about whether internal coaching is a vital part of the mix for you.

Potential challenges of using internal coaches

Chapter Three outlined some of the challenges of being an internal coach from the perspective of the coach. But what about the downsides of using internal coaches, as opposed to external coaches, from an organisational perspective?

Status/credibility

In the course of the past three years I have met and talked to very many internal coaches and have never failed to be impressed by their levels of commitment and professionalism. A number of them had been coaching for many years and even those who were fairly new to it were fired up with enthusiasm and clearly giving it their all. I therefore feel a little wary of raising the issue of credibility but it is important to do so because:

- It is often mentioned in the literature; and
- It has been raised, too, by some of my interviewees as an irritant.

Frisch (2005), Jarvis, Lane, and Fillery-Travis (2006), and others have mentioned that one of the key challenges for internal coaches can be their potential lack of credibility with senior managers. Yedreshteyn (2008) expresses it like this:

> External executive coaches come into organisations with advanced degrees, training and broad coaching experience, which is likely to afford them immediate credibility, something that internal coaches may not receive. (p. 29)

Wrynne (2011) raises a related idea that coaches can be perceived by some as a status symbol and that an internal coach confers less of that status than an external coach does. The issue from the coaches' point of view is that there can be a perception among potential clients that external coaches are "better" and this can be bound up, for some coaches, with the notion that they are not always appropriately valued and their services properly recognised. This was expressed by one internal coach as: "The organisation does not recognise internal excellence, but appears to see external coaches as more professional."

Given how experienced some internal coaches are (and the fact that ten per cent of the internal coaches that took part in my research coached executives in the top team) one can readily see how galling this must be. It is a known phenomenon that prophets are not always honoured in their own land and that more credence is often given to the utterances of external consultants than to executives who have been saying the same thing for years. It is something that you need to be aware of and to take care to position internal coaching as a high quality service, to provide your coaches with excellent training and continuing professional development, and to ensure that there are champions within the business who can market the coaching service with enthusiasm and authority.

Increased scope for ethical dilemmas

Chapter Three described the numerous varieties of dilemma that can arise for internal coaches. Frisch (2005), Wasylyshyn (2003), and others have drawn attention to the fact that some managers have concerns and negative perceptions around a possible lack of confidentiality if they have an internal coach. Internal coaches themselves acknowledge the difficulties that can flow from coaching someone who is not sufficiently distant from them in the organisation:

> "Internal coaches provide a value for money form of coaching. However, there are more potential dilemmas, particularly for those coaches like myself who sit at the centre of the organisation."
>
> "I prefer to coach people from outside my own department, as it is easier to remain objective if I do not know the people or the situations personally."
>
> "I feel I do my best coaching when I know nothing about the individual or their area of work."

This is something that you can address as part of the matching process for coaches and clients (or ask the coach to check out in any chemistry session if it is a client-led system). On the confidentiality front, though, the evidence suggests that while some very senior leaders may decide that they would prefer to discuss their personal and professional issues with an external coach rather than an internal one, the actual issue of confidentiality is not something that most managers have serious concerns about.

Despite the challenges that exist for internal coaches relating to ethical dilemmas, as Hawkins (2012) says, all problems for internal coaches "can be addressed by an organisation that is willing to invest in the appropriate training, development and supervision of internal coaches" (p. 62).

One approach that can alleviate potential problems on the confidentiality and role conflict fronts is to explore reciprocal arrangements with other organisations. At the end of this chapter I give some examples of successful collaborations.

Being part of the same culture

Being part of the same system as their coaching clients can be a two-edged sword for internal coaches. There are some significant benefits but also challenges. As Hunt and Weintraub (2006) put it:

... the internal coach does swim in the same political and cultural waters as the coachee, at least to a degree. While this can be informative, it can also represent a trap for the unprepared. (pp. 2–3)

Or as an internal coach expressed it:

"In some ways we can be less objective, as the issues that affect all staff also affect us. It can be more difficult to step back and take a third party view about an issue that also causes concern for you as an employee."

The restructuring that many organisations have been forced to implement in the world recession can really test internal coaches' ability to put their own concerns to one side and give their full attention to the client. Below is an extract from *The Listener*, a coaching journal developed by Ken Smith, who used to be an internal coach in a government department before setting up his own coaching practice. It illustrates the real difficulties that internal coaches can find themselves in, by virtue of being part of the same system as their clients. Smith is a very experienced coach with a sophisticated understanding of the dynamics. Less experienced practitioners might be less aware (or unaware) of how their own feelings about their organisation being in turmoil may be playing out unhelpfully within the coaching relationship—particularly if they do not have access to supervision.

Internal coaches are of course caught themselves in the change net. It may easily be that our own futures are very uncertain and we must deliver a professional coaching job while at the same time knowing that we are at risk of redundancy. So how good are we at recognising our own emotions and managing them productively within the coaching session, drawing on them only in a way that enhances rapport and avoids a parallel process of distress? We need to learn from the emotions we ourselves experience in uncertainty that can deepen our self-knowledge and so help build our practice. The challenge of this can be compounded when the psychological contract we have as employees within our organisation is broken. When this happens, how then can we, as internal coaches, congruently represent our organisation to our clients, no matter how directly or indirectly we are asked to do so? We need to ask ourselves honestly: "Where is my own energy right now and where do

I want to put my energy?" and from the answer conclude whether we can take the coaching assignment. (K. Smith, 2011)

Issues when using external coaches

It is no part of my brief to talk at length about external coaches. As an external coach myself I believe, of course, that there are many excellent external coaches who do a great job. However, two issues were mentioned time and again by internal coaches so should at least get a mention.

Financial imperative

Internal coaches often mentioned that there was one variety of ethical dilemma peculiar to external coaches: the conflict of interest inherent in the fact that their livelihood depends on attracting and keeping clients. This could mean, for example, that they might be tempted to encourage clients to purchase additional sessions that they do not need or to take on ethically dubious assignments such as coaching the direct reports of someone they are already coaching. This issue also appears in the coaching literature (e.g., Maccoby, 2009).

Dependency issues

The sorts of ethical dilemmas that arise for internal coaches, associated with knowing many of the people in the organisation, can also arise for external coaches if they work for a significant amount of time in an organisation and become familiar with the key managers. Some coaches may also be leadership consultants or OD specialists and find themselves working in an organisation over a number of years and in a variety of capacities. Internal coaches point out that in these cases such individuals will be subject to the same sorts of boundary and confidentiality issues as those encountered by internal coaches. One of the internal coaches who took part in my research wrote:

> "Most of the dilemmas the research seeks to explore can be found in the life of an external coach. I have come across external coaches who work only with one or two organisations and can have unhealthy dependency issues with them."

Reciprocal arrangements

Given the downsides in terms of potential role conflicts, confidentiality issues, and the coach being part of the same system as the client, an increasingly popular alternative approach is to set up reciprocal arrangements with other organisations, sometimes termed "coach trading".

The reciprocal arrangements work as networks of organisations that pool resources; share training, supervision, and CPD arrangements; and release their coaches to coach in each other's organisations. In the UK a number of regional networks have been set up. The initial drive has come from the public sector, particularly local authorities: for example, an early network was the West Midlands Coaching Pool Partnership established in 2007, involving thirteen local authorities. There are now a number of networks around the country including the North West Employers' Coaching Network, the Suffolk Coaching and Mentoring Partnership, and the Kent Coaching and Mentoring Network. Companies in the private sector are now also setting up informal networks that may develop into something similar.

Below are two case studies that illustrate different approaches to running a coaching network—one was informal and the other is formal, with both operating across central government: hence they offer interesting alternative models.

Case study 5.1: Coaches in government network

One afternoon in December 2006, Ken Smith (then head of L&D in the Department for Culture, Media, and Sport) started wondering why, in spite of the strong reputation his team had for one-to-one work, more people were not taking up the offer of coaching. Perhaps one reason was that they were reluctant to be coached by a colleague in the same organisation. So he sent an email to a few L&D practitioners in other government departments, asking them if they were wondering the same thing—and the Coaches in Government Network was born. Five years later there were 227 members from over fifty organisations.

It worked very informally. To be a coaching member of the network—that is, to work with a client in another member's organisation—a coach had to have a coaching qualification and complete a simple coach profile, giving information to prospective clients on their experience, credentials, and approach. Members managed their own development and made their own arrangements for supervision. Each coach could decide how much coaching they wanted to, or could, contribute.

Ken himself managed the informal brokering system with most referrals coming from L&D managers in government bodies or self-referrals. Clients chose their own coach from profiles sent to them. Ken describes the process of coaches and clients finding the network as "viral marketing" because people became aware of it through word of mouth and through occasional references in coaching publications. In the five years of its life the network provided nearly 1,000 hours of coaching.

The network was a community and not an initiative: an example of how something can grow organically and emergently. With minimal structure, it gave members the freedom to choose how to develop their practice, autonomously and in line with their own interests. And by not charging each others' organisations for the coaching provided, the coaches removed a barrier to access, achieved a substantial saving in fees, avoided adding an unhelpful administrative burden, and maximised the available coaching resource.

The network also offered CPD: a journal called *The Listener* was published regularly with contributions from members and the wider coaching community and Ken also organised occasional half-day conferences with speakers who donated their services. Katherine Tulpa, chief executive of the Association for Coaching Global, came to the launch of the network. Speakers at later conferences included Dr. Alison Whybrow, past chair of the special group in coaching psychology of the British Psychological Society, who ran a session on cognitive behavioural coaching and Wendy Sullivan of the Clean Change Company talking about clean language. Later, Ken and Elizabeth Crosse, head of L&D at the Legal Services Commission, provided *pro bono* supervision for individuals and groups.

Two dilemmas hovered around the network: whether to insist on a common framework of coaching standards for members; and whether to secure senior sponsorship. The first might have added to the network's credibility and given its clients additional assurance; but it would have worked against its community ethos and was anyway unfeasible given that the network was run by Ken voluntarily around his day job. Similarly, carrying out systematic evaluation, though highly desirable, was not practicable: there was no time to do this and it would, to a degree, have worked against the preferred light touch co-ordination of the network. In retrospect, not routinely calling in evaluation data feels to Ken like a lost opportunity. The second, securing sponsorship, would have raised the network's profile across members' organisations and perhaps have brought additional resources for CPD but although sponsorship was sought early on, it was not forthcoming.

A number of things made the Network possible and unique but two critical features stand out: a committed and active person at its hub who understood the organisational culture within central government and found a way to work "underneath" it, in order to create a new community; and the presence of widely distributed, independent nodes of expertise and interest, in the form of the L&D practitioners located in the multiplicity of government agencies across the UK. The network closed late in 2011 when Ken left the Civil Service, at a time when the L&D function in the service was radically redesigned and centralised.

Case study 5.2: Civil Service Learning

The summer of 2012 saw the launch of an innovative internal coaching scheme across the UK civil service, developed by Civil Service Learning (CSL)—part of the UK government. Available to any civil servant in a leadership role, up to 120 internal coaches are listed in an online coach management system that permits potential coaching clients across government to search for a coach by several criteria, including region and type of coaching required (e.g., holding difficult conversations; career development; transition coaching) and allows a chemistry meeting to be set up. The coaching scheme is led by James Pritchard, a learning consultant in CSL, who has designed and implemented the scheme in partnership with a group of stakeholders from across government. It has a number of interesting features:

- The coaches are already qualified, experienced coaches with a range of qualifications up to Masters level. CSL did not get involved in training them—they invited applications from coaches who already had a track record and put them through a rigorous validation process.

- Internal coaches who are existing civil servants are listed in the same database as "approved" external coaches. The biographies detailing approach, qualifications, experience, and so forth are presented in identical formats, the only difference is that the external coaches' fees are quoted whereas the internal coaches are free for clients to use.
- The scheme is technology enabled. CSL does not get involved in any matching—potential clients contact a coach directly (or maybe two or three for comparison purposes).
- The coach management system, which was developed specifically for the scheme, includes a personal area for each coach to list their clients, which department they work in, the dates of coaching sessions, etc. While the names are confidential, the data about numbers of coaching clients, numbers of sessions, and departmental usage feed into a management information system which Pritchard and his team can analyse for return on investment purposes.
- Departments register and pay an annual sum to CSL in order to have access to all the learning services CSL provide, including internal coaches. At the outset some departments already had a cadre of trained, experienced internal coaches while many others did not.
- Two supervision days *per annum* are offered to the coaches (a morning of CPD and an afternoon of group supervision) plus two one-to-one telephone sessions with an external supervisor.
- The coach management system automatically sends an evaluation questionnaire to the client when the coaching programme is completed. It is in two parts: a) a report by the client on achievement of aims/goals and an assessment of the coach and b) an assessment of progress by the client's line manager (which is discussed with the client who then submits the line manager's comments). The client knows that their comments will be shared with the coach as part of the coach's development.

Pritchard has a high opinion of the standard of the internal coaches and has taken care to position them as of comparable quality to the external coaches that have been approved by CSL. This driver is behind the decision not to differentiate between the internal and external coaches on the database. He is also careful with language, describing the internals as "internal executive coaches".

His confidence in their quality is underpinned by the rigour of the half-day "validation process" (run by Oxford Brookes University) that successful applicants for the scheme had to successfully negotiate. Applicants had to satisfy four criteria:

- *Knowledge and understanding*: Could candidates articulate their coaching model, show an understanding of other models, and explain their choice?
- *Coaching competence*: Candidates held a half-hour coaching session with a colleague. They were assessed on whether a) they worked in a way that reflected their espoused coaching model and b) they were effective.
- *Psychological mindedness*: Interviewers assessed this through questions around candidates' awareness of their own biases/values/appreciation of boundary issues etc.
- *Developing coaching capability*: Assessors looked for candidates' attitude to learning and the extent to which they were constantly looking for opportunities to develop their skills.

Time will always be an issue but there is an expectation that internal coaches will have around three clients at any one time and have their manager's agreement to release them for their coaching work for around one day a month. This ensures that they keep their skills fresh and justify the investment in them.

And the future? Pritchard also hopes to hold an annual conference where internal and external coaches exchange stories, share experiences, and see what organisational learning emerges.

Summary

There are distinct advantages to organisations in using internal coaches. They provide good value and, in addition to providing a coaching service, internal coaches become better managers and leaders themselves and make a significant contribution to the development of an organisational culture that fosters high performance. As long as care is taken to address the challenges around confidentiality, boundaries, and role conflicts, an internal coaching service can provide many benefits. Becoming a member of a coaching network can provide more flexibility of resource as well as reducing some of the downsides associated with the coach and the client being part of the same system.

QUESTIONS TO REFLECT ON

Factor to consider	What are the implications for your organisation?
Advantages of internal vs. external coaches	
There are a number of factors that make internal coaching an attractive option. Are they sufficiently compelling? How can one ensure the benefits are optimised?	In thinking about whether internal coaching is the right path for my organisation: • Is there a financial benefit from using internal vs. external coaches when training, on-going support, time away from the day job, etc. are taken into account? • What value do we place on our coaches having a shared knowledge of the environment, people, culture, internal politics, etc.? • Can an internal coaching resource add value to other business initiatives that are going on in our organisation? • How can the business "leverage" the investment in the coach's development as a manager and leader which comes about as a result of training and working as a coach? • What mechanisms do we need to create to ensure feedback from internal coaches contributes to organisational learning? • How could the matching process be used to improve communication and understanding between different business areas?

(Continued)

QUESTIONS TO REFLECT ON   *(Continued)*

Factor to consider	What are the implications for your organisation?
Potential challenges of using internal coaches How might the following potential downsides be minimised? • Status/credibility issues for internal coaches • The increased scope for ethical dilemmas • The challenges associated with coaches and clients being part of the same culture	• What do we need to do to ensure that our coaches are as seen as professional, credible, and on a par with external coaches? • What do we need to take into account when matching coaches to clients to set our coaches up for success when coaching senior personnel? • How do we see the disadvantages of our coaches being part of the same organisational culture as their clients? Are there any aspects of this issue that need to be addressed in the training and support we give our coaches?
Reciprocal arrangements Collaborative arrangements where organisations that are geographically close pool resources, share training, supervision, and CPD arrangements and "trade" coaches are becoming popular	Would our organisation benefit from a reciprocal arrangement? If so: • How could we find out more about the pros and cons? • Who would our natural partners be? • Is there already a local network that we could join? • What needs to be in place to ensure that the costs to our organisation are reflected in the benefit gained?

CHAPTER SIX

Developing a coaching strategy

If you fail to plan, you are planning to fail!

—*Benjamin Franklin*

What this chapter is about

This chapter explores:

- The need for a strategy and what needs to be included
- Governance and getting commitment from the business leaders
- Identifying the strategic purpose for developing an internal coaching resource
- Harvesting organisational learning
- Targeting your coaching resource
- Positioning the scheme to best effect
- Scope and approach of the coaching scheme
- Budget allocation
- Factors that impact on sustainability.

Why have a strategy?

Some people have trouble with the word "strategy" and find the word "plan" less off-putting. Also some people are natural planners while others take a more emergent approach. Whatever your natural preference, some kind of strategy or plan is essential, both to help you to think through what you want to do and how you want to do it, and as a vehicle for getting everyone on board who needs to be—and all moving in the same direction.

Internal coaching schemes come in all shapes and sizes. Your internal coaching resource may consist of two people who were already experienced coaches when they joined the organisation; who co-supervise each other and are members of a coaching professional body, so subscribe to its code of ethics and access CPD through it. Their coaching activities may cost your organisation virtually nothing. Or you may be lead coach for a multinational company with many internal coaches; run a sophisticated coach management system; provide regular supervision for the coaches from an external provider; arrange bi-monthly CPD sessions; put on an annual conference; and so forth. Clearly your strategies will look very different in their scope, scale, and sophistication. While I hope your thinking will benefit from reflecting on the issues raised in this chapter, obviously your response to them will be proportionate to the scale of what you are already doing or proposing to do.

Some organisations simply provide interested managers with a few days of coach training, match them up with anybody expressing an interest in being coached, and say "Go to it!" with no clear strategic framework for what they are doing or any further support for the coaches. You might argue that a) any coaching in an organisation is better than no coaching and b) systems and processes can add little to the good work that the coaches are doing. But such a hands-off approach:

- Fails to maximise impact by not articulating any strategic context or purpose for the coaching
- Misses a trick by not getting the coaches together and developing a community or garnering organisational learning
- Risks grievances or employee tribunals if a coaching relationship goes wrong with no process for dealing with it

- Neglects the continuing growth and development of your coaches and
- Provides no data to tell you whether the coaching is effective (or even ethical).

In most organisations you will need to make a business case for the coaching scheme in order to get approval for the funding—the processes will vary from organisation to organisation. If you have not yet done so, this chapter should provide you with some thoughts as to what you might put in that too.

Governance

At the outset, decide if you need a steering group. I have heard numerous arguments for and against. Lead coaches in the "for" camp see a steering group as a crucial aspect of governance: that is, ensuring some clarity around who is accountable to whom and for what. If the group includes influential managers from across the organisation then it can provide: heavyweight input to and critiquing of the coaching strategy; champions for the scheme around the business; a process for ensuring that the coaching is linked to business needs; a valuable channel for keeping in touch with client requirements and any changes in organisational strategy; support if the scheme comes under threat when budgets are tight; necessary challenge around effectiveness and value for money; and a spur for the lead coach to keep on top of monitoring and evaluation measures. One coach lead told me that if she were to start from scratch again then she would "pay much more attention second time around to governance".

An alternative point of view is that if the scheme is run by a proactive, energetic lead coach with the freedom to make decisions; the ear of influential people at board level; buy-in from a strong champion who can provide support if required; and good lines into stakeholders around the business, then all a steering group would add is a layer of bureaucracy that needs to be serviced with papers and attention, taking the lead coach away from "the real work". Perhaps the key to this issue is scale. If it is intended to develop a substantial number of coaches in the future, even if the scheme has small beginnings, then it might be worth setting up a steering group from the outset. The value of having individuals from around the business invested in the success of the scheme should not be underestimated.

Case study 6.1: Successful use of a steering group

In 2005, Southern Railway built on their investment in leadership development for 250 managers and external coaching for sixty managers by working with Buornacorsi Consulting to pilot an ILM5 coaching programme with eighteen managers. The aim was to develop accredited coaches to act as role models. Every coach worked with three clients.

The original steering group was made up of the managing director, L&D manager, and the two consultants from Buornacorsi; but from the second cohort this morphed into a larger group led by the new HR director, and over three or four years Buornacorsi gradually stepped back. By the fourth run of the programme, the coaches became part of a formal internal coaching service.

The steering group became the key driver and focused at each meeting on:

1. What was happening on the programme
2. How to improve the programme
3. Ways of getting buy-in from senior leaders across the business
4. Ways to measure the success of the programme
5. Spin offs into other L&D initiatives: such as, using coaching skills in performance conversations
6. Continuous professional development for the internal coaches
7. Recognition for the programme from external awards.

In 2008 research showed a statistically significant correlation between managers who had been on the programme and high employee engagement scores, and in 2009 the programme won a National Training Award.

The factors that helped the steering group to be a positive influence on the shape, progress, and results of the internal coaching service included:

- A diverse membership to represent all areas of the business
- An external perspective, in this case from Buonacorsi Consulting
- Robust discussion to really find out what would work in the existing culture
- A strong link between the HR director (chair of the group) and the managing director and executive—with regular updates both ways
- Regular review, feedback, and evaluation
- Regular celebration of achievement, with award ceremonies at the end of each programme.

Commitment from the business leaders

Having a senior champion is important to your success, if you can get one. As Dr. Martin Read said, in his foreword to the CMI/Penna report on the business benefits of management and leadership development (McBain et al., 2012):

> We cannot leave management development solely to HR teams and training specialists. They have an important role to play, but throughout my career I have seen the difference that the chief executive's commitment to development can make. So I urge CEOs and MDs—of companies large and small, of public services, and of charities—to look closely at how they personally promote better management and leadership throughout their organisations. (p. 3)

Support could take the form, say, of the CEO, or another board member, agreeing to chair your steering group; or saying publicly that they have benefited from coaching; or promoting the service at a staff event. One professional services firm has a short video clip on their intranet of a board member talking about the impact that coaching has had on him. Another route to securing visible commitment from senior figures is to train them as internal coaches. When the NHS introduced internal coaching, the first cadre of coach trainees included a number of CEOs of health trusts who became energetic advocates.

You need to nurture that commitment from the top through regular meetings and reports—written or oral—either to the steering group, if there is one, or to an influential senior figure such as the CEO, COO, or HR director so that the added value being provided by the internal coaching is always kept front of their mind. The lead coach at one large consultancy provides a quarterly report that is sent to lead partners across the business including the COO. It includes:

- a summary of coaching activity (how many being coached; at what grades; from what parts of the business)
- what proportion of the budget has been spent
- evaluation results
- a "forward look" which could cover things like plans for training more internal coaches, running a conference for the coaching community, or expanding the scope of the coaching into a new area (e.g., maternity coaching)
- insights about systemic issues gained from feedback.

At the other end of the spectrum, many lead coaches simply go and see the key champion at regular intervals to keep them in touch with developments.

Strategic purpose

An early series of questions to address is:

- What is the purpose of setting up an internal coaching resource?
- What problem is it seeking to resolve or organisational benefits is it hoping to deliver?
- What benefit is the client going to get from it?
- What are the drivers?
- Who is it for?
- How does it fit with your organisation's mission, business strategy, existing leadership development, or learning and development strategies and plans, and talent management processes, and so forth?

Perhaps your internal coaching strategy is part of a broader strategy, together with the use of external coaches and training managers in coaching skills, to build a coaching culture? The answers to these questions form your strategic purpose.

Hawkins (2012) points out that some surveys—though they were principally looking at external coaching—have suggested that "relatively few organisations believe that they are deriving the full benefits of executive coaching" and the reasons given included:

- Lack of clarity of the purpose of coaching in the organisation
- Lack of focus on where and when coaching would be most beneficial. (p. 22)

Similarly, some evaluation research carried out on behalf of the Learning & Skills Improvement Service (LSIS) that listed the "top ten essentials" that internal coaches working in further education said they needed, showed that seventy-seven per cent of the coaches needed a "clear organisational purpose" (Turner, 2012, p. 8). Hunt and Weintraub (2006), too, say: "We have found that those internal coaching programmes that seem to be most successful have a job to do" (p. 4). Attention given to getting proper clarity about your purpose really is time well spent. The two case studies below provide examples of some quite broad strategic purposes.

Case study 6.2: Strategic purpose in the NHS

In the NHS they asked the question: "How can we best support the changes going on in the NHS?" and the strategic health authorities overwhelmingly supported a plan to set up a cohort of internal coaches to support people who were transitioning to different roles, leaving the service, or being promoted into new roles. Those at board level tended to be supported by a register of external coaches but there was a need below that for the managers who were operationally implementing the changes, and the internal coaching cohort was built to fulfil that purpose. This was gradually reinterpreted as "supporting talent management", for if you are developing your best people they will manage the changes better than they would have done otherwise.

Case study 6.3: Strategic purpose in the BBC

In the late 1990s, some people from within the L&D and HR communities in the BBC became interested in and learned about coaching. This led, at the end of 2000, to formally setting up an internal coaching service. The purpose was "to provide professional, executive, leadership and management coaching to support the BBC strategy, equal to or better than that which is available externally. And at a fraction of the cost to the licence payer".

They identified the following benefits to the organisation:

- The impact of clients being able to address their own leadership performance and effectiveness
- Quicker results from new appointments coached to maximise impact, influence, and effectiveness
- Application of learning from leadership development to organisational life by considering course input to client-specific situations
- Inexpensive means of providing executive coaching, accredited coach training, supervision, and development to high numbers of staff.

Targeting your coaching resource

There are a number of benefits, also, to having clear objectives for the internal coaching sitting under the broad purpose. They include: giving focus to the coaches; simplifying the task of explaining the rationale for the scheme; making decisions around selection and training easier; and helping the targeting of appropriate evaluation measures and metrics.

Hunt and Weintraub (2006), amongst others, are doubtful about the unfocused approach. They say:

> Organisations would do well to make sure that they don't have internal coaches without portfolio, wandering around, looking for work. Coaching in an organisational context needs to be tied to organisational goals and needs, otherwise it will ultimately be viewed as a fad and lose its credibility. (p. 4)

This section offers examples drawn from many, many internal coaching schemes of targeted support, under the headings:

* Support for transitions
* Support for HR initiatives
* Support for L&D programmes
* Support for business change.

Support for transitions

* *Transition to partnership/director level*: There were many examples of coaching people who had gained promotion but before they made the move—so that they could plan for hitting the ground running—and also for the "first 100 days". Some support was very specific, for example, coaching people to become better at chairing formal meetings (where the services of an internal coach, who may be able to sit in on meetings to observe the new promotee in action, can be particularly valuable).
* *Onboarding*: New recruits at a senior level find it especially helpful to be supported by an internal coach, as their familiarity with the system and the culture can help the client up the learning curve fast.
* *Maternity transition*: Losing high-flying women mid-career is costly for organisations and maternity coaching is gaining in popularity, particularly in high pressure legal or consultancy environments

where it can be difficult for recent mothers to balance their family commitments with client-facing roles. The period between six months and eighteen months back in the role is often the crunch time when the employee decides whether staying in the role is sustainable or not. In one consultancy firm there are a number of "returners" who have trained as internal coaches and specialise in maternity coaching.

Support for HR initiatives

- *Improved retention*: Sometimes organisations hit a period of losing staff at a rate beyond normal wastage. Sometimes this can be because managers have lost sight of what their options are within the organisation and internal coaches can help to re-engage them.
- *Career development*: Internal coaches can be used very productively in career coaching as they understand the organisation and what the opportunities might (or might not) be. Research by Levenson, McDermott, and Clarke (2004) in fifty-five large organisations found that using external coaches actually increased the risk of losing staff that had "derailment risks". Internal coaches are often in a better position to help a client think through their options within the organisation and assist them to develop a career plan.
- *Encouraging diversity*: Coaching can play a particularly helpful role in supporting, for example, emerging Black, Asian, and minority ethnic (BAME), and female managers who are trying to break through the glass ceiling.
- *Embedding new HR systems*: Organisations have found internal coaches to be a valuable resource when managers are struggling to implement new HR systems such as managing sickness, or a new methodology, or competence structure for appraising staff. Problems can range from managers not having engaged with a new system at all to their not appreciating the opportunity that it might offer to manage their staff more effectively or even save them time.
- *Improving implementation of existing systems*: Many organisations expect managers to conduct end of year development interviews with their direct reports. Managers can fail to grasp this opportunity and either ask their staff to write their own development objectives or interpret the word development simply as "training courses". Where an HR department decides to have a push on conducting such interviews properly, internal coaching can make a significant contribution

to helping managers reflect on how they might approach the task more positively.

Support for L&D programmes

- *Board member development*: Ten per cent of the internal coaches in my research coached board directors. In some consultancy firms, internal coaches routinely coach very senior partners. Even if main board directors opt for external coaches, subsidiary board members may not. Experienced internal coaches can make a significant impact by coaching people at this level.
- *Leadership/management development programmes*: It is common for managers to bewail the fact that a colleague or direct report has been on a development programme and does not seem to have learned anything from it. Equally, participants on such programmes can find themselves completely overwhelmed by the volume of theoretical material that they are exposed to on such programmes and then return to the office to be overwhelmed again by an overflowing in-box. It can make a significant difference if participants are allocated a coach to help them to embed and explore what they have experienced; to think through how they can translate what they have learned back into the workplace; and to have some support for experimenting with trying out new approaches or behaviours. Internal coaches' understanding of the context in which they are operating can be invaluable.
- *Talent management schemes*: These can take many different forms. Often they involve a mix of access to training (internal and external); work shadowing with senior people; development opportunities such as short-term secondments and regular meetings with a mentor. Continuing support from an internal coach is a very helpful component and can be the "glue" that maintains the focus throughout. Some talent management schemes may be for comparatively junior managers but they deserve top notch coaching. As Hunt and Weintraub (2006) put it:

> … pushing coaching down the organisation does not mean that the coaching can be of lower quality. When providing a coaching resource to high potentials or middle managers, the organisation is coaching its future. (p. 3)

- *Specific initiatives*: From time to time learning and development departments recognise a systemic need. One organisation whose lead coach I interviewed had identified a problem around leadership development. They had acquired a 360-degree feedback instrument focusing on leadership competences and she had trained half a dozen internal coaches specifically to focus on delivering the feedback to dozens of managers and then helped to put together a development plan for each of them. The plan was to test-drive it with the board and then introduce it through the rest of the management layers. Another example was where a pharmaceuticals company was instituting a push to improve success rates for their sales teams. They gave them some advanced training then used internal coaches to help them to embed the learning and put their new skills into practice.

Support for business change

- *Strategic support*: One London-based consultancy offers its internal coaches for what they call "thinking partnerships": that is, to support partners in thinking about business and people issues. The lead coach is pleased at the take-up. She specifically positions her internal coaches as "change agents".
- *Supporting business critical projects*: A number of organisations have focused some of their internal coaches' efforts on supporting individuals heading up major change programmes.
- *Supporting new teams*: Examples here have included coaching the manager responsible for leading a new product development team; another, leading a project to improve the way that customer relationship managers interacted with customers; another, to transform the way that the manufacturing and sales teams worked together.

These are all examples of ways of targeting coaching support. It is desirable, when identifying specific programmes as part of your overall coaching strategy, to frame outcomes that are measurable. Chapter Ten, which focuses on evaluation, explores this issue further.

Organisational learning

Do not forget, when thinking through your strategy, the opportunity it offers for harvesting systemic learning and feeding it back into the business. Hawkins (2012), Fletcher and Macann (2011), and others have all written about the benefits. As Alison Maxwell said in a particularly colourful metaphor: "Coaches can reach into the bowels of the organisation in a way that other interventions cannot" (Maxwell, 2013). However, you need to decide on a) the gathering mechanism that works best for your organisation and b) where the information can be fed back for maximum impact and utility.

Facts and figures 6.1: Mechanisms for feeding back organisational learning

Some examples:
- In the NHS, the ten strategic health authority coaching leads would meet quarterly as the "SHA Coach Network". As part of the meeting anonymised themes from the centrally funded telephone coaching supervision would be circulated for discussion. This would be used to inform commissioning CPD for internal coaches.
- In one pharmaceutical company, the lead coach met with the management development director twice a year to talk non-attributably about themes emerging from the coaching sessions provided to participants on leadership development programmes.
- A lead coach in a legal firm told me that she regularly picked three themes to feed back to the lead partner. This was done in an *ad hoc* way. "Sometimes he listened, sometimes he didn't. I would know if he'd listened because I'd hear about some conversation that he'd had or some action that he'd taken."
- At one media organisation, the supervisor asked the supervision groups to come up with the "top three organisational issues" every six months and then shared these with OD.

There seem to be two main categories of helpful data: a) information that suggests ways in which delivery of the coaching could be improved and b) information that suggests ways in which the organisation could work more effectively.

Examples of harvested themes for improving the coaching service

- Several supervisors in one large organisation reported back that some of the coaches were struggling to get enough clients and felt that they were becoming deskilled. The lead coach took steps to increase publicity of the scheme and to streamline the "matching" system.

- A supervisor spotted that issues around boundaries kept cropping up and suggested a refresher CPD session around that.
- A number of coaches fed back to a lead coach that their line managers were becoming disgruntled at the amount of time that the coaching was taking up. The lead coach spent the next few months systematically contacting the line managers of all the coaches to remind them of the benefits and also to express personal gratitude for the contribution their direct reports were making to the organisation.

Examples of harvested themes for improving the organisation

- Coaches in an engineering company noted a significant number of senior clients needing support in taking decisions. Managers appeared to be afraid to put their heads above the parapet in case they got it wrong. The issue was fed into a board awayday.
- Coaches in a consultancy company became aware of conversations at all levels around the poor gender mix in recent promotions to partner and, in particular, a) how this was demotivating high flying women and b) the negative message it was sending throughout the organisation about attitudes towards diversity generally. The partners took it on board.
- Senior managers coaching clients in a local authority reported feeling that top-level decisions were being taken without being properly communicated to them. This left them feeling disengaged. It resulted in more attention being given to internal communications.
- Coaches in a professional services company who were coaching "returners" after maternity leave were able to feed back some very specific problems: when women reached the "unpaid" element of their maternity leave, their security passes and email access were automatically disabled as though they had left the company. Plus, on their return to work they had to be escorted into the building as though they were a visitor. They found this very dislocating and unwelcoming. The company acted on the feedback.

Sometimes coaches can pick up on issues that people are disgruntled about which can shed light on a dip in retention rates or poor employee engagement scores.

However, the fact that data is collected does not ensure that it is actioned, so it is important to check that a) the information is reaching the people who can act on it and b) that they are actually doing something with it. I came across one example of an organisation that was dutifully feeding data into OD quarterly and only discovered after some years that it was not actually being used.

Case study 6.4: Gathering organisational learning

One firm, where the coaching effort is distributed around a number of business units, has developed an approach to gathering organisational learning that draws on a variety of sources.

- The coaches working within each business unit meet regularly with their lead coaches and share knowledge including any organisational themes emerging.
- They have a number of supervision groups for their internal coaches that meet four times a year led by two external supervisors. Each supervisor agrees with their groups at the end of each session three to four organisational themes emerging from the group discussions that are fed back to the overall coach lead for the business.
- L&D runs a variety of programmes including coaching skills for managers' training. Data about systemic issues can surface from these too.
- There is an annual all day coaching conference to which all internal coaches (and external coaches) are invited. The question "What are we seeing in the organisation?" is asked and all contribute to sense-checking some high level organisational themes.

Once a quarter the lead coach synthesises the learning from all these different sources to feed back to the steering group.

Positioning

The success of your internal coaching scheme will partly depend on how you position it. Once it is up and running its reputation will be built on how valuable the coaching proves to be and how its success is communicated, but managers will form some opinion about it from the word go, based on who will be eligible to receive coaching, where the scheme sits within the business, and how you communicate that. Your strategy therefore needs to give some thought to these aspects.

Eligibility

Selecting who will be eligible to access your internal coaches will flow from your strategic purpose. Sometimes it will be very obvious: if your key purpose is to support your talent pool then they are the ones who will be eligible. If, however, you have settled on a much broader purpose, such as developing the leadership potential of managers, then you will need to find a way of identifying who is entitled within that group. Do you want to publicise the availability of coaching, then leave it in the hands of interested individuals to apply, ask managers to identify people who might benefit, or hand pick people in business critical areas?

Many lead coaches position the coaching as being an investment in the organisation's talented people to help them to reach their potential. One lead coach commented that they do not have the resources to make coaching available to anyone who might like it so have identified certain groups who are eligible such as:

- all executives above a certain level
- managers on specific development programmes and
- those making transitions to director level.

Another approach though is to recognise that building an internal coaching pool offers the ideal opportunity to accelerate the development of more junior managers, not merely the senior élite.

Remedial coaching: Is there a place in your internal coaching scheme for remedial coaching? Most of the lead coaches that I interviewed said, in effect, "Absolutely not". They were usually thinking of situations where they felt that a line manager was ducking their responsibility for performance management and that they should step up to the plate rather than handing the problem over to a coach. However, not all internal coaching schemes exclude this kind of work: coaches can support significant turnarounds working with poor performers who have been given a six-month improvement plan to work on. Some internal coaches successfully specialise in it and become highly sought after.

Where the scheme should sit

Most coach leads are experienced, trained coaches who already work in OD or L&D roles in a central function. The coaching effort is often therefore most naturally sited there. Depending on the size of the organisation, OD and L&D may or may not sit within HR—some organisations have a separate L&D or talent management operation. Then again, some organisations work on a distributed leadership model and have HR/OD/L&D business partners all around the business with some coaches attached to each cluster. There are therefore a number of places where responsibility for the coaching scheme might naturally be sited.

It is important to give some thought at the outset to the best place for your coaching scheme to be in the light of the messages that this may transmit to your key clients. Two specific aspects of this raised by a number of my interviewees were a) whether to have the coaching scheme within a "central function" or distribute it around the organisation and b) the downsides of having a coaching scheme sitting within HR.

Coaching as a central or distributed function: There were felt to be some specific upsides to situating lead coaches within business units: they can fine-tune provision to the needs of their client group and work in tandem with the business head to ensure that the focus reflects business priorities. However, this will result in an individual approach in each unit so a casualty can be consistency. Managers can learn that colleagues in another unit can access a particular type of coaching, such as help with transitioning to a new role, which they cannot. One way to mitigate this is to get the coaches together regularly to exchange information about what they are doing and report back to their business heads. This will also help to build a community of coaches across the organisation.

Most lead coaches, however, felt that their natural home was sitting at the centre, within or alongside HR, OD, and L&D.

Coaching sitting within HR: One school of thought argues against siting the coaching function within HR. One lead coach pointed out that HR can play different roles within different businesses. Where they are proactive, strategic, and operate a "business partner" type model there is no problem associating HR with the coaching effort. However, where they are more reactive and transactional, or are only really prominent when there is a big redundancy programme, then the association with coaching can be unhelpful. As the same lead coach put it: "Most L&D people try to distance themselves from HR and perceive them as driven by rules and process." This view seems to reflect the wider debate within the HR profession about its future and, in particular, its capacity to play a strategic role.

An article in *People Management* magazine, entitled "HR: the damning verdict" (2013), reads:

> HR wants to be a trusted adviser to business leaders. But most chief executives regard their HR heads as the poor relations at the top table, according to a new survey. An Oracle/IBM "C-suite perspectives of HR" study, carried out by the Economist Intelligence Unit, found that 30 per cent of Chief Executives and senior leaders in western Europe felt that their HR Director was "not of the same calibre as other C-level executives". More than 40 per cent thought the HR function was "too focused on process and rules" and over a third said that it did "not understand the business well enough".

One could argue that, in those firms where HR is not really rated, siting the coaching function there would not be getting it off to a flying start. However, if you, as lead coach, are also an HR manager (or you are yourself head of HR) and you are looking to make the function more proactive in helping to drive business effectiveness, you might consider whether setting up a well-regarded internal coaching resource could in itself send a helpful message about HR to the rest of the business.

Scope and approach of the coaching

Your strategy needs to make clear what you are expecting from your coaches:

- How results-driven do you want them to be?
- Will they mentor as well as coach?
- Will they involve the client's line managers?

Business objectives vs. personal objectives

How "results-driven" are you expecting your coaches and their clients to be in their coaching relationships? Are you happy for coaching sessions to be a rare opportunity for the client to draw breath, reflect on their work, and go wherever their thoughts take them? Or are you keen for specific, work-oriented goals to be agreed, perhaps in a three-way meeting with the line manager, at the outset and not to be deviated from? Are you looking for the clients to get professional development or personal development or both? Where, as an organisation, do you want your coaches to put the boundary between the needs of the organisation and the needs of the individual client, in the sense of work *vs.* personal issues? Chapter Three included a brief discussion of the issue of "Who is the client?" from the perspective of the coach. It is something that you too, as lead coach, need to think about, and it would merit a place in your coaching strategy. Would it concern you if a client devoted a whole coaching session to their attempts to lose weight, because they felt that their size was having an impact on their self-confidence? Or spent time on their concerns about whether their teenage daughter might be developing anorexia, because anxiety about it was making them short-tempered at work?

To some of you this might seem like a non-issue—you train your internal coaches to "be professional" and to use their judgement as to what it is reasonable to spend work time discussing. However, uncertainties around this issue frequently appear in research on internal coaching and it often came up in interviews. Lack of clarity around the scope is illustrated by this quotation from an internal coach supervisor:

> "The purpose is often pretty woolly—or it may have started off by being clear but then that purpose disappeared and the coaches just turned their hands to whatever came up. Coaches often had to make it up as they went along when deciding whether a personal issue could be on or off the agenda. As a supervisor I would often ask my coaches 'How clear is your mandate and how could you find out?'"

Coaches often tell clients that the agenda is theirs, without necessarily putting much of a boundary around that except perhaps to say something about "as long as it is about your development". This can translate into clients' believing that any topic is permitted. Snape's (2012) research about the internal coaching client perspective mentions: "… everyone was clear that the coachee should be able to discuss anything they wanted to" (p. 50) and Wrynne (2011) says: "All the coachees either display a tension between their personal goals and organisational goals or express difficulty in separating the two" (p. 42). As lead coach you may want your internal coaches to put rather tighter boundaries around what coaching time can be used for. Or not!

Wrynne points out that the CIPD's definition of coaching talks about aiding an "individual's private life" but, as he says:

> [This] indirectly asks the question as to whether the organisation is responsible for an individual's broader development and if this should be facilitated on organisational budgets. This problematic notion, whereby individuals might engage in learning or development outside the parameters set by the organisation, channels into the broader debate on the tensions between individual and organisational learning. (p. 2)

A relevant and interesting piece of research was undertaken by Carter (2009) when she analysed some eighty-eight client action plans as part of a wider evaluation study of internal coaching in an organisation. The plans had been completed by clients during the first or second coaching session. Some 225 objectives were listed—an average of 2.5 each. She categorised the objectives by primary outcome expected into "individual" or "organisation" objectives. The "individual" category included self-awareness, personal effectiveness, and career and skills development outcomes. The "organisation" category included customer service, reputation, and culture change and business strategy outcomes. Only thirty-seven objectives (seventeen per cent) were fully aligned to business outcomes.

When I interviewed Carter about this research she said that there had been a lot of reaction to that article, both positive and negative. She recognised that there was a chain of impact—that working on a personal goal such as raising the client's overall confidence is likely over time to impact on the client's work performance. However, she felt that a key issue that can be overlooked by organisations when setting up coaching schemes was the line of sight with business strategy: "If your company is looking to accelerate the personal development of its people, that's fine, but be clear that's what your coaching programme is about. If on the other hand your organisation expects specific business impact, then I suggest thinking about giving guidance to your coaches and line managers to encourage their clients/staff to include relevant business oriented goals" (Carter, 2013).

She suggested some dos and don'ts for getting the best value for money from internal coaching.

Top tips for better business focus

DO	DON'T
Select clients carefully. What business impact will you get from people unready for change?	Adopt a no-barriers approach to accessing a coach. You need clients from business critical roles to have an impact.
Be clear at the outset what business benefits are expected and how/when they are measured.	Give clients the sole responsibility for selecting areas for work—organisational needs may not be included.
Brief everyone that at least one area to work on should be for business benefit. Spend time to get and keep managers and sponsors involved. They should ensure the coaching has a real link with business needs.	Assume managers know how coaching works or that they assess outcomes.
Encourage successful clients to share their experiences. This will help promote the coaching to the wider organisation.	Produce management reports with routine scheme efficiency data. You must build in evidence of effectiveness, performance, and productivity benefits. Ease off using your volunteer coaches' time. When coaching use is high, payback grows and the scheme is better value.

Source: Carter, A. (2009). "Your best bet". *Coaching at Work*, 4(6): 46 (www. coaching-at-work.com). Reproduced with permission.

One other aspect of the "Who is the client?" question is how coaches should deal with situations where the interests of the organisation and the individual clearly seem opposed. As Peltier (2001) put it:

> To whom does the coach owe loyalty? What happens when a client's interests or intended behaviour are at odds with those of the company? For example, what if a client wants to focus on skills that the company clearly does not need—or skills that the client would

like to use in her next job or as an entrepreneur? What happens when the client is angry and contemplating legal action against the company, or is plotting his next move to a new company? (p. 226)

These sorts of issues will be seen as a no-brainer by some and an ethical dilemma by others but the bottom line is: are you happy for the client to be setting the agenda and for the coaches to use their judgement in the moment? Or do you want to be providing your coaches with any guidance?

Mentoring vs. coaching

Another aspect of putting boundaries around the scope of your internal coaching effort is how you feel about your coaches including a little mentoring along the way. What kind of coaching do you want from them? Chapter Three discusses some of the issues from the coach perspective. Coaches often find that their clients want them to play the mentor role and sometimes put pressure on them to do so. They can feel put in an invidious position, as that was not usually what they were trained to deliver and they are not sure if it is "allowed". Snape (2012) quotes one client responding, on the subject of whether a coach should give guidance or advice: "I know they're not meant to, being a coaching session, but I would still like it" (p. 50). Yedreshteyn (2008), too, notes this topic being discussed by clients who were being supported by internal coaches on a leadership programme:

> There was a lot of conversation about preferring to work with coaches or mentors. Some clients wanted an independent and objective coach from another business while others were disappointed not to have a more senior leader from their function, someone who could also serve in the role of mentor and help them grow in the corporation.

Some would argue that internal coaches are uniquely well placed to pepper a little mentoring into their coaching. There is evidence (Macann, 2012a) that coaching clients are increasingly looking for coaches with experience of their business area and perhaps, rather than "pure" coaching, they would welcome elements of mentoring in the coaching conversations. Should an internal coach who has skills in, say, OD and who may easily be able to offer a consultancy perspective, be allowed to go there if a client is struggling with managing a change programme? That may not be what you want—and you may have a thriving mentoring scheme to meet this need—but it is worth sharing with your coaches how flexible (or not) you expect them to be in this regard. Many organisations provide written guidance about what clients can expect from their coaches and this would be the place to put the results of your reflections. Some organisations specifically use the term coach-mentor for their coaches to signal that they can wear both hats.

Involvement of line managers

What role do you, as lead coach, want line managers to play in the coaching? Of course, where they are the boss of a potential internal coach they will need to give permission for that person to take the time for coach training, and subsequently for coaching clients, receiving supervision, and undertaking their continuing development as coaches.

Many businesses look, too, for the active involvement of the clients' line managers in the coaching process: beginning with authorising participation in the scheme then possibly involvement in a three-way meeting at the beginning of the coaching assignment; a check-in part-way through the process and then feedback at the end on any changes or progress they had noticed. For line managers to be able to play their part, it is important that they are given guidance about the process and what is expected of them.

The scenario just painted, however, is of a fairly "hands on" variety of coaching scheme. In some organisations the line manager may have little or no part in the process at all, or even know that their direct report is being coached. In that scenario, based on the principle that individual managers take responsibility for their own learning and development, the starting point might have been a 360-degree feedback report initiated by the client; an end-of-year interview with their boss that identified areas for development; or even feedback from an unsuccessful interview for a new role. You will want to think about what makes most sense in your organisation. How much line manager involvement do you want?

Budget allocation for the coaching scheme

Your strategy will need to include a section on what budget will be required to set the internal coaching scheme up and then run it. Implementation will inevitably involve a lot of administration and day-to-day decision-making. However, the budget requirements will depend on a myriad of factors including the following:

- How large the initial cohort of coaches is going to be
- Whether they are to be part-time or full-time coaches
- How high profile the initiative will be
- Whether the coaches are to be trained from scratch or whether you can draw on experienced coaches already working within the organisation. If the latter, whether they will be formally validated and, if so, whether the validation (e.g., in the form of an assessment centre) and/or the training will be delivered internally or externally
- Whether a qualification to a certain level is required of the internal coaches and, if so, to what level. Also whether accreditation will be sought
- How the matching is to be done: that is, individually (which is time-intensive for the lead coach) or via an electronic coach management system (which involves a set-up cost if custom built or an ongoing cost if leased from a provider)
- Whether a major and on-going communications/marketing exercise will be needed or if the coaching is to be "by invitation only"
- The volume of written guidance/policy development planned
- Whether supervision will be one-to-one or group and whether it will be delivered in-house or outsourced
- Whether energy will be invested in building a coaching community
- How much CPD or other types of event will be on offer to the coaches
- Whether corporate membership of a coaching professional body will be invested in or whether individual membership will be offered to the coaches (currently typically around £100 p.a. per coach in the UK)
- How monitoring/quality assurance will be carried out and how evaluation is to be done
- How much resource will be required to service a steering group, if used.

Many of these issues will be explored in some depth in Chapters Eight to Ten.

There is a school of thought that says that people only value what they pay for. This argument can translate into a view that if internal coaching is paid for from a central budget, managers will not think really carefully about who would benefit most from it and how they might best support that manager through the process so that they get the maximum value from it. I have not identified any organisations where this line of thinking has been followed through and individual business units or divisions "pay" for the coaching through a system of cross charging to their L&D budgets but a handful of my interviewees said that they were thinking about it. For consultancy and law firms, where employees are used to accounting for their time through time sheets and there are already sophisticated systems for charging time to different clients or cost headings, this can be fairly straightforward to do. For many other organisations where this is not the norm, setting it up could be quite an administrative chore. However, in terms of positioning the offering, ensuring that the business units or divisions "pay" for it is making this statement to the organisation: "This is a service that contributes to the bottom line, not a central overhead."

Piloting your scheme

One useful approach, if you want to prove the concept before devoting significant funds to an internal coaching scheme, is to pilot your coaching scheme first in one part of the organisation, conduct an evaluation into its effectiveness, and only then roll it out across the organisation. The following case study is an example of this.

Case study 6.5: Piloting your coaching scheme

In 2007, a large public sector organisation decided to pilot an internal coaching scheme within one business area. The trigger was a staff engagement survey that showed that staff in that part of the business (numbering some 2,000 people) were noticeably less engaged than in others. The head of L&D for that business partner suggested that an internal coaching scheme could contribute to the solution and a business case was made for training eight staff as internal coaches—the role to be on top of their day jobs. Until the pilot, only senior staff had had an opportunity to receive one-to-one coaching (and always from an external supplier) and the decision to go for an internal coaching scheme was partly driven by a desire to bring the same coaching benefits to staff at lower levels. The business benefits identified were:

- developing the leaders at the top and
- empowering those managers further down the organisation and making them feel more supported and valued.

ICF accredited training (to qualify for Associate Credentialled Coach level) was chosen; contracts were drafted and agreed, between the organisation and the coaches, and between the coaches and the coaches; expectations by all parties were clarified; and boundary issues discussed. Eighteen months on, the pilot was expanded to train a further thirty-six coaches. At this point the importance of ongoing support for the coaches was recognised and the programme added in coaching circles and two days per annum of CPD (including group supervision and triad work).

In 2010 an evaluation questionnaire was launched for clients to complete. Most of the questions involved a seven-point Lickert scale (from strongly agree to strongly disagree) and covered a lot of ground (feedback for the coach; the coaching process; personal learning development; impact on the job; organisational impact; and support received). Those running the scheme were conscious of the need to demonstrate its value and were therefore very pleased when consistently ninety per cent of the clients answered "Strongly agree" to the following two statements:

- Coaching, compared to other learning activities, is a worthwhile investment in my development.
- Coaching, compared to other learning activities, is a worthwhile investment for the organisation's development.

Responses to the statement: "The provision of coaching demonstrates to me that the organisation is committed to developing its people" were also very positive, demonstrating that clients were feeling more valued. Clients reported feeling more motivated, engaged in their job, empowered, and able to take actions forward. Some line managers who were interviewed similarly reported that their wider teams had benefited from a staff member's coaching because of the client's positive behavioural shifts and the impact these had on ways of working.

In the two years following the pilot more internal coaches were trained and in early 2013 there were over 100 internal coaches coaching throughout the organisation. Much effort has since gone into the development of marketing materials to explain what coaching can offer and to promote the reputation of coaching. They are now developing a team coaching approach.

Sustainability

When thinking through your strategy, make sure you build in features that make your scheme's sustainability more likely. Over the past two years of listening to stories about successful and less successful coaching schemes, and asking lead coaches about what has gone well and what less well, I have been struck by the theme of sustainability that has come up in a number of different guises. Where schemes have faltered, the dominant narratives have been: a) schemes set up by a passionate advocate for coaching (almost always a coach themselves) who then moves on or is made redundant and is replaced with someone who lacks the seniority, or energy, or influence, or personal experience of coaching to keep the profile high; b) schemes which start with a burst of enthusiasm but then hit a wall because staff cuts mean that the coaches have less time available in which to coach and, if they have not felt their contribution was particularly valued by the organisation, lose motivation and impetus; or c) schemes which had a senior champion, and thus the lead coach did not feel the necessity to collect evaluation data but, when that champion left the organisation, found themselves high and dry with no data to demonstrate that the coaching was providing benefit. The following represent a few thoughts on strategies that some organisations are employing to ensure the sustainability of the internal coaching resource.

Leadership

One key benefit of having a steering group is that the energy behind a coaching scheme does not rest simply with the lead coach. If it is run well, it should form a nexus of people committed to ensuring that the scheme flourishes. Members of the group can help to make sure that the purpose is kept fresh and relevant to the needs of the organisation and to support the lead coach if they show signs of flagging. It can also help to have not one lead coach, but a small team of them, either distributed through the organisation or in a cluster at the centre. They can support each other and take it in turns to take the strain when activity in their day jobs is particularly demanding. It also means that even if one of them moves on for whatever reason, the infrastructure will not collapse.

Balancing supply and demand

It seems that organisations can concentrate on the supply side: that is, selecting and training the coaches to the detriment of the demand side: that is, recruiting clients. From my interviews, I can corroborate the fact that there are many organisations out there with underemployed internal coaches. Quotations include:

> "My organisation's invested a lot of money in training me but has then failed to give me anyone to coach. I feel as though I'm deskilling and already need a top-up. I'm losing confidence."
>
> "We were trained up and only then did my firm start looking for coachees so there was a hiatus. It should be a seamless process—not leaving us twiddling our thumbs."
>
> "I feel a lack of connectedness with the infrastructure (i.e., the people who are running the scheme). They don't seem to be marketing internal coaching—perhaps to protect us from being overwhelmed by requests—but it's bad news from where I'm sitting. I'm losing motivation, enthusiasm, connectedness."

Many lead coaches are nervous of being swamped by demand and therefore under-market the scheme, so the initial sign-up can be very slow. The result of that can be: a) that the coaches become deskilled or lose interest and b) that anyone who asks for coaching gets it, even if they are not in an influential position or wanting to work on business critical issues, because the coaches want the practice. So the payback is less. One approach for balancing supply and demand better is to market enthusiastically and maintain a waiting list if demand outstrips supply. This is likely to result in a more sustainable service.

Building a coaching community

On 14 January 2013, a meeting of the EMCC's public sector coaching and mentoring forum, which I chair, discussed another aspect of sustainability: how an internal coaching community can continue with useful work even when the L&D function which ran it has been completely dismantled (so that the coaching community is, in effect, leaderless). In the public sector, there are sadly a number of examples of where this has happened and the internal coaches are left wondering how to deal with the situation.

The discussion was around self-managed groups and how, if the internal coaches have been encouraged to become a real community, they have a much better chance of making a go of being self-managed and continuing to deliver coaching within their organisation. This could include making referrals to each other; getting together regularly for co-coaching or coaching practice sessions; or perhaps taking it in turns to organise a lunchtime CPD session with an external speaker happy to donate their services. But if they have been isolated from each other that is most unlikely to happen.

There are many good reasons for building a coaching community—this is just one of them. If you work in a well-resourced organisation then finding yourself in this situation may seem inconceivable, but for some coaches it is all too real.

Valuing your coaches

Retention of coaches can be another sustainability issue. They may leave the organisation because restructuring or staff cutbacks lead to redundancies or because they want to work as a freelance external coach or join a coaching consultancy. Or their job may change shape so they have less time available for coaching. Training new coaches takes time and resources and you want to keep them—with their experience and knowledge of the organisation and the people in it—for as long as you possibly can.

Given that you do not have the lever of offering them promotion or a pay rise, the best way of keeping your coaches is to make them feel valued and supported. As Long (2012) puts it:

> In many organisations, the internal coach has to fit coaching around their day job. Their contribution as an internal coach may not even be recognised at appraisal. While coaching can be a rewarding "escape" from other parts of their role, unless there is encouragement and support from somewhere within the organisation then it is easy to see how the commitment to coach can wane, and for internal coaches to go off radar. (p. 3)

So what kinds of ways are organisations finding to demonstrate that they value their internal coaches? The following are some examples:

- The lead coach taking every opportunity to say thank you to the coaches (examples were at CPD days or regular get-togethers), affirming what they do, and acknowledging the commitment they show by coaching on top of their normal jobs.
- Some lead coaches collect the feedback from evaluation forms and hold regular one-to-ones with their internal coaches to pass on the feedback and thank them for their commitment.
- A senior champion, ideally at board level, sending an annual thank you email to all the internal coaches for their contribution to improving organisational effectiveness. One HR director sends a handwritten Christmas card annually to every internal coach.
- One organisation has a "coach of the year" award. Clients are invited to nominate their coach for it. The winner and several runners up receive book tokens for varying amounts and there is a little ceremony. Other organisations to whom I have fed back this idea did not like it at all, as they felt it was divisive. However, a by-product of the award is publicity in the organisation's monthly newsletter, raising the profile of the overall scheme.
- In some organisations the coach's development objectives as a coach will form part of their overall individual development plan, so their coaching work is being acknowledged in that way.
- Investing in supervision, holding regular CPD sessions, and arranging get-togethers for the internal coaching community are all seen by coaches as demonstrating that the organisation values what they do.

Demonstrating value

A tried and tested way of ensuring that a coaching scheme continues to be funded is by demonstrating its effectiveness. I worried about the lead coach, one year into his role, who told me that he did not plan to do any evaluation, rather trusting to: a) his coaches to do a professional job and b) his very influential champion to argue successfully for the funding each year. What will he do if, in two years time, his champion moves on and the finance director asks for evidence that the money was being spent well before committing any more funds?

There are many other good reasons for evaluating the effectiveness of your internal coaching scheme but ensuring that it is sustainable is one of them. Evaluation is explored in depth in Chapter Ten.

Summary

This chapter has examined the need for a coaching strategy and the areas you might cover. A good strategy becomes your blueprint for implementing your internal coaching scheme and ensuring its success. We have discussed a number of different issues ranging from how you will ensure the commitment from the business which is essential for sustainability, through to the scope of the scheme, including eligibility and targeting your coaching resources and the need to evaluate it. If you have clarity on these issues your communication to the business will be clear and consistent, and that is paramount to the success of your internal coaching programme.

QUESTIONS TO REFLECT ON

Factor to consider	What are the implications for the organisation?
Do we need a coaching strategy? A coaching strategy provides clarity around: • the purpose of internal coaching • governance arrangements • key stakeholders and intended recipients • intended "deliverables" • resources needed • positioning and communicating • monitoring and evaluating • creating sustainability	• If our scheme is currently small, what are the consequences of not writing a strategy for the future? • Who is my audience for the strategy? What do I need to consider so that it is best positioned to gain their support? • What is going on in the organisation at present that has relevance for the coaching strategy: – other development initiatives – talent management – change programmes
Governance Is a steering group desirable for the implementation of the coaching strategy? It can provide: • influential input from across the organisation • champions for the scheme	If a steering group is appropriate for my organisation: • Who would be best to chair it? • To whom should we be accountable?

(Continued)

QUESTIONS TO REFLECT ON   (*Continued*)

Factor to consider	What are the implications for the organisation?
• a channel for ensuring that the coaching is linked to business needs • support if the scheme comes under threat when budgets are tight • challenge around effectiveness and value for money	• How can I ensure that the members have credibility within the business and are able to influence it? • How does the makeup of the group reflect our coaching strategy? • How will I frame the members' role? • What will their practical commitments be? • How often will I need to review the group? • What needs to be in place to address turnover, ensure commitment, etc.?
Commitment from the business leaders How will we gain commitment and support from business leaders?	• Who in the senior management team are likely to support internal coaching? How can I use their influence to bring other members of the senior management on board? • What needs to be in place to ensure continued support for internal coaching if: – our business champion leaves? – I leave?
Strategic purpose Do we have clarity on: • the key business driver for an internal coaching resource? • the benefits the coaching will deliver to the organisation?	What do I need to take into account when defining the strategic purpose of internal coaching: • What are the problems or issues that coaching could help resolve? • How could coaching contribute to business priorities?

(Continued)

QUESTIONS TO REFLECT ON   (*Continued*)

Factor to consider	*What are the implications for the organisation?*

• how internal coaching fits within our culture, business purpose, etc.?	• What are the key benefits to:
	   – potential clients?
	   – the organisation as a whole?

Organisational learning Coaching offers the potential for gathering "intelligence" from the business and synthesising it into valuable organisational learning	• How might we go about harvesting organisational learning? • Who could make best use of it? • Do we need to communicate our process to clients so they are reassured about the confidentiality?
Positioning The internal coaching scheme needs to be positioned to best effect in terms of: • who will be eligible for coaching • whether we exclude poor performers • where the scheme should sit within the organisation	• Have I focused on communication as part of my coaching strategy? • What channels of communication are most effective in my organisation? • Who are my key stakeholders for internal coaching? How do I need to tailor my messages to engage different groups? • Do we need to target clients in any particular area of the business to ensure we align with our strategic purpose? • How can we ensure the principles of equality and fairness underpin our approach to eligibility? • What are the pros and cons to the business of using coaches to work with individuals who are underperforming?

(*Continued*)

QUESTIONS TO REFLECT ON *(Continued)*

Factor to consider	What are the implications for the organisation?

	• Which area of the business would be best positioned to "own" coaching, taking into account:
	  – the size of our organisation?
	  – functional role of individuals in a section?
	  – credibility of HR?

Scope and approach of the coaching
What is expected of the coaches in terms of:
• driving results
• including or excluding mentoring
• involving line managers
	• Do we want to link clients' coaching objectives with:
	  – their operational objectives?
	  – their personal development plan?
	• Are we expecting our coaches to do any mentoring?
	• Would three way meetings between client/ coach/line manager be beneficial? If so what support and guidance needs to be in place to make the process easy for all?
	• How can we engage line managers in supporting members of their team who are internal coaches?

Targeting your coaching resource What are our objectives for internal coaching? How can we make best use of our internal coaches to meet business need?	• On which areas of the business or on-going business programmes do we need to target our coaching resource? • How will we review and re-evaluate our targeting of coaching resource?

(Continued)

QUESTIONS TO REFLECT ON   (*Continued*)

Factor to consider	What are the implications for the organisation?
Budget allocation for the coaching scheme How will the coaching scheme be funded?	• Will we fund the internal coaching training centrally or expect individual business units to contribute? • If we have central funding do we want to "charge" business units for the use of an internal coach?
Sustainability It is important that: • the energy behind a coaching scheme does not rest simply with the lead coach • supply and demand of coaches is balanced • a self-managing coaching community is built • the coaches feel valued and therefore give their services for many years	• What am I doing now to ensure internal coaching is owned by the operational units and does not just sit with the "lead coach"? • Is there a succession plan for my role of lead coach? • How am I engaging with the business to ensure internal coaching will continue even if there is a change in top management? • Would a pilot be beneficial to give an idea of demand before we commit to training a larger cohort of internal coaches? • How should we promote our internal coaching service? • What are the "drivers" that will help create a proactive coaching community? How can we help to build it? • What do we need to put in place to sustain the energy and enthusiasm of our internal coaches?

(*Continued*)

QUESTIONS TO REFLECT ON   (*Continued*)

Factor to consider	What are the implications for the organisation?
	• Would we want to have "coaching sabbaticals" to allow internal coaches to drop out of the pool for a specified time to meet increased demands from their functional role? • What do we need to do in terms of "succession planning" to ensure we deal with attrition?
Demonstrating value To ensure continued funding it is important to provide evidence of impact.	• What are the different ways that we can demonstrate the impact that the coaching is having? • Who needs to know? • What evaluation methods will best fit our coaching scheme, given its size, scope, and purpose?

CHAPTER SEVEN

Building the organisational framework

If you can't describe what you are doing as a process, you do not know what you're doing

—*W. Edwards Deming*

What this chapter is about

One of the lead coaches I interviewed as part of research for this book mentioned that if a supervisor for one of his coaches were unavailable, internal coaches would come to him if they had an ethical dilemma to talk through. I queried whether this arrangement was covered in the coach's initial contracting with the client, and he realised that it probably was not. In the contracting conversation, the coaches only talked about sharing information with the coach's supervisor, not with the lead coach. Potentially, these situations could lead to a breach of confidentiality and need to be thought through.

When using internal coaches, issues can arise that are beyond the scope of individual contracting. You need some corporate policies and processes. This chapter offers some thoughts for drafting these, and for communicating with the rest of the business. While you will not want to build an unnecessary edifice of documents, there are a number of considerations to take into account when setting up the organisational framework. This chapter covers:

- Roles, responsibilities and accountabilities
- Contracting
- Record-keeping and the legal implications
- Procedures for selecting coaches, pairing coaches with clients, monitoring, and evaluation
- Venues
- Guidance
- Standards, ethics, and quality of service
- Communication.

Roles, responsibilities, and accountabilities

The purpose of articulating what the key roles comprise is to clarify everybody's expectations of, and obligations to, each other. These roles are:

- Steering group, if any
- Lead coach/scheme administrator
- Line managers/sponsors
- Coaches
- Coaching clients.

Role of the steering group

If you do decide to have a steering group then its terms of reference should cover issues such as: What is its remit? Who should be its members? How, and to whom, will it report on its activities? What kind of data will it monitor? How often will it meet? In some organisations the lead coach chairs the steering group; in others, it is chaired by a "champion", perhaps a board member.

Role of the lead coach

It is the responsibility of the lead coach to ensure that you select the right people to be coaches, train them in the appropriate skills, set up a robust administrative infrastructure and policies to underpin the process, and provide the support necessary for your coaches' continued development. In most organisations, the lead coach will also be a practising internal coach. The breadth of the role varies widely depending on matters such as how large the scheme is; whether the lead coach also delivers training for the new coaches, or is a coach supervisor who also delivers supervision; how "hands-on" the matching process is; and whether there will be a mechanism for capturing organisational learning.

Another variable is whether the lead coach is responsible for the whole coaching strategy including the use of external coaches. In one consultancy firm, there is a lead coach for each part of the business and the process is that they meet up with prospective clients in their area to assess their development needs. On the basis of that conversation they may decide that the individual's needs would best be met by allocating an external coach, an internal coach, a company mentor, or some other kind of intervention. In this context it clearly helps to have a lead coach, tied into learning and development, with knowledge of the resources available.

Role of the line manager

Line managers have two distinct roles in a coaching scheme:

a. Agreeing to release someone to be trained as a coach, and
b. Playing their part in supporting a direct report who might benefit from having an internal coach.

In the former role it is important that the line managers understand what they are being asked to authorise in terms of the commitment that the potential coach will be making. It would be short-sighted to underplay the time commitment at the outset since the investment in training and developing a coach will be wasted if the line manager insists at a later date that the coach must withdraw. Remember that the coach will be committing to:

a. Training
b. Preparation and reflection time
c. Delivering coaching sessions
d. Supervision
e. CPD
f. Coaching community events.

However, line managers also need to understand the benefits to the effectiveness of coaches in their day job of acquiring these additional skills.

You will need to decide how much of an involvement you want from the line managers of the clients. Many organisations involve them as much as possible, for example:

- Asking them to authorise the coaching
- Involving them in the goal setting
- Asking them to be as clear as possible with the client about what success would look like
- Taking responsibility for feedback, and
- Taking an active role in supporting their continuing development.

The Ridler Report (Ridler & Co, 2013, p. 12) showed that seventy-four per cent of the 145 participating organisations had three-way contracting around coaching objectives (meeting between the coach, client, and line manager) at the outset of each coaching relationship. It is also common to have a three-way discussion at the end of the relationship, which can form the basis of an evaluation.

The purpose of the first three-way meeting is to ensure that there is a common understanding on all sides of the purpose of the coaching. There may be both public and private goals: that is, some goals agreed with the line manager and others that are agreed just between the coach and client. It is common, for example, for the client to want to do some work on their relationship with their line manager but they may not want to be explicit about that in this forum. At this meeting it can be useful to agree what, if any, feedback will be given by the coach to the line manager. In some schemes, line manager involvement is minimal—indeed the line manager may not even know that someone whom they manage is receiving coaching.

Role of the coach

How you describe the role of your coaches will partly reflect the training that they have received and the model of coaching that your organisation has adopted. If you have decided to recruit people from within the organisation who have already trained as coaches, and thus have trained in a variety of models, you might offer a more generalised description of what they do. This is the point at which to consider whether you are happy for your coaches to play any kind of mentor role as well as delivering "pure" coaching. The sorts of areas you might cover in any description of your coaches' role include:

Activities

- Managing the process (e.g., number and duration of meetings and where to meet)
- Using relevant diagnostic psychometrics or a 360 feedback instrument (if required)
- Helping the client to articulate coaching goals and what success would look like
- Supporting the client in exploring their options and the implications of each
- Inviting the client to reflect on their learning from past experiences
- Giving feedback
- Supporting the client in identifying actions
- Holding the client to account for agreed actions and helping them to identify any reasons holding them back
- Helping the client to identify any additional support they may need beyond the coaching relationship and how to source it.

Approach

- Showing respect
- Asking penetrating questions to help the client explore issues in depth
- Active listening
- Openness and honesty
- Helping the client to work things out for themselves
- Balancing support and challenge
- Being alert to the multiparty nature of the coaching relationship
- Being aware of the potential for conflicts of interest .

Role of the coaching client

An important aspect of the role of the client is the degree to which they are ready to be coached. It is common for lead coaches to focus mainly on the coaches, and less so on the clients and their suitability. Research strongly indicates that "coachability" is an important consideration. Stokes (2007), Yedreshteyn (2008), and Haden (2013) all suggest that the success of coaching assignments relies to a significant degree on the readiness of the client. This is therefore something to think about when establishing the organisational framework. How might you assess the clients' readiness? Stokes introduces the concept of the "skilled coachee" and the skills and attributes that are desirable (see table below).

Personal attributes desirable in a skilled learner/coachee	Skills desirable in a skilled learner/coachee
Is open to and seeks out feedback	Ability to work things out for themselves
Wants to progress and develop	Ability to identify benefits
Prepared to be open and honest about themselves	Takes responsibility for their own learning
Openness to challenge	Takes responsibility for own solutions
Welcomes and values forming relationships	Able to check out own understanding and ask questions to ensure they learn properly
Has a positive attitude	Maintains ground rules
Persistence/determinedness	Gives feedback to coach
Receptiveness	Ability to understand questions
Honesty	Picks things up quickly
Diligence/proactivity in following through	Responds to feedback
Commitment to the process	Good listener
Prepared to take risks to make progress	Can distinguish between things they have to memorise, things they need to understand and things that are best learned by doing
High integrity	
Capable of focus/concentration	
Is confident to take on new learning opportunities	

Stokes, P. (2007). *The Skilled Coachee* (p. 2). Table reproduced by kind permission of the author.

Some organisations ask the client to sign an undertaking. An example is:

Outline agreement between client and coach

I agree to work with my coach to shape the coaching relationship to best meet my needs by:

- Sharing what I know about my motivation
- Sharing what my values are and what is important to me
- Co-designing approaches that will support me
- Asking for changes when a strategy does not fit me
- Thinking before each session what I want to get out of it.

I give my coach permission to:

- Challenge me with powerful questions
- Request I take action when I have identified something that is important to me
- Hold me accountable for actions that I commit to
- Provide questions for me to think about.

Contracting

In some organisations the arrangements are pretty informal, particularly to start with, but putting something on paper is time well spent. Ideally aim for an agreement between coach and employer, as well as between coach and client.

Agreement between coach and employer

A contract is optional, but it is generally desirable to have something written about the expectations that coach and organisation have of each other, covering issues such as: a tailored code of ethics; any limits to confidentiality; what development they can expect; guidance around referrals to other professionals; supervision/support arrangements; and so forth.

Facts and figures 7.1: Contract between coach and employer

When it came to the question of contracting between the coach and the organisation:

- Thirty-three per cent of the internal coaches indicated that there was a formal contracting document between them and their organisation describing their responsibilities and obligations as a coach and the organisation's obligations to them.
- Where there was no such document, comments mainly fell into three categories:
  - there were plans for one
  - a much more limited kind of document did exist
  - formal contracting was limited to the coach-client relationship.

What level of time commitment are you expecting from your coaches? Do you have an expectation around the minimum number of clients that they should have at any one time (the norm seems to be one to three)? Are supervision and CPD mandatory? Some organisations make them mandatory and say that their coaches can no longer practice if they do not attend; some specify a minimum number of hours of CPD per year, and leave it to the coach to arrange it for themselves; others leave the number of hours entirely to their discretion. If the training you have provided offers a route to accreditation, do you expect your coaches to follow through? Are there any quality assurance arrangements that the coaches need to be aware of or to sanction: for example, observations of sessions or feedback from clients about their effectiveness? What are the evaluation arrangements?

Another area for consideration concerns the expectations the coaches have of you as lead coach: for example, whether you commit to regular one-to-one meetings, formal recognition, or giving support when they face a dilemma. Other expectations might be for giving feedback, ensuring there are sufficient clients for them, and information on the complaints system. These are all issues to cover in a contracting document.

Agreement between coach and client

It can be helpful to provide your coaches with an outline of a contracting document for them to discuss, amend, and agree with the client. It can include the issues outlined above that describe the roles of the coaches and their clients. In addition, what do you actually want them to be saying about confidentiality, boundaries, action if role conflicts arise, cancellation arrangements, and where the meetings should take place? This document (see Guidance, below) could also be the place to include something about the purpose of the coaching scheme; the organisation's definition of coaching and how it links to the overall business and development strategies; and the coaching approach being adopted.

Facts and figures 7.2: Contract between coach and client

- Approximately fifty per cent of coaches had some kind of written agreement with the client about their expectations of each other. Of these agreements, twenty-five per cent involved the client's line manager too.
- Contracting between the coach and client was often oral and only one third of the coaches reported that the content of that contracting conversation was provided by the organisation.
- Around fifty per cent had developed their introductory contracting conversation with the client based on previous experience or what they had learned in training—meaning that there might well be an inconsistent approach to it across the organisation.

Record keeping

K. M. Rogers (2011) examined the legal considerations in coaching and concluded that there are only two aspects for coaches to be careful about: confidentiality and data protection. Both of these are relevant to record-keeping.

Confidentiality

Rogers explains that a breach of confidentiality is demonstrated by means of a three-stage test:

1. The information disclosed by the client to the coach must have a "quality of confidence about it";
2. That information must have been disclosed in a situation where "there was an obligation of confidence"; and
3. The coach must have made "an unauthorised use of that information". (p. 181)

Interestingly, the client does not have to demonstrate that he or she has actually suffered any damage. Clearly, unauthorised sharing of client information with another party would be caught by this provision so ensuring that any records kept are safe is important.

Data protection

The UK's Data Protection Act 1998 (DPA) places requirements on people, including coaches, to protect personal data. The act has eight data protection principles in schedule one:

1. The data shall be processed fairly and lawfully
2. It is only obtained for one or more specified and lawful purposes
3. It shall be adequate, relevant, and not excessive
4. It is accurate and up to date
5. It is not kept for longer than necessary
6. It is processed in accordance with the data subject's rights
7. It is kept secure using technical and organisational methods
8. It is not transferred out of the European Economic Area (EEA) unless there is an adequate level of protection for data subjects.

Principles Five, Six, and Seven seem of particular relevance to coaches.

Taking Principle Five, for example, do you have a view on what notes your coaches should keep? Might you suggest, as many do, that coaches keep separate notes of content (which may include personal information such as problems with the client's marriage or children or relationships with colleagues) and process (which will cover interventions made and the intent behind them)? And how long do you expect the coaches to retain the records?

Facts and figures 7.3: Coaching records

Ninety-three per cent of the participants in my research kept some kind of records of coaching conversations.

- Around one third had a fixed period after which records were destroyed
- Around one half took an ad hoc approach
- Around one sixth did not know if there was a set period or not.

The period that coaches keep their records for varies widely, from destroying the notes after the final session to three years or more after the end of the coaching. While the safest approach might be to destroy them as soon as the relationship has reached a conclusion, coaches are often reluctant to do this in case the client returns for coaching at a later date. Electronic records that are "deleted" may still be accessible somewhere on the server. And how should the coach dispose of written information? Are shredders easily available?

Considering the data subject's rights (Principle Six), the client has the right of access to his or her personal data—which means that they can ask their coaches to see any notes they have taken. Coaches should be made aware of this. Some coaches, I know, do share their notes with their clients as a matter of course.

On the matter of how to keep records secure (Principle Seven), consider: where should coaches keep their client notes? Do you plan to have an area on the intranet that can only be accessed by the coaches and where they can store them? You need to consider a range of security factors: such as availability of locked filing cabinets; who has access to the key/code; data on a computer should be password protected; and so forth.

You could also consider giving guidelines to your coaches about use of the company email system. In my research, just under half (forty-seven per cent) used internal email for confidential exchanges with clients and this can be risky (see Case study 7.1).

Case study 7.1: Secure records and the use of company email

Michael T is an experienced internal coach of six years' standing who coaches senior people in his organisation. At the outset of each coaching relationship he checks with his client whether anyone else has access to the client's emails. If someone does, he suggests to the client that he uses their personal email address for any correspondence relating to the coaching. Michael himself has sole access to his work emails. Michael has around twenty staff and recently he has had to give a formal warning to three of them who were using their PCs for unauthorised purposes. He reported this to the head of HR who, unbeknownst to him, asked the IT department to monitor for a few weeks the use of *all* the PCs in Michael's division, which included Michael's own. One day the IT director called him down for a meeting and explained, with much discomfort, that when he went to investigate the cause of much hilarity in the IT room, he discovered IT staff reading an exchange of emails between Michael and his senior coaching client which related to very personal information indeed about the content of a particular session.

Question: What action would you take if you were Michael?

Use of coaches' notes in court cases

There is no recognised coach-client privilege comparable to the lawyer-client privilege, priest-penitent privilege, or doctor-patient privilege (Williams & Anderson, 2006). As a result, while coaches may promise to exercise confidentiality, they can still be compelled to reveal their written notes in a court of law. Coaching notes can be subpoenaed: for example, if the client becomes involved in an employment tribunal case. It is thus advisable that coaches include in their contracting process the arrangements for keeping client data safe but also explain the legal limits to that protection. One of my interviewees became involved in an HR investigation following a grievance procedure relating to her client. They said she must share her coaching notes and she felt that she had no choice. As a result she now keeps separate notes about content and process and just writes initials if another person has been discussed. She makes it very clear in her notes what interventions she has made during a client session.

Coaching venues

In Chapter Three I discussed some of the considerations concerning selecting venues. It is helpful if this is covered in your policies. This section draws on research by Linehan (2011) with fellow participants at Ashridge Business School. Linehan concludes that this is more than a simple "hygiene factor", like providing a glass of water. If either the coach or the client is not comfortable in their surroundings, this is likely to get in the way of reaching any depth or meaningful outcomes. The client might not realise it at the time or might not like to say—assuming that the coach will have chosen an appropriate venue. Conversely, the perfect environment for a session can make a major contribution to a client's shift in thinking—as those of us who have occasionally coached outside or walking along the seafront can attest.

Coaches and clients alike often prefer to avoid the formal feel of meeting rooms as they can inhibit open and relaxed interchanges.

Linehan notes that it is also worth thinking about what the location represents or symbolises to the client. If their issues relate to difficulties with colleagues, or a lack of self-confidence, say, does meeting in the work environment reinforce these feelings? Meeting the client in their own office can provide insights into their day-to-day reality, but holding the session in a cluttered, interrupted environment can stifle the flow of conversation. Some on-site meeting rooms can provide more tranquillity for reflection and privacy than a coffee shop or hotel lounge, but does your organisation have a tranquil room? Would confidentiality be jeopardised if people knew its purpose?

It is advisable to check if the venue provides real privacy; for example, that the conversation cannot be overheard, and that the coach and client are not visible through glass walls. Peltier (2001), says: "In clinical practice, both the fact of the counselling relationship and the content of the relationship are confidential" (p. 227). Some clients may not want it known that they have a coach. The venue should be quiet enough to encourage reflection. If the client feels emotional, the venue should not inhibit them from expressing their feelings. It should also be conducive to the coach's giving their full attention: for example, without canned music which the client may be unaware of but which bothers the coach.

There are also practical aspects, such as access to refreshments and lavatories; and convenience factors, in terms of location: a private on-site meeting room might be the least-bad option.

You may decide that the issue of where coaching sessions take place is purely up to the coach and their client. But make sure that they have given some thought to the considerations and options.

Coaching by telephone or Skype

Linehan's research also acknowledged the increase in remote or virtual coaching. If your organisation is spread across many sites, perhaps globally, this may be the most cost-effective option. Is there any guidance that you need to give your coaches? Office environments do not necessarily provide access to Skype, and video conferencing facilities may be in large meeting rooms not conducive to intimate one-to-one conversations. Linehan suggested that most coaching relationships involve at least an introductory session that is face-to-face. The coaches Linehan contacted found that coaching by telephone often enhanced their listening, and meant that they could take notes without distracting the client. There were mixed views on video: many saw the camera image as a distraction in itself, especially if the quality of the picture was poor. Interrupted connections fracture the coaching session; and video conferencing facilities can sometimes have a disconcerting time lapse.

You may want to consider whether training is needed for those who use the telephone or Skype so that they a) prepare well and get their space distraction free (including putting a note on the door to say "do not disturb"); b) practise deep listening; c) seek feedback and review their practice; and d) have supervision which looks specifically at the issues for this way of coaching.

All these considerations indicate the importance of coaches discussing venue options during the contracting phase with their clients and later revisiting the issue.

Processes

The next three chapters explore in depth issues around selecting, training, validating, and accrediting coaches; options for matching coaches and clients; providing supervision and CPD; and how you might go about evaluating your scheme. The processes you need will develop from decisions on these areas.

An early decision is whether to opt for an automated coach management process. I have spoken to coach leads successfully running schemes using a highly automated system and others successfully using a completely unautomated, personalised process. Your choice will obviously depend on what resources you have available to you, your needs, and the scale of your scheme. Here is a description of both ends of the spectrum.

Highly automated

Some organisations have invested in custom-built coach management systems. Most seem to work well, though some involved more investment to set up than was claimed by the providers. An alternative approach is to go down the route of subscribing to a service offering a fully developed coach management infrastructure that you can link into. A web search of "coach management systems" reveals several of these companies and I have heard some good reports but it is always important to get references.

A fully automated system might provide a range of services, including guidance to clients on the coaching scheme and a coach register. It may also feature a mechanism to arrange a "chemistry meeting" with two or three of those coaches and for existing clients to schedule sessions. Other features may be space to set up records of agreed goals, time and place of sessions and milestones, and to log CPD and supervision. There will be a reporting system providing monitoring and evaluation data for the use of the lead coach, and often an automatic request for coach, client, and line manager to complete evaluation questionnaires at the conclusion of the coaching.

Highly personalised

At the other end of the spectrum, the lead coach would interview the prospective client (and sometimes the line manager too) to explain the purpose and process of coaching, get an idea of their needs and coaching goals, and help them to decide if coaching is the best intervention. They would then match the client to a suitable coach, organise the "chemistry meeting" and talk to them after this meeting. Lead coaches would check in at regular intervals, meet with line managers who did not seem to be supportive, and request monthly returns from each coach, covering the number of sessions, clients, and time spent coaching. They would also chase missing data, analyse statistics, and follow up anomalies. They would meet with the coach and client at the end of the coaching relationship, send evaluation forms to all parties, and analyse them.

My descriptions are illustrative rather than comprehensive and obviously there will be examples from both ends of the spectrum and all stations in between. Some lead coaches want to be very much managing the process and informed of what is going on. Others just set up the system, let the prospective client select their coach, and only intervene if a problem arises.

Guidance

How much or how little written guidance you decide to provide is obviously up to you. It does not replace contracting at an individual level, but will set its parameters, in line with agreed company-wide policies. The provision of guidance is not just to ensure that your coaches, the clients, and the line-managers are well informed: as an employer, you have a duty of care towards all concerned. Maxwell (2011) says that "coaches are always potentially implicated at a deeper level". She quotes a passage from the British Psychological Society's special group in coaching psychology's 2007 "Guidelines for supervision for coaching psychology":

> Some forms of coaching applied in work settings are described as being largely performance-based … However, even when services do not involve working with underlying issues, they can impact on clients at a very deep level or require that the practitioner has a sophisticated understanding of the deep motivational drivers to succeed in implementing the "surface" level of implementation. (p. 191)

Some organisations have a series of fact sheets or handouts covering different issues. Others focus on who the different audiences are and write targeted guidance for each. Different approaches may be equally valid, but it helps to have a considered and agreed approach. As stressed at the beginning of this chapter, there is a need for organisation-level guidance, as well as individual contracting, but obviously the two are linked.

For the coaches

Frisch (2005) referred to the need to "over-engineer" processes for the internal coaches relating to contracting, dealing with conflicts, and so forth and to set up processes and forums to help coaches to deal with dilemmas. In addition, you could think about providing information for your coaches on the following topics:

- The organisation's coaching strategy, including the purpose of the internal coaching scheme and how it aligns with the corporate strategy
- The organisation's expectations of its internal coaches (see the contracting documents section earlier in this chapter) including time commitment
- A draft contract for them to use with their clients, including guidance around confidentiality, boundaries, the role of the line manager in the goal setting process, and so forth
- The ethical code to which they need to adhere and any complaints handling arrangements

- The process if they hit an ethical dilemma and want to talk it through with someone, such as the lead coach or a supervisor
- The nature of support available to them including access to supervision, CPD, and "coaching community" events
- How systemic themes of value for organisational learning will be harvested
- Evaluation arrangements
- Guidance around what to do if a client wants to discuss leaving the organisation
- Guidance on how to deal with information concerning bullying. In a number of organisations the guidance is for the coach specifically to mention this issue at the contracting stage; to coach the client to sort it out for themselves but, if they will not or cannot, to take the issue to the lead coach to resolve on a case by case basis
- Where they can refer clients for professional help beyond their competence, such as mental health issues, alcoholism, financial problems, marriage guidance, or bereavement
- Policies such as the taking and destruction of notes and appropriate venues for sessions.

A note about confidentiality—in some organisations the limits to the confidentiality offered varies from coach to coach; and what can be shared with the line manager, if anything, can be a particular issue. It seems sensible for the formulation to be consistent across the organisation so you might like to consider the actual wording you would like your coaches to use. The following quotation from an internal coach illustrates how important confidentiality—and the perception of how confidentiality is handled—is to internal coaches:

> "I take the approach that if it is confidential then any perceived breaches (whether they have happened or not) are a reflection on my personal professional status. In the past when this has happened I have challenged, stood my ground as it is about the client's information and my reputation. Once a reputation is lost in terms of confidentiality it is lost forever. I am quite clear about this dilemma—confidentiality means just that and it has to be adhered to. Setting up a clear contract saves any ambiguity on everyone's part, it is about managing expectations and as a coach I see that as a key part of my job."

For the clients

Clients need to feel comfortable and informed about what they are signing up to. You could think about providing information on the following:

- The organisation's coaching strategy, including the purpose of the internal coaching scheme, how it aligns with the corporate strategy and who is eligible for it
- The definition of coaching that the organisation employs and an explanation of what coaching is and is not
- A description of the process from the initial "chemistry" session to the conclusion of the coaching relationship, including the line manager's role
- The ethical code to which the internal coaches adhere and any complaints handling arrangements
- Where to go for further information
- The process for terminating the coaching if the relationship isn't working. Snape (2012) quotes a client as pointing out that with an internal coach "it could be awkward to terminate the coaching" (p. 55). What guidance can you offer the clients to take the embarrassment out of it?
- How they can best prepare for the coaching so that they get the best possible benefit from it (see section earlier in this chapter on the "skilled coachee")
- Their part in the evaluation process.

For the line managers

Many organisations put together a "Guide for line managers" to help set their expectations of coaching and enlist their support for helping the client through the process. Topics might include:

- The organisation's coaching strategy, including the purpose of the internal coaching scheme, how it aligns with the corporate strategy and who is eligible for it
- The definition of coaching used (see section above on the client), and how it should be positioned as a development activity and not part of the line manager's performance management responsibilities

- Their role in helping the client to develop coaching goals and supporting them in reaching them, including giving them regular feedback
- Their role in any evaluation process.

Standards, ethics, and quality of service

Ethical code

Subscribing to an ethical code is something that every coach must do as it is fundamental to what being a coach is all about: how they see their role, how they carry out their work, and how they address any ethical dilemmas that might arise. The EMCC's and ICF's codes emphasise the importance of coaches' highlighting their adherence to a code of ethics with the client prior to the start of the coaching. However, despite that, the Ridler Report 2013 shows that only fifty-six per cent of the 145 organisations that took part include a reference to an ethical code in their contracting process.

An internal coach needs to take their duty of care towards the client very seriously because a) they may hold privileged information about the client; b) the coaching relationship is an intimate, self-revealing, trusting context; c) they may in addition have some kind of position power; d) they may be perceived by the client to have a hotline to the line manager or HR; and e) the client may be emotionally or psychologically fragile or in an unresourceful state. It is therefore essential that they operate to an ethical code.

In addition to the moral imperative, Williams and Anderson (2006), who take a legal approach to ethics in coaching, underline the professional relevance of internal coaches subscribing to an ethical code:

> Ethical behaviour is a choice to conduct oneself in keeping with a set of core values and the Code of Ethics of a profession is a form of self-governance defined by high standards based on those values. (p. 93)

They point out that the derivation of the word profession is the Latin for "bound by an oath" so the idea of a code of ethics to which members are bound is central to the idea of coaching being a profession. One route that you could follow is to pay for your coaches to be individual members of a coaching professional body. Or have a look at what the benefits might be of corporate membership, if available.

Within the UK, a document produced in February 2008 by AC, APECS, EMCC UK, and UK ICF (the UK Coaching Round Table) included the aim that "every coach needs to abide by a code of governing ethics and apply acknowledged standards to the performance of their coaching work" (Townsend, 2011, p. 143). Then in April 2009, a statement of shared professional values, collated by the UK Coaching Round Table, was signed. It covers crucial elements such as boundaries, confidentiality, and diversity (more information at www. coachingcircle.co.uk). At the EMCC's Bilbao conference in December 2012, the AC, EMCC, and the ICF announced an alliance. A unified code of ethics will no doubt follow in due course.

If you have decided to source training for your coaches externally, then that training (depending on what you choose) may take them down the path of ICF or EMCC or AC accreditation, in which case it would make sense for your organisation to adopt the ethical code of that particular professional body. But if the training is not leading to accreditation, or you are going to be using coaches who are already trained in a number of different traditions, it would make sense to draw up your own code of ethics so that all your coaches are working to the same one. Most organisations adopt or base their code on that of one of the coaching professional bodies.

Complaints process

Complaints about coaches are very rare, but as the lead coach it is in your interests to sort out a clear procedure at the outset rather than being caught on the back foot if one arises. The ethical codes of all the coaching professional bodies include a complaints process so they could act as your starting point.

Facts and figures 7.4: Complaints processes

- Twenty per cent of coaches said that there was a separate, specific procedure for dealing with complaints about coaches, sitting outside the normal grievance or disciplinary procedures
- Fifty-five per cent said that there was not
- Twenty-five per cent did not know.

Examples of comments made, in the event of a problem, illustrating both ends of the spectrum were:

> "There is nothing established, and I don't think the organisation has considered this possibility—I suppose it would be via the usual grievance policy."
>
> "If these were to arise the contracting document with the coachee specifies whom they should contact, so the procedure is set out."

Once you have decided on your code and complaints processes, it is important that you communicate them clearly to the coaches and their clients—they are for the protection of your coaches as much as their clients. In my research, over one third of the coaches did not know whether they were bound by an ethical code, so make sure that you highlight it with them.

Quality assurance

Some lead coaches adopt the "no news is good news" approach, when it comes to monitoring coaching standards: the approach that, if no-one complains, it must be going well. Most, however, adopt a more active approach. Some lead coaches make it part of the supervisor's role to report back any concerns they may have about an individual coach. Some external coach supervisors would not be prepared to do this, believing that it compromises the supervisory relationship. It is a conversation that should be had. Sometimes, the lead coach is also a trained supervisor and supervises groups of internal coaches so it is recognised by all parties that they have a dual function. If they pick up that a coach is struggling, then this could be a signal for additional training or, at the very least, a conversation off-line with the lead coach.

Other quality assurance methods cited in my research include:

- Making it clear to clients at the outset what the route is for giving feedback about how the coaching is going
- Contacting the client from time to time to check that all is well
- Asking the coaches to gather some feedback from the client at regular intervals to pass on to the lead coach

- Asking the client to provide qualitative feedback directly to the lead coach at the completion of the coaching
- Asking the client and line manager to complete a formal questionnaire at the completion of the coaching that includes questions about outcomes, and for the client, specific questions about the coach's perceived effectiveness
- Asking a client from time to time if they would be prepared for their session to be observed by the lead coach, purely in the service of learning for the coach
- Asking the coaches to record a session from time to time for discussion with the lead coach.

Bear in mind that qualitative feedback from the coaching client, whether mediated by the coach or not, will sometimes be affected by the syndrome of the client wanting to please or protect the coach. It is a feature of coaching relationships that an intimacy develops and this can militate against an analytical approach on the part of the client to working out what progress is being made and to what it should be attributed.

Something to think about is: are you prepared to stop someone coaching if they do not seem to be developing into a competent coach? How would you deal with this situation? How great is the risk to the reputation of the coaching scheme if you do not address it?

Communication with the business

If your coaches are only available, say, to support specific leadership programmes and for managers in transition, you may not see a need to spread the word more widely about coaching, as this might simply stoke demand from managers who are not eligible. One lead coach said:

> "I push back if I get feedback that I should communicate more about coaching on the grounds that: we do not have enough capacity to serve more clients; it would affect a delicate supply/demand balance; there is value in coaching being something special: it's brokered in by special conversations; and I'm not building a business."

However, in many organisations there is wide eligibility, and the process depends upon managers becoming aware of the scheme's existence. Some internal coaches do not have enough clients. As mentioned, some organisations have an automated process with a coaching space on the intranet that is accessible for people who are interested.

Businesses tend to look on their coaches as being the advocates for coaching, but actually it is the coaching clients who are the real advocates. One consultant who advises organisations on how to set up an internal coaching scheme said that she suggests asking the coaches to save part of the final session for asking their clients: "Who will you tell about your coaching, now that you understand what it is all about and what it can offer?" She recommends that the coach and client should write a short, agreed statement on what they have achieved together which can be put on the intranet, included in a company newsletter, or form part of any marketing material.

Ideas for publicising and marketing the coaching that organisations have used include the following:

- The lead coach having regular catch-up sessions with heads of divisions to remind them what is available
- Having a regular coaching slot in an "all staff" regular email briefing
- Having an annual "coaching week" featuring messages from senior executives, such as the CEO reporting the value that coaching has had for them; an information desk in the lobby; and so on
- Putting together case studies and stories on coaching
- Instituting a "Coach of the Year" award with a small awards ceremony
- Instituting a "Coaching Division of the Year" award based on:

  - how many people they had released to do the coach training
  - how many clients they had put forward
  - how many people had done a manager-as-coach skills course.

- Putting on the intranet a short video of a coaching session to help people to understand what is involved (there are a number already on YouTube)

- Holding a coaching event—possibly during the lunch hour—modelled on "speed dating" where a number of coaches are available to spend no more than ten to fifteen minutes coaching managers who come along to get a feel of what it is like to be coached.

Summary

The policies and processes you create will translate your strategy into deliverables, building the infrastructure that will drive a sustainable programme of internal coaching. They underpin how all the different parties involved will behave with each other, and the key to it all is clarity. The aim is to ensure that great coaching is delivered in a safe supportive environment, that all involved in internal coaching understand their roles, and that there are mechanisms in place to provide on-going quality assurance.

Case studies unpacked

Case study 7.1 (see page 161)

Michael had a discussion with the heads of IT and HR. He wanted an investigation into why:

- *all* the accounts in Michael's team were being monitored, not just the suspect three
- he had not been consulted about the arrangements, and
- the members of the IT department had been so cavalier in their treatment of confidential emails.

An investigation was carried out into the behaviour of the IT staff, as there were clear guidelines on confidentiality in the IT policy about monitoring staff's email accounts. The member of staff who had forwarded the emails for others in the team to read was given a final written warning and the others who read and discussed the email were given written warnings. Michael shared with his client that the emails had been read by members of the IT team and that disciplinary action had been taken. The learning Michael took forward was only to use email for exchange of logistical details, for example, meeting times, and to use the telephone if he wanted to exchange anything that would have implications for client confidentiality.

QUESTIONS TO REFLECT ON

Factor to consider	What are the implications for the organisation?
Roles and responsibilities Getting clarity about who is responsible for what, i.e., • Steering group, if any • Lead coach • Line managers • Coaches • Coaching clients	• Have we created clarity for the business on the responsibilities and accountabilities of the key roles involved in delivering the internal coaching scheme? • What are my challenges in persuading line managers to allow coaches to have time away from their functional role? • Do we need internal coaches to have an operational objective around delivering a coaching service so this contribution to the business is valued as part of the "day job"? • What level of involvement do we want from line managers whose team members are receiving coaching? • Will we require line managers to authorise coaching for team members? • Will we require coaches who are trained in psychometrics and 360 feedback to use these skills as part of the coaching process? • What do we need to do to "educate" our potential clients on what coaching is and what it is not? • Are we going to try to assess the "coachability" of potential clients?

(Continued)

QUESTIONS TO REFLECT ON   (*Continued*)

Factor to consider	What are the implications for the organisation?

Contracting documents
How do we want to "contract" with our internal coaches?
 	
How do we want our internal coaches to "contract" with their clients?
	• How formal do we want the contracting process between the organisation and internal coaches to be?
	• What are the specifics of contracting that we need to cover in regard to:
	  – signing up to a code of ethics
	  – the limits to confidentiality
	  – training and accreditation requirements
	  – number of coaching hours
	  – CPD requirements
	  – referrals to other professionals
	  – supervision/support arrangements
	  – quality assurance
	• What should we have in place if we need to take a coach "off the register"?
	• How will we support coaches if a grievance is brought against them by a client?
	• How formal do we want the contracting process between the coaches and clients to be? Do we expect a piece of paper to be signed?
	• What do our coaches need to make clear to clients in their contracting around:
	  – sharing themes from coaching for organisational learning
	  – what they will take to supervision
	  – feedback to line managers?

(*Continued*)

QUESTIONS TO REFLECT ON   (*Continued*)

Factor to consider	What are the implications for the organisation?
Record keeping What do we need to consider in regard to the two aspects of record keeping: confidentiality and data protection?	• Do existing organisational policies cover confidentiality and data protection adequately or do we need to provide specific guidance for our coaches? • What might we need to include in our brief to the training providers around data protection and record keeping? • What do we need in place if a coach leaves the business to ensure any confidential information is dealt with appropriately? • What are the considerations for storing information on the organisation's computer network? Who has access?
Coaching venues How can we create a confidential, quiet and "safe" environment for the coaching?	• What capacity do we have for providing suitable rooms for coaches to meet clients? • If meeting space is at a premium what priority do we need to give to booking rooms for coaching sessions? • If coaches use Skype are there any security considerations? • What are the implications for our training programme if we are to encourage telephone coaching?
Processes What type of coach management system suits our coaching scheme?	• What specifically do we require from our coach management system?

(*Continued*)

QUESTIONS TO REFLECT ON   (*Continued*)

Factor to consider	What are the implications for the organisation?

	• Would a personalised system be good use of the lead coach's time?
	• Does the size of our coaching scheme justify an automated system? If so, would it be more cost effective to:
	  – develop a custom built coach management system
	  – subscribe to a service
	• How will we ensure that our coaches understand how the system works?

Guidance
What guidance do we need for our coaches, clients, and line mangers?
	• Thinking about guidance for the three groups—coaches, clients and line managers:
	  – what is common to all?
	  – what needs to be tailored for the specific audience?
	  – what is the best route for communicating it?
	• What do we need to put in place to ensure our guidance is regularly reviewed and updated to meet emerging needs and changes?
	• What "supporting resources" may we want to make available via our intranet for coaches, clients, and line managers?

Standards and ethics What needs to be in place to ensure internal coaches are meeting their "duty of care" towards their clients and that standards are high?	• Shall we develop our own code of ethics or adopt one of the professional bodies' codes?

(*Continued*)

QUESTIONS TO REFLECT ON   (*Continued*)

Factor to consider	*What are the implications for the organisation?*
	• If there is a complaint against a coach will our organisation's grievance process suffice or do we need to create a specific complaints process? • How will we ensure coaches, client, and line manager are clear about the system we have in place to deal with complaints? • What do we want to assess or measure that will give the assurance that our coaches are delivering a high standard of service? • How can we communicate our quality assurance process to our internal coaches so they see it as positive rather than feeling that their competence is being questioned? • How will we deal with coaches who are not competent?
Communication with the business Judging how much publicity to give the coaching scheme	• Are we going to target eligible groups of potential coaching clients or will all managers be eligible for coaching as long as their line manager authorises it? • How widely do we want to publicise the scheme? Can our steering group be advocates? • Which is likely to be the greater challenge, too many coaches or too few? • How can we make best use of clients to be advocates for the coaching scheme?

CHAPTER EIGHT

Selection and training

Those organisations that scrimp on the careful selection, training and supporting of internal coaches run serious risks. Ultimately their greatest risk may be that they undermine the perception of coaching as a learning tool because of the lack of credibility of their internal coaches

—*Hunt & Weintraub*, 2006, p. 4

What this chapter is about

Generally it is the responsibility of the lead coach to select people with the potential to make good internal coaches and provide them with the right length, depth, and scope of training to enable them to do a good job.

This chapter explores:

- How you can identify and select potential coaches
- Options for training
- Qualifications and accreditation
- Considerations for matching coaches with suitable clients.

Selection

Routes to identifying potential coaches

The method you use to recruit your coaches will depend on a number of factors, including how many coaches you need; for what purpose; and how much resource you have at your disposal for running the recruitment process. One tip offered by experienced lead coaches is to select and train more coaches than you initially think you need to allow for an inevitable process of attrition. Some coaches will fall by the wayside during training; some may not make the grade; some may be made redundant from their day job soon after they complete their training; some may move to a new, very heavily loaded role and no longer have time for their coaching role. If you train your coaches as a cohort then the unit cost of adding a few additional trainees may be fairly low.

Most of the lead coaches whom I interviewed had amended their method for identifying suitable candidates over time. One key piece of learning for some was: beware of simply sending an email to all staff asking for volunteers unless you have the time to separate the wheat from the chaff (though the benefit of this method is that it offers everyone in the business an equal opportunity to apply). However, an all-staff email can work if you help potential candidates to screen themselves out by making clear: a) what coaching involves; b) what kinds are attributes you are looking for; c) the time commitment that would be involved; and d) the need for any application to be authorised by the applicant's line manager.

A filtering method used by McBride in the case study below is the "Readiness to Coach" questionnaire.

Case study 8.1: Readiness to coach

McBride, Europe's leading provider of private label household and personal care products and a multinational with more than 4,500 employees, has been developing an internal coaching service and uses a "Readiness to Coach Questionnaire" as part of the application process to filter potential applicants and to help them to examine their own readiness. The questionnaire includes thirteen statements. Here are three examples:

- I am good at seeing below the surface to what is going on
- I make a conscious effort to listen actively (i.e., paying full attention and ignoring distractions)
- I give regular and timely feedback to others.

Applicants are requested to a) give a copy of the questions to a colleague and their line manager for them to rate the applicant on a scale of 0–10, and b) rate themselves. The application form asks what prior coaching experience they have had; what they will contribute to the McBride coaching programme; and what they expect to gain from being a coach. Their line manager needs to provide comments in support of the application.

The completed questionnaires are distributed with no "personal identities attributed" to be reviewed by at least two accredited coaches. Thereafter there is a conversation with the applicant with a view to "sponsoring" their application with a recommendation to an internal coach panel. In 2012 they had thirty-nine applicants. Thirty-one were invited to join the programme for training and eight were offered alternative developmental options including working with a coach.

Ian Jenner, Group Head of Learning and Development, is very pleased with the quality of the applicants. The questionnaire does the job well and seems to provide a good indication of readiness for future coaching practice.

The application form has been used for the last four cohorts as part of their process for selecting internal coaches. McBride has fifty-six active coaches from seven European nationalities. Some of the coaches have been practising for more than seven years.

An alternative approach to the all-staff email for identifying potential coaches is to send a carefully worded invitation to business heads/ heads of divisions explaining that a pool of internal coaches is to be set up (with an indication of what is involved, the time commitment required, and the likely benefits to the individual in their day job), that you are looking for certain listed qualities, and could they put forward anyone they think suitable. The benefits of this approach are that:

- From the start you are engaging and partnering with the business
- You send a clear message about targeting resource to meet business need

- The quality of the proposed candidates should be high, as you have benefited from an initial level of screening
- The business heads are already invested in the process
- The potential coach will feel valued and complimented by their line management by being nominated.

Two words of warning though: a) using some form of nomination by line managers may have equality and diversity implications and is more likely to be challenged by unions and b) one coach lead said, with hindsight, that they had trusted the views of the heads of division rather more than they should have done. Even though they had specified attributes such as interpersonal skills, a learning focus, self-awareness, and listening skills, some divisional heads were more skilled at identifying such attributes than others. It also turned out that some took a different view about seniority from others so it was necessary, in future runs, to specify that grade was unimportant. On the other hand, in terms of credibility, you may work for an organisation where seniority actually is important—so you do need to make clear what you are looking for in that respect.

Some lead coaches personally handpick some or all of their trainee coaches. Some talked of choosing experienced learning and development specialist colleagues. Another fruitful route was identifying managers from across the business who enjoyed developing people, evidenced by having a) volunteered in the past to be mentors or b) attended and responded well to "leader as coach" or "coaching skills for managers" type training. Once your training pool is up and running you may well find that your coaches become advocates within the business for coaching and start to recommend others to be in your subsequent cohorts of trainees.

If you are not extending the invitation to train to all staff, and you are in a unionised environment, it is important to engage the business and the unions in your process from the start. You may also need to consider carrying out an equality and diversity impact assessment on your final list of people to reassure the business that there has been no discrimination.

Recruiting from HR

In Chapter Six I included a brief discussion about the pros and cons of siting the coaching scheme within HR. The key issue was HR's reputation within the business. Whether to recruit your coaches from within HR is a separate though related issue. Clearly the scope for ethical dilemmas relating to role conflict can be greater for HR internal coaches but this need not rule them out as long as they contract carefully and are very alert to potential conflicts. On the one hand is the view that HR is an obvious source of internal coaches:

> HR professionals are a logical choice when an organisation considers developing a cadre of internal coaches ... HR professionals bring important resources to the table. They typically have the well-developed interpersonal skills that are fundamental to solid coaching relationships. Many HR professionals have specialised skills training, such as in change management, communication and problem-solving: these are also foundation skills for coaches. In addition, HR professionals have in-depth understanding of the immediate system in which their executives operate, along with knowledge of their corporate culture and specific industry. (Figlar, Adams, & Hornyak, 2007)

On the other hand, some lead coaches said that they specifically avoided recruiting coaches from HR on the grounds that they "are some of the toughest people to train". This view seemed to arise from a perception of the HR profession as majoring on problem-solving and decision-taking and being peopled by managers who were task, process, and action oriented and therefore found it hard to wean themselves off moving their clients too swiftly to solutions. However, there were plenty, too, who were in the middle ground of looking to recruit coaches from all parts of the business, including HR.

What about the clients' perceptions? The clients in the large American company that was the focus of Yedreshteyn's (2008) research had no doubts:

> Clients expressed three main concerns, that the coaching would not be pragmatic, that it would not address relevant issues extensively, and that they wanted someone with experience in the business ... not an HR professional as their coach. (p. 76)

> Clients suggested that the coaches should be more credible, meaning not HR professionals. (p. 82)

However, they were expressing preconceptions rather than experience of actually being coached by an HR professional.

Figlar, Adams, and Hornyak (2007) published research on the introduction of an internal coaching scheme in Lockheed Martin involving the training of 275 coaches and specifically examined the issue of using the development of HR professionals as internal coaches as a strategy for enhancing the credibility of HR within the organisation.

They identify some very helpful questions to determine the readiness of HR professionals for a coaching approach which include:

1. Strategic HR direction—Does the idea of having your HR professionals develop themselves in a way that is more consultative match your strategy? If so, what is the best way to promote inquiry skills in an advice and action-oriented profession like HR?
2. Internal credibility—Does your existing HR population have the credibility to begin work with executives or high potential leaders in this capacity? Do you have a small group of individuals you could start with to begin to build that credibility?
3. Time—Are your internal HR professionals committed to the time it takes to build their individual and the organisational capability of executive coaching? Coaching is a recognised profession: hence most professionals just focus on this area. Realistically, is your company committed enough to allow coaches to take the time to coach?
4. Sustainability—Are you prepared to sustain the coaching programme including ongoing skills development, education and feedback?
5. Accountability—Are you prepared to take coaches out of the coaching pool for ethical violations or lack of effectiveness? (p. 6)

They conclude by saying:

> Investing in one's HR professionals to provide critical coaching services can be an effective strategy for strengthening the leadership pipeline while promoting HR professionals as strategic partners within the business. (p. 8)

As lead coach you might want to give some thought to the role of HR professionals in your coaching squad. Depending on the function and reputation of HR within your organisation, training HR professionals as internal coaches could serve a strategic purpose.

Recruiting union representatives

Unions are normally supportive of development opportunities for staff. However, there are opportunities for resistance if they do not fully understand the benefit for their members, particularly if it is perceived to be an élitist programme that only benefits a small group. Several organisations have selected and trained union representatives as internal coaches as a way of gaining their buy-in and support for the programme. In one, this approach had an unexpected benefit: improved employee relations. As these individuals trained alongside members of HR and management they built rapport and understanding and developed solution-focused communication skills.

Selection process and criteria

Process: Having decided what method you are going to deploy to reach candidates for your coaching pool, what process and criteria will you use to assess suitability? Lead coaches use a wide range of processes. At one end is a single-step process involving a simple application form asking for information such as: how long the applicant has worked for the organisation; why they want to train as a coach; authorisation from their line manager; and a commitment to devote the necessary time to the process. Some lead coaches take the view that they do not want to screen people out of the process too early since trainees can develop so much during the training—though there are obvious cost implications if they turn out not to be suitable. If you take this view, it is important that you are prepared to fail people at the end of the training. You may be able to give unsuccessful candidates ideas for how to develop themselves so that they can try again another time.

Many organisations use a two-stage process involving a detailed application form designed to test out a variety of attributes and experiences desirable in a coach—and perhaps also asking applicants to complete an "aptitude for coaching" or "coach readiness" questionnaire—followed by an interview. You may also ask them for references, including one from their line manager, testifying to their interpersonal skills and so forth. It is important that candidates realise that they can cite experience outside their work lives in support of their application. A number of lead coaches mentioned the high desirability of managers who had experience of being Samaritans or holding other voluntary roles requiring advanced listening skills.

A more resource intensive, expensive, and sophisticated process used by some larger organisations is to run an assessment centre for their applicants. One lead coach said that they ran a full-day assessment centre to test out people's skills, and that the most common reason for failing this process—though not many did—was an inability to shake off the temptation to provide solutions. If you use an assessment centre approach it can offer a useful two-way process in that it helps the candidates to decide if coaching is for them by giving them some first hand experience and understanding of what it involves. It also offers the opportunity, for second and subsequent cohorts, to ask some of the coaches from an earlier cohort to be present to answer questions from candidates about what it is like in practice. Some may decide at that point that it not for them or that they would be more suited to being a mentor.

Criteria: When recruiting your coaches you will clearly need to decide what attributes, skills, and competences you are looking for. These may depend to some extent on the stated purpose of your coaching scheme. A good place to start is to cast your eye down the competence frameworks of the coaching professional bodies. However, it is important to bear in mind that those frameworks are aiming to assess the competence of coaches who are already practising, whereas you are looking for potential.

The sorts of things you are likely to be interested in include:

• What is their value set around learning?
• Do they exhibit curiosity?
• Do they seem interested in people's potential?
• How self-aware do they seem?
• How committed are they to self-development?
• Do they view people as being capable, resourceful, and able to solve their own issues?

A number of researchers have identified attributes that make for good coaches. Stern (2004) suggested that the coach needs to be perceived by the client as:

• credible
• confident
• experienced in business practices
• patient yet action-oriented
• trustworthy
• able to keep their confidences
• genuinely interested and engaged

- professional
- not intimidated by an executive
- not likely to shy away from confrontation.

In some ways it is particularly important to check out those last two attributes. It is common for would-be coaches to be more aware of the support aspect of a coach's role than the challenge aspect. Yedreshteyn (2008) has some interesting things to say in relation to clients who had been disappointed in their coaching experience:

> They offered several explanations for this. They primarily said their coach was not a good match and they wanted … a professional with more experience in the business. Clients also reported wanting more candour, criticism and "push back" from their coaches. (p. 77)
>
> Many clients said that their coaches would have been more effective had they followed up more, understood the client's business better, offered more criticism, challenged the client, confronted them at times to help them face challenging issues, and held them accountable for their actions. (p. 80)

Your criteria are likely to be wider than whether the candidate looks to have the attributes desirable in a coach. Other criteria include:

- *Time commitment*: Do you believe that they will be willing and able to give the necessary time to their role as a coach? Some organisations require their coaches to sign an undertaking to have a minimum of two coaching clients at any one time; to undertake the prescribed supervision and CPD; to contribute to organisational learning; and be prepared to promote coaching within the organisation.
- *Credibility/reputation*: Do they have the experience and reputation within the business to make a credible coach? Credibility is an interesting issue because it is in the eye of the beholder. To different people credibility can mean any or all of the following:
  - seniority
  - a recognisable qualification
  - the reputation that the coach has in their day job
  - the personal presence or interpersonal skills of the coach in front of them.

There are mixed views about whether a coach needs to be a high performer in their day job in order to make a credible coach. One of my lead coach interviewees had actually resigned over this point of principle: a coaching champion was insisting that potential coaches should already be in the "top right hand corner" of a nine-box talent management grid (that is, a high performer with high potential) whereas the lead coach took the view that a middle of the road performer in their day job could still make an excellent coach. However, another lead coach believed that each coach's reputation within the business was very important indeed and, in the scheme he ran, the line manager was required to confirm that the applicant was a good performer.

- *The need for a broad mix*: Many organisations take great care over getting a broad range of candidates even if this means that a good applicant must wait to be trained as part of a future cohort. A good mix generally means trying to ensure that the coaches are representative of the organisation in terms of function, geography, ethnicity, and gender.

Training

If you have decided to take the path of enlisting the skills of existing employees, who are already trained coaches, to form all or part of your internal coaching pool then you will need some method of validating their skills. There is a short section relating to this later on in this chapter. However, if you are planning to train some or all of your coaches from scratch, there are a number of issues to think through:

- What content do you want the training to cover? What depth of training do your coaches need to do the job? Will any of them need specialist training on top?
- Is a specific qualification necessary or important in terms of the coaches' and the scheme's credibility? Do you want your coaches to be accredited and, if so, do you plan to support them through individual accreditation with one of the coaching professional bodies?
- Who is going to train them? Do you want to send your coaches on open programmes so that they share experiences with a wider range of trainee coaches or run a dedicated course for your cohort that will have the benefit of kick-starting a "coaching community"?

Whatever the answers to all these questions, it is crucial that your trainee coaches are able to devote enough time to the training. It must be made clear up front to them and their line managers what the time commitment will be. Most training will involve considerably more learning hours than simply attending the training modules whether it is writing assignments, practice coaching with "guinea pigs", writing a learning journal, or reading books and articles.

There is also the issue of funding the training. Some organisations have a funding policy for training of any kind—particularly if participants will gain an external accreditation that will be of personal benefit to them in future employment—that requires coaches to commit to being with the organisation for a specified time after training or repay a proportion of the cost of the training. Two years seemed to be a common period specified.

Content

What do you want your coaches to know and to be able to do? Whatever content you decide on will need to build on and develop the sorts of skills and aptitudes that you were using as criteria during your selection phase, and you will probably have already looked at the competence frameworks developed by the coaching professional bodies. If you go for a specific qualification—see below—then the content will be laid down, though there may be flexibility in how it is delivered.

Coach training would normally include:

a. An explanation of what coaching is and how it differs from counselling, mentoring, and consulting.
b. An exploration of the basic coaching skills such as rapport building, active listening, powerful questioning, goal setting, and giving feedback.
c. Ideas around the "self as coach": that is, encouraging high levels of self-awareness in the coaches so that they are in a better position to distinguish between their own "stuff" and that of their clients.
d. A simple coaching model such as GROW (Whitmore, 2002), CLEAR (Hawkins & N. Smith, 2006), or OSCAR (J. Rogers, 2013).
e. Some basic psychological concepts such as motivational factors, needs-driven behaviour, and limiting beliefs.
f. Content for the contracting conversation with the client, including confidentiality, boundaries, and ethics.

g. Considerable practice of coaching each other. This is normally done in triads (coach, client, and observer) with the trainees taking it in turns to play each role, using real issues, and providing structured feedback to each other.

h. Some trainers also offer coaching demonstrations at an early stage, with time out for questions and discussion mid demonstration, which are always very popular with trainees and help to build confidence.

Most training programmes will include exposure to some of the theories and concepts around adult learning, management development, psychological-mindedness, and so forth. However, a focus on skills-based training is essential as the aim is for coaches to conduct effective coaching sessions.

Ethics in practice: I make no apology, given their importance for internal coaches, for making a special plea for considerable attention to be given to a) the role of ethics in coaching practice; b) the importance of tight contracting; and c) giving the trainee coaches plenty of opportunity to discuss ethical issues that they may encounter. Some coach training still being delivered in the UK was originally developed

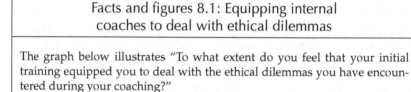

Facts and figures 8.1: Equipping internal coaches to deal with ethical dilemmas

The graph below illustrates "To what extent do you feel that your initial training equipped you to deal with the ethical dilemmas you have encountered during your coaching?"

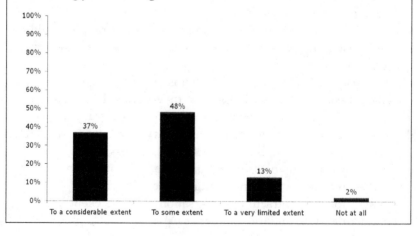

for independent external coaches and may not yet have entirely adapted to reflect the particular issues that internal coaches can face.

What depth of training?

How academic or practical do you want your programme to be? And how comprehensive? You and your steering group will need to discuss what you are looking for. You may decide at the outset that you want your internal coaches to be considered to be on a par with external coaches and put all your trainee coaches through a diploma level programme lasting, say, nine months. Or you may decide to take things one step at a time and start with basic coaching skills followed by regular CPD to build on that. Some new coaches, if they have considerable management experience and are "natural coaches", may be ready to coach, even at senior levels, after a comparatively small amount of training. The reality is that the coaches in an internal coaching cohort will have variable experience and competence: in a personalised scheme the lead coach can talk to the clients about their needs and find someone suitable; and in an automated one, the coach biographies can provide potential clients with a sense of how much experience and training the coach has. Each coach can gradually take on more demanding clients as they gain experience. Lockheed Martin (Figlar, Adams, & Hornyak, 2007) gave more advanced training to a small cadre of senior coaches. They were deployed with the most senior clients and had responsibility for advancing the effectiveness of the internal coaches in their business areas as well as for delivering coaching.

A further aspect is whether you expect your coaches to be capable of coaching clients on virtually every issue or if you will make space for some coaches to specialise. Some coaches particularly enjoy coaching on a specific set of issues, such as maternity coaching, sales support, or career development. If you decide to go this route then you may need to think about the relevance of any specialist training or opportunities for group discussion with other coaches specialising in the same areas to get maximum organisational learning.

Qualification/accreditation

I encountered a wide range of views about whether it was necessary for internal coaches to have a specific coaching qualification or to be formally accredited. Some organisations felt that it was essential for the credibility of their coaches to have one or the other or both. Others did not think it was an issue at all. The coaches themselves, however, tend to like being able to cite a qualification or accreditation.

Qualifications: There are a number of routes to qualification—you can use a training provider whose course offers a qualification or, if you are the lead coach, you can be trained to deliver, say, an Institute of Leadership and Management (ILM) qualification programme. ILM5 provides a basic, national qualification that can be delivered by any provider who is qualified to do so (currently around 2,000 in the UK). The trainee coaches have to be practising managers. One tip that a lead coach offered was that these programmes can sometimes be delivered rather drily. It is essential that programmes such as the ILM's are delivered by practising coaches who know what coaching is like in real life so can deal with the inevitable questions and wobbles from the trainees. So if you are not running it yourself, it is important to talk to the tutor who will actually be delivering the programme and not just to a salesperson. Check whether they are really listening to your needs and the purposes for which you are setting the coaching scheme up. Are they prepared to do any fine-tuning to meet your requirements?

Accreditation: Training leading to ICF accreditation is also popular. There are three levels: the basic level (Associate Credentialed Coach) involves sixty hours of training—four blocks of two days—plus twenty hours of coaching. It takes around four months and at the end candidates' skills are validated against eleven ICF competences.

The AC and EMCC both take a competence/evidence-based portfolio approach to accreditation and if you want your coaches to go through that process after they have trained and acquired the necessary hours of experience then you may need to offer them some support for that. You may also want to think about paying for your coaches' membership of one of the professional bodies.

A number of the larger coach training organisations have had their coaching programmes accredited by a university so that is another route to accreditation.

Some organisations, such as the BBC, have developed their own internal coach training and then subsequently undertaken the process to have it accredited by the EMCC, so that their coaches have a recognised accreditation that is portable. A different approach is for you to simply designate managers who successfully complete your coach training as a "certified [organisation name] coach". However, it is also worth thinking in advance if you particularly like the approach or competence framework of one of the professional bodies (EMCC, AC, ICF) because if, at some later date, you would like your coaches to go for accreditation by that body, then the training they have will fit better with one or another. Some lead coaches talked about the training they had arranged as being "ICF aligned" or "EMCC aligned".

The Ridler Report (Ridler & Co, 2013) reported that while fifty-four per cent of participating organisations expected their external coaches to be accredited, only thirty-seven per cent expected their internal coaches to be accredited. In practice, the driver for some kind of qualification or accreditation often comes from the coaches themselves and Yedreshteyn (2008) explores why the coaches like it:

> There are several potential reasons why the internal coaches were interested in having Executive Development create a Certificate program for them. They said that it would help them gain credibility in the eyes of clients, help them learn more about coaching, help all of the coaches have the same knowledge, but there may also be other reasons. Coaches whose clients do not return their calls or seem uninterested in the services they are offering may need to be recognised elsewhere and having a title of "Certified" Internal Executive Coach may give them the affirmation they are looking for. (p. 101)

Delivering the training

Having decided broadly whether you are looking for a practical, skills-based coaching programme that will get your coaches up and running quickly or if you are looking for something with more theoretical and/or psychological input, you will need to decide who is to deliver it.

In-house vs. open programmes: There are many training establishments in the UK—colleges, universities, business schools, and specialist coach training establishments—that offer coach training programmes at certificate (or foundation), diploma, or Masters levels. The EMCC lists on its website those training courses that have been awarded their European Quality Award (EQA). Some coach leads believe that there are benefits to training their internal coaches on open programmes in terms of a) broadening their managers' horizons from learning alongside external coaches and managers from other organisations; b) little administrative input apart from booking someone onto the programme and paying the invoice; and c) their coaches receiving a specific qualification. However, there are also drawbacks to taking the open programmes route:

- It is usually more expensive;
- The course dates are fixed way in advance so there is no flexibility in terms of timing;
- There is no opportunity to fine-tune the content to the needs of your organisation.

Many of those organisations—and others—will be willing to put together a programme to deliver the same training, or something fine-tuned to your specific needs, to a cohort of your trainee coaches. This is likely to provide better value, though if you want many changes from what they usually deliver then clearly the development time will raise the costs.

Delivering in-house using an external provider: Delivering the training in-house, even if you use an external provider, means that you can ensure that the content is exactly what you want and that you can "top and tail it" to make it very organisation-specific, including sessions on:

- Your organisation's coaching strategy
- The part that your coaches will be playing in helping the organisation to achieve its business strategy and leadership and talent management plans
- The coaching policies that you have developed
- The coaching processes that you have developed
- Taking them through the way you expect them to contract with their clients
- Taking them through the ethical code that you have developed or adopted.

One or more of your coaching champions can also talk to the trainees about the value of the work they will be doing and, in future cohorts, practising internal coaches from your organisation—and maybe coaching clients too—can talk about the challenges and rewards that they have experienced. If your organisation has adopted a particular 360-degree assessment instrument based on your management competencies, then the coaches could also be trained in how to use and interpret this instrument and use it in their coaching.

One of the biggest benefits, though, of training all your coaches in-house as a cohort is that you will have got your coaching community off to a great start. Learning to be a coach is an emotional experience. At the beginning, most managers find themselves way out of their comfort zone—having been used to identifying and providing their staff with solutions for most of their working lives—and there is nothing like sharing deep emotional experiences with colleagues for quick and lasting bonding.

If you are looking to train a considerable number of internal coaches, you may need to embark on a competitive tendering exercise. This will involve specifying with considerable clarity exactly what you want—otherwise comparing like with like will be difficult. For smaller contracts, you may decide to approach two or three training providers with whom you have had good experiences in the past and work out with them, in a series of iterations, what you want. There is also always a lot to be said for asking around for recommendations.

One lead coach said:

> "We were clear that we wanted something that was very practitioner based, not too academic. We went for a six-day programme, in three two-day modules spread over six months, that was aligned with EMCC standards but was not a full qualification as we were concerned that people might leave once they had completed the training. It was the equivalent of a foundation programme but we made it clear to the trainees that it was the beginning of the journey, to be followed up with lots of CPD and supervision."

The relationship that you have with your training provider may well turn out to be a long-term one so it is really worth checking out that there is a fit. Many providers, in addition to training your coaches, will be in a position to:

- provide supervision to your coaches or recommend supervisors
- train your most experienced coaches to be internal supervisors
- develop CPD programmes for you
- support your coaches through an accreditation process
- source expert speakers for you
- help you monitor take up and support your internal marketing.

Developing and delivering the training in-house: Your organisation may be in the fortunate position that you, as lead coach, have the background and experience to develop and deliver the training yourself—or perhaps you with some of your colleagues. A number of the lead coaches whom I interviewed had a learning and development background and were already experienced in delivering training in-house to managers in how to use a coaching approach. Such courses tended to be called: "Coaching skills for managers" or "The manager as coach". Training a cadre of internal coaches was for them simply the next logical step. This approach has all the advantages of using an external provider to deliver the coaching to your first cohort in-house but also retains all the learning within the organisation and will probably be better value. Another key benefit is that by observing the trainee coaches through the programme, you will have a pretty good idea of the strengths and weaknesses of different coaches and who the really talented coaches are. This will be helpful later on if your matching process is a personalised one.

Validation

The most cost-effective approach to setting up an internal coach cadre quickly can be to put out a call for employees who are already fully or partially trained. However, if you are to be sure that these coaches are of good quality, you will need to establish some kind of process for validating their skills.

At the minimum, you will want to interview them about their training, their experience, their approach, and so forth. A more rigorous approach is to set up an assessment centre and ask the candidates, for example, to: a) articulate their coaching model and approach; b) do some observed coaching; c) critique the session afterwards with the observer; and d) be interviewed about such issues as their ethical framework, their experience of supervision, what they have learned from supervision, and so forth.

Some organisations have taken a hybrid approach and recruited both trained and untrained coaches and put them all through the same training on the grounds that they will then share a common vocabulary around coaching; will be exposed to a common approach (say if the training takes an appreciative enquiry or a neuro-scientific approach); and will form the basis of a community of coaches.

Matching

The key decision in deciding your matching approach is whether you want the driver of the process to be you or the client or some combination of the two.

Hand matching: Some lead coaches make the process extremely personal and interview both the potential client and their line manager to get an accurate sense of their development needs. They may decide that some other intervention is more suitable (say mentoring, training, or a job move). If coaching does seem the best option then they may: a) hand-pick a suitable coach and set up a chemistry meeting, or b) identify two or three possible coaches and provide the client with their contact details and biography so that they can choose. In one organisation that employs some full-time internal coaches as well as a number of lead coaches, a decision is taken whether to allocate the client a lead coach, a full-time coach, a part-time coach, or an external coach. The interview with the line manager offers an opportunity to check out that the client's needs are not really a dressed up performance management issue that the line manager is trying to avoid. In that situation, a lead coach might instead say to the line manager: "Rather than getting a coach for X, would you find it useful if we had a conversation about how you might address this issue with him?"

Mukherjee (2012) has written about a large internal coaching initiative where it was considered to be essential for the coaches and clients to be hand matched. This was because the coaches were all very senior managers, so it was felt that many of the clients would have been keen to connect with specific managers whom they judged could make a difference to their career prospects. The HR department used the following broad criteria:

- clients should not be from the same functional domain (to avoid overlapping of mentoring with coaching);
- the coaches should not have clients working under them directly (to avoid boss-subordinate relationship); and
- clients should be known as high performers and not going to retire within the next ten years.

A key benefit of so-called "hand matching" is that the lead coach is choosing the coach that they believe would best meet the needs of the client in terms of experience, background, and style. However, the lead coach would also be taking into account issues such as:

- the development needs of the coach
- the availability of the coach, as in how many clients they were already coaching
- where in the business the coach works, so as to reduce to the minimum the likelihood of role conflict or the coach knowing many of the colleagues with whom the client works.

There are additional reasons why it is best to find a coach who works in a very different part of the organisation from the client:

- It is easier for the coach to be objective in their dealings with the client if there is no pre-existing relationship. They can give feedback in a more honest way and be challenging, if necessary.
- Misuse of power is less likely if the coach and client work in very different areas. So if there is a need for difficult and candid feedback the coach need not fear that their job could be in jeopardy at some later date.
- Colleagues may be less likely to take advice or be open to developmental suggestions from a colleague than he or she would from someone from elsewhere in the organisation.

Client-driven matching: The alternative approach is for the client to be the initiator. In this scenario there would be a register of internal coaches—it could include approved external coaches too—which would be stored on the company intranet. Sometimes a register of coaches might be open to all employees to view but often a manager would only be given access to it once approval had been given for them to have a coach. It is usual for such registers to include biographies of the coaches, to a template, including past experience in the organisation; coaching experience; any qualifications or accreditations; any specialities (career development, transitions, change management, sales); coaching approach; and sometimes a space for any testimonials from former clients. The coaches normally write their own biographies. The client would select one or more coaches from the register and arrange to meet them.

Since the inception of the relationship is not mediated by the lead coach in this approach, it is generally the responsibility of the coach, during the chemistry session, to check out whether they and the potential client have colleagues in common. If they do, it is better for the client to look for another coach. In some organisations the coach register may be no more than a listing but it could be part of an automated coach management system that logs relationships, sessions held, evaluations completed, and so forth. Chapter Seven provides more information about automated coach management systems.

What next?

Something to be aware of is that when coaches finish their training they can experience a sense of isolation. It can feel as though that "wrap-around" support that they have while training is abruptly withdrawn. The skill is to keep them feeling as though they are part of a community of coaches with access to continuing support. The next chapter is devoted to supervision and CPD, which play a large part in providing that sense of support. Particularly important too is to get your coaches up and running with a coaching client as soon as possible.

Summary

Identifying, selecting, and matching coaches to clients are essential elements of any internal coaching programme. These elements will be guided by your coaching strategy and strategic purpose. However, training is probably the deciding factor that will determine the programme's success. The credibility of your coaches will depend on their capability, which will be a reflection of their training and experience. In addition, training is likely to be the area that requires greatest financial investment, so you will want to demonstrate value for money. It is important that the content and method of delivery reflect what you require your coaches to deliver and help build your coaching community.

QUESTIONS TO REFLECT ON

Factor to consider	What are the implications for the organisation?

Selection

- What are the routes to identifying internal coaches in our business?
- How will we invite potential candidates to apply?
- What process and criteria will we use to assess suitability?

- Do we want to pilot one cohort of internal coaches before rolling out a programme?
- How can we ensure applications from a diverse pool of individuals?
- What information do potential coaches need to help them self-select?
- How can we use the selection process to engage the business in internal coaching?
- Who needs to be engaged in the selection process?
- Would an application form meet our purpose? If so, what needs to be included?
- Do applicants need line managers' authorisation?
- Who will assess the application forms?
- What will be the "appeals" process for potential coaches who are rejected?
- If we want some sort of assessment process:
  - what do we need to use to assess applicants "aptitude for coaching"?
  - what will we be looking for in an interview process?
  - how will we deal with those that are unsuccessful?

(Continued)

QUESTIONS TO REFLECT ON   *(Continued)*

Factor to consider	*What are the implications for the organisation?*

	• How will we ensure individuals selected:
	  – will be able to commit the required amount of time?
	  – are credible and have a good reputation?
	  – are representative of the business as a whole—we have a broad mix?

Training What are the considerations for training our internal coaches in terms of content?	• How can we ensure the training builds on the skills and aptitudes we used as criteria in the selection phase? • What do we want our coaches to be able to do once they have finished training? What implications has this for the balance of theoretical and practical elements of training? • What depth of training needs to be provided? Do we need to consider providing any specialist training?
Qualification/accreditation Will it improve the credibility of our internal coaches if the training provides them with a qualification or accreditation?	• If we decide on a coach training that leads to accreditation, what type of qualification best reflects our organisational requirements? • Does the organisation have a funding policy for training? If so what are the implications if a trained coach leaves shortly after becoming qualified?

(Continued)

QUESTIONS TO REFLECT ON   (*Continued*)

Factor to consider	What are the implications for the organisation?
Delivering the training Would in-house training be more effective than sending potential coaches on open programmes?	• Do we have sufficient coaches to justify an in-house training programme? Do we have the expertise to deliver it ourselves? • How do we need to work with suppliers to ensure the programme reflects our organisational needs? • What may we also need in terms of CPD/supervision that we need to take into account when commissioning the training? • What do we need to specify if we are to carry out a competitive tendering exercise?
Validation Can we use people in our organisation who have been fully or partially trained in the relevant skills but have not gone through our coaching programme?	• What would give us the assurance that these individuals have the relevant expertise to be successful coaches? • Would it be beneficial to put them through the training anyway?
Matching What process for matching—hand matching or client driven—will best meet our organisational need? What are the criteria that we will use to guide the matching process?	• Taking into consideration the size of our internal coaching programme, would hand matching or client driven matching best meet our needs? • How does our coaching strategy inform the criteria we will use for matching coaches? • What information do we need our coaches to provide to help with the matching process? Will we put this information into the "public domain" or will it just be available for potential clients?

CHAPTER NINE

Supervision and continuous professional development

If you don't provide supervision for internal coaches ... the sustainability and return on investment of your coaching initiative is in jeopardy

—*Hawkins & Schwenk*, 2006, p. 17

What this chapter is about

Learning to be a good coach takes training, practice, and support in the form of supervision and continuous professional development. There is no "quick fix". Some trainee coaches will have so many transferable skills and aptitudes from former roles and life experience that they will hit the ground running. Others will need longer to settle into the role. But either way, a three-day training programme—or even a diploma programme spread out over six to nine months—is not enough to support the development of your coaches. A programme of supervision and continuous professional development (CPD) is essential for refining your coaches' skills; maintaining ethical standards; providing opportunities for them to reflect on and learn from their practice; giving them exposure to different approaches; and staying current on issues and practices within the profession. Anything less is exposing your coaches and their clients to unnecessary risks.

This chapter is all about supporting your coaches once their formal training is complete. It explores:

- The purpose and benefits of coach supervision
- The three aspects of supervision: normative, formative, and restorative
- The advantages and disadvantages of one-to-one and group supervision
- Managing confidentiality in group supervision
- Using external or internal supervisors
- Typical supervision issues for internal coaches
- What good supervision looks like
- Models of supervision
- Finding a supervisor and procuring services
- Alternative approaches to supervision
- Continuing professional development, the benefits and options for delivery.

Supervision

It is widely recognised within the coaching profession that supervision makes a significant contribution to coaches' continuing development. Organisations that procure external coaches often make regular supervision a requirement but then fail to enforce similar standards of support and quality assurance for their own internal coaches. Money may be tight but failing to support internal coaches is a false economy. One would hope that practice has improved since Hawkins and Schwenk's (2006) research showed that while eighty-eight per cent of organisations using internal coaches believed that they should have supervision, only twenty-three per cent actually provided it. However, anecdotal evidence suggests that provision is still poor.

Some internal coaches felt that once the training was over, they were on their own. One said:

> "I loved the training but once it was done I never heard from anyone again apart from the odd telephone call from an administrator to give me the contact details of a possible new client. We had no supervision, no events when we could all meet up and share

experiences and no CPD. In the end I joined the EMCC at my own expense and attended their CPD events but I would have much preferred to have the support and company of other internal coaches from my firm."

However, while many internal coaches expressed the wish for supervision, there will be others who may not appreciate its value. Maxwell (2011) noted that: "There is a suggestion that (internal) coaches see supervision as only necessary in a crisis … or as a time expensive luxury … rather than a necessary form of on-going learning, reflection and quality control" (p. 191). Several lead coaches told me that with hindsight they wished they had been firmer about insisting that coaches attended supervision sessions.

What is the purpose of supervision?

The concept of supervision came originally from therapeutic practice and it has taken a while for the term to be accepted in the coaching world. Attempts have been made to coin different words to describe both the person who does the supervision and for the practice (supervision groups, for example, are called "shared learning groups" in one organisation) because the words, for some, have uncomfortable overtones of policing or controlling. However, over the past few years the debate about finding alternative terminology seems to have died down and the terms "coach supervisor" and "coach supervision" are widely recognised.

There is a variety of definitions of what constitutes coach supervision. Here are a few:

> … a formal process of professional support which addresses the coach's development and the effectiveness of his or her practice. This is done through interactive reflection, interpretive evaluation and sharing expertise. (BPS's Special Group in Coaching Psychology, cited by Moyes, 2009, p. 161)
>
> … a structured formal process for coaches, with the help of a coaching supervisor, to attend to improving the quality of their coaching, grow their coaching capacity and support themselves and their practice. Supervision should also be a source of organisational learning. (Hawkins & Schwenk, 2006, p. 2)
>
> Supervision provides a protected and disciplined space in which coaches can reflect on particular client situations and

relationships, the reactivity and patterns these evoke in them and, by transforming these live in supervision, can profoundly benefit the coachee, the client organisation and their own professional practice and development. (Hawkins, 2011, p. 287)

Supervision is a forum where supervisees think about their work in order to do it better. (Carroll, 2006, p. 4)

The EMCC's guidance on supervision refers to a supervisor "assessing competence and supporting development" and offers a three-cornered model for defining the nature of supervision based on work by Proctor (1986). The same three aspects appear in research by Kadushin (1992) who examined the purpose of supervision in a social work context, but I am using Proctor's terminology. The three aspects are:

- normative—the supervisor shares with the supervisee responsibility for ensuring that the supervisee's work is professional and ethical, operating within whatever codes, laws, and organisational norms apply
- formative—the supervisor acts to provide feedback or direction that will enable the supervisee to develop the skills, theoretical knowledge, personal attributes, and so on that will mean the supervisee becomes an increasingly competent practitioner
- restorative—the supervisor is there to listen, support, confront the supervisee when the inevitable personal issues, doubts, and insecurities arise—and when client issues are "picked up" by the supervisee.

(EMCC Guidelines on Supervision: Interim Statement)

Normative: This facet of the supervisor's role equates most closely with the natural meaning of the word "supervision" because it requires the supervisor to uphold the standards of the profession, model good practice, and assure the quality, professionalism, and integrity of the coach's practice. Chapter Four puts considerable emphasis on the role of supervision in helping coaches to resolve dilemmas ethically. This draws on the "normative" part of the supervisor's role. As Carroll and Shaw (2013) put it:

There comes a time when the voices of others enter the dialogue and weave their influence ... Different perspectives can provide wider vision and help us to make mature choices. (pp. 353–354)

From the perspective of the employer, the "normative" aspect of supervision provides a degree of quality assurance. If the coach wishes to discuss a dilemma, then the supervisor is expected to help them to arrive at the most ethical way forward; if the coach struggles with an aspect of coaching practice that seems to the supervisor to put the client or organisation at risk, the supervisor would be expected to address this; if guidance as to how the coach might practise more safely is needed, the supervisor should provide it. Most coaches very much value this aspect of the supervisor's role as they want to be sure that they are operating ethically and professionally.

As a lead coach you would do well to think carefully about what you actually expect from your coach supervisors in this area and to discuss it with them. Supervisors have responsibilities towards the coach, the coach's client, and to the organisation (and ultimately the organisation's clients) but what does this mean in practice? How do you want them to discharge their obligation to you, as representative of the organisation's interests? If supervision is partly about improving and evaluating the internal coaching service for the ultimate benefit of the clients and the organisation then should there be some line of communication between the supervisor and the lead coach? I have spoken with external supervisors of internal coaches who say that they do not see themselves as having an obligation to talk to the lead coach about, say, suspected performance issues. They regard their supervisory conversations with internal coaches in the same way as they would those with external coaches: that is, a confidential space where the responsibility for making any changes rests squarely with the coach. But if the external supervisor is not that familiar with the organisation, has little contact with the lead coach once the contract has been signed, and has no obligations to signal any concern they might have about the quality of a coach's practice, how confident can the lead coach be that the coaching is all that they might wish?

In her session on supervision at the 2012 EMCC conference in Bilbao, Katherine Long (Director of Development and Supervision at OCM, who leads on OCM's Certificate in Organisational Coach-Mentoring Supervision) posed the question: "What should a supervisor do if they think that a coach is really underperforming?" If the coaches feel that their supervisor may be making some kind of judgement of their competence that will be reported back, what impact will that have on which issues they bring to supervision and the extent to which they feel they can expose their vulnerabilities? Experienced coaches recognise that it is all about their learning but new coaches may feel less robust.

Formative: This aspect of the supervisor's role is about developing the coach's knowledge and skills through the encouragement of reflection, helping them to explore their practice through discussion of their client work, and providing ideas, tips, techniques, and knowledge. The supervisor may give the coach direct feedback, introduce them to a relevant theory or model, or invite them to role-play. The aim is for the coach to become an increasingly competent practitioner. Butwell's (2006) research noted that all the coaches in her small-scale study of a supervision group highlighted skills acquisition as being a key benefit of their group supervision. It would probably be useful for the supervisor you select, if external, to know what models of coaching your coaches have been introduced to during their training. This allows the supervisor to know what vocabulary and approaches they are familiar with.

Hawkins (2011) argues that supervision should certainly be partly about developing the coach but points out that: "In our training of several hundred coach supervisors we have found that generally they are less skilled at attending to the supervisee's capacity than they are at attending to the current client work" (p. 286). When supervising internal coaches, building capacity is particularly important because, compared with external coaches, they usually have many fewer clients—which translates into fewer issues to bring up directly from their client work. Coach supervisors of internal coaches also remark that internal coaches sometimes have no clients at all for a period so that the sessions can focus much more on keeping their skills fresh and have more of a CPD feel to them.

Supervisors talk about how supervision sessions tend to change in style and content as coaches become more experienced. When they begin, new coaches tend to want a lot of input and ideas and can get "hung up on techniques". As they get more experienced, they tend to be more interested in talking about underlying themes, about themselves as coaches, and about patterns that they have noticed across their practice. Supervision is not just about discussing client issues—it can also be purely reflective. A generative question that many supervisors ask is: "Which of your clients do you enjoy working with most/least and why is that?" Or: "With which clients do you feel you do your best/worst work and why might that be?"

Restorative: The third aspect is providing practical and psychological support to the coach. They may be finding it hard to cope with the competing pressures of their work and coaching roles; may have doubts and insecurities around their competence (particularly if they have no clients for a period); or may be psychologically taking on board the concerns and worries of their clients.

I can still remember my shock, many years ago, the first time that a client wept during a session. This possibility had not been mentioned at all during my training though I understand that it is more common now for this eventuality to be covered. Clients often cry. There are many reasons: they may be feeling huge relief in acknowledging their situation and responding to a feeling of having been really "heard"; they may be accessing a painful time in their past when reflecting on what is contributing to current feelings; they may be overwhelmed by a very demanding job and feelings of being unable to cope or they could be worried, for example, about being made redundant and the impact that would have on themselves and their family. If a coach has a series of clients who are highly stressed it can take its toll. Moyes (2009) wonders how essential the supportive element is for coaches as compared with, say, social workers and suggests that "the level of support coaches need is arguably qualitatively different" (p. 163). That may well be so, but one lead coach, who was moving on from a role in an organisation under high pressure, told me that with hindsight she would have done much more around "how coaches self-regulate": that is, how they manage their resilience. It can be challenging being part of the same system in an organisation that is in crisis. The coaches continue playing their role while in distress themselves and this can have an impact on their ability to be fully present for their clients.

Tehrani (2010) carried out some interesting research into the area of "compassion fatigue" where workers in the caring professions can "experience symptoms similar to those of the people they are supporting" (p. 133). She notes emerging evidence to suggest that where a professional has the opportunity to create meaning from what is going on, then personal growth is a real possibility. Among the personal and professional activities that she cites as helping the individual to translate the distressing experience into personal growth are "using reflection, meditation or other form of reflective practice" and "accessing professional supervision or consultative support" (p. 134) thus highlighting the value of coaches being able to access supervision and acknowledge the emotional impact on them of their coaching work.

Patterson (2011) talks about the four tasks of coaching supervision:

1. Assuring professionalism, integrity, and ethical practice of the supervisee
2. The personal and professional learning and development of the supervisee
3. The rest, refuelling, and restoration of the supervisee
4. Celebrating and honouring the work of the supervisee. (p. 123)

I really like the addition of "celebrating and honouring the work of the supervisee". The constraints of confidentiality mean that coaching can be a lonely business and the supervisor is in an ideal position to affirm a coach's work.

Some of the reasons given by organisations for not providing supervision (Hawkins & Schwenk, 2006) were that:

• it is too expensive
• they could not find a supervisor or
• their coaches did not need supervision.

Benefits of supervision

Researchers have noted that the benefits of supervision are perceived differently by the various parties involved. Hawkins and Schwenk (2006) pointed out that while "coaches are interested in making themselves more effective" (eighty-eight per cent of the coaches in their research were interested in developing their coaching capability), those organising coaching services "put more emphasis on quality assurance" such as "protecting the client; minimising the organisational risk of unethical or unprofessional practice; ensuring the coaching is focused on work objectives and within the boundaries of the coach's capability [and] … raising coaching standards by continually improving quality and effectiveness". They also highlighted the fact that in the case of internal coaches: "benefits include bringing geographically dispersed coaches together to share good practice, improving collaborative learning and identifying organisation themes and issues" (p. 7).

Liz Macann, formerly lead coach for the BBC's internal coaching service, highlighted the following positives about supervision:

- a sense of community and connectedness with other coaches
- a belief in the coaching process being stimulated
- ongoing personal development that informs coaching practice
- more effective working with "sticky" clients
- confident coaches who are better equipped to deliver high-calibre, time-effective coaching
- an organisational safety net to help coaches maintain boundaries and minimize any organizational risk. (Hawkins & Schwenk, 2006, p. 10)

Recent research by Humphrey and Sheppard (2012) found reported benefits as in the table below.

Reported benefits of supervision

For coach	For coaching organisation	For clients
Increases rigour	Generates generic issues	Keeps the coaching clean
Enhances professionalism	Highlights the development needs of the organisation	Provides quality assurance
Extends coaches' repertoire/ development	Builds confidence in our profession	Protects and represents clients' interests
Acts as a safe pair of hands		Maintains confidence in the process
Builds confidence		
Provides challenge		

Table reprinted by kind permission of the authors. Humphrey & Sheppard (2012), "Supervised behaviour", *Coaching at Work, 7*: 6 (Autumn 2012), p. 49.

One-to-one supervision vs. group supervision

Any coach who has had both group and one-to-one supervision with a trained supervisor would agree that they are both valuable but offer very different experiences. How do you decide what to offer your coaches? Hawkins and Schwenk (2006) point out that all supervision has its limitations:

- Individual supervision with a senior practitioner can lead to dependency
- Group supervision can be overtaken by the dynamics of the group and leave insufficient time for each individual
- Peer supervision can become collusive. (p. 15)

One-to-one supervision: In one-to-one supervision the coach has the supervisor's undivided attention. Many coaches say that they prefer one-to-one supervision as you can get much deeper. You can also spend longer on an issue. In a one-hour one-to-one session you can really bottom something out. You have the privacy to role play or really get into personal material—such as deep-seated patterns that may be holding you back or getting in the way with a particular client—that might be difficult, uncomfortable, or feel "unsafe" to share in a group session. Keen adherents of group supervision would counter that by saying that once a group is well established, feelings of safety will evolve, but that takes time. One internal coach summarised the benefits for her of one-to-one supervision:

- It's time efficient and easy to organise (only two diaries)
- There's more confidentiality
- All the time is mine!

Several lead coaches suggested that those receiving one-to-one supervision should be given a new supervisor every couple of years to minimise collusion and dependency and offer them a new perspective.

Group supervision: There are numerous different approaches to running a supervision group but the common features are that groups tend to be for around five to six coaches (minimum three, maximum eight) and meet at regular intervals with constant membership. Some supervision groups run for a whole day, others for half a day or two to three hours. Group members bring issues to the group—which is run by a trained coach supervisor—about their own development as a coach or client-related matters for discussion and learning.

Benefits for the coaches: Key benefits of group (as opposed to one-to-one) supervision, articulated by a variety of experienced and less experienced internal coaches, are:

- The richness of the learning as there is "more than one supervisor in the room": that is, the coaches in effect supervise each other, with increasing levels of skill as they become more experienced, under the guidance of a trained supervisor
- By hearing what issues other coaches bring to supervision, you learn from other people's experiences things that you have not yet encountered yourself
- The support you get from knowing that other coaches have experienced the same setbacks that you have and are empathising with you
- Being able to "benchmark" your practice by hearing other coaches talking about their experiences can be reassuring and affirming
- A sense of community and connectedness with other coaches. Some coaches talked about the importance of feeling part of a network, even if they did not contact the others between sessions
- Help with recognising boundaries within the organisation. Being supervised with other coaches working in the same system can be really helpful because they may be dealing with the needs, expectations, and internal politics around the same group of stakeholders.

Benefits for the lead coach/organisation: Lead coaches sometimes train with the first cohort of coaches and are often part of a supervision group with their coaches. Some lead coaches have reported the value of getting to know their coaches better through this route and how it can help them for the matching process. It can also assist them to spot those that may need additional support or some issue taken offline (but also see the section below on *Challenges in using internal supervisors* for the difficulties that this dual role can pose for lead coaches). There can be value in the lead coaches moving groups every so often.

Other benefits are:

- The potential for harvesting organisational themes that emerge from coaching across the organisation. This will be need to be specifically contracted for with the supervisor and a process established
- Building a community of practice
- Making connections across silos as coaches from different parts of the business get to know each other
- It generally costs less to employ a trained supervisor to run a group for six people than for those six each to have one-to-one supervision.

However, if the one-to-one supervision is by telephone this may not necessarily pertain.

Drawbacks of group supervision: However good a supervisor is at making sure that everyone around the table is engaged, group supervision can allow individuals to coast. While the coaster may be learning from what they are hearing, their lack of contribution reduces the value of the experience for the others. At the other end of the spectrum, most groups do not have time for every coach to present an issue at every session and this can be frustrating for a group of fully engaged coaches, all of whom may want some airtime. If the groups meet monthly this may not present too much of a problem but if they only meet quarterly or less then some coaches may feel that they are not getting enough attention.

Butwell (2006) explored the experience of internal coaches in a supervision group. They met quarterly so it took some time for the participants to get to know each other and feel "safe" and this was reflected in concerns they had about letting down their guards. Butwell reports a participant saying: "I've got working relationships with half the people around that table … Has that held me back in any way though? It might have done" (p. 49). There can be fears associated with self-disclosure: whether revealing their vulnerabilities as coaches might affect colleagues' views of their capability more generally.

Confidentiality: However, the issue that gave rise to most discussion in interviews, by a considerable margin, was the boundaries around confidentiality. In short, the problem is the extent to which discussion of client cases in group supervision sessions may compromise the confidentiality of the client. Many coaches had experienced situations when a coach had held up their hand and said: "I know who you are talking about". The issue can be compounded if the group is supervised by an internal supervisor as they are part of the same system. One internal supervisor told me that she was also working as a coach with the CEO and one of the coaches in her supervision group came up with an issue that his client had with the CEO. She dealt with the situation by saying "I would be compromised if we carry on with this. I'll arrange for you to have a supervision session with someone else to discuss that issue."

Two examples from coaches of inter-relationships were: "One of my clients was a friend and colleague of the coaching supervisor", and: "I am in the same talent programme as some of the people whom a colleague in the supervision group coaches."

Some organisations were so large that the likelihood of coaches knowing whom a fellow supervisee was talking about was low. In others, the internal coaches were a very close-knit group working in a fairly small world and the likelihood was high. Most supervisors were intensely aware of the inherent risks, and devised ground rules to try to protect the confidentiality of client information. Examples were:

- Reinforcing before every supervision session: "What's said in the room, stays in the room"
- Ensuring that clients are never named or their job titles mentioned
- Making it clear that the coaches are there to discuss behaviours not people
- Contracting that if someone recognises who is being talked about, and it is a problem for them (e.g., the client issue being discussed relates to another coach's boss), then they leave the room
- Having the option of the issue being taken off-line (e.g., a one-to-one session for the coach to discuss that particular issue).

Some internal supervisors are pretty robust and pragmatic about this issue. One said to me that he had never had an issue with confidentiality because:

- They have a code of conduct around confidentiality
- The subject is the coaches' *practice*—the data is rarely sensitive
- In a group you might guess who it is but you could be wrong
- The way he contracts is by asking the coaches at the beginning of each session:
  - what do you need to leave behind?
  - what do you need from this session?
  - are there any issues around the data you're bringing that you need to contract with others around?

This is all well and good but some coaches are still uncomfortable about this issue. One wondered:

> "Even though we contract to leave the room if we recognise who the client is, no-one ever actually does. Might not someone's curiosity occasionally trump their professionalism and they end up being privy to something that affects their view of a colleague and which they should not really know about?"

A thought that this leaves me with is: when your coaches contract with their clients, do they make clear that they may take an issue relating to that client to group supervision and that other coaches may therefore become privy to it? How transparent should this reasonably be?

A final two points: a) a number of organisations have decided that the process that best meets their coaches' needs is a combination of group and one-to-one supervision. Where resources allow, a popular formulation is to alternate the two and b) both one-to-one and group supervision can be conducted by telephone. The latter helps to keep the costs down.

Internal vs. external supervision

As lead coach you will need to decide how to source supervision for your coaches, irrespective of whether it is group or one-to-one. Will you bring in external supervisors or train one or more of your most experienced internal coaches as a supervisor? Or perhaps you, as lead coach, are already qualified, or plan to qualify, as a supervisor yourself. There are some distinct pros and cons to using internal or external supervisors and they mirror the arguments for using internal or external coaches.

Benefits of using external supervisors

- An enhanced sense of confidentiality—that the supervisor is unlikely to know the person about whom the coach is talking
- They offer a different kind of challenge, as they will not have the same blind spots. Internal supervisors may take things for granted about the culture while externals are freer to ask a question that opens things up
- They bring fresh ideas and different models in—additional to those learned by the coaches during training
- They are more accessible (internals have a day job).

Disadvantages of using external supervisors

- The costs are likely to be higher overall (though external supervisors tend to cost less than external coaches)
- The organisation may not have contracted for them to be available *ad hoc* for discussion of any ethical dilemmas, thus leaving coaches without access to support between supervision sessions

- They do not always understand the language and the culture, so time is taken up explaining (though this should diminish over time).

Long (2012) has identified some additional disbenefits:

- The fact that it is a commercial relationship can lead to collusive behaviours with the external supervisor less willing to challenge and unconsciously behaving more as an ally to the coach.
- The supervisor may hold strong views that are at odds with the vision for coaching within the client organisation so that they stop behaving as a partner to the client organisation "and take on a role as an unofficial consultant".
- Because of the inherent power imbalance, particularly with an inexperienced coach, an external supervisor using a different perspective or imperfect understanding of the organisational agenda, could cause real confusion for the coaches about the "right" way to coach. (p. 2)

Benefits of training internal supervisors

Despite the fact that they have day jobs and the time pressures associated with that, internal supervisors—particularly if they are also the lead coach—are more likely to make themselves available to coaches for a quick consultation about an ethical dilemma. While to some it might seem counter-intuitive, one highly experienced internal coach also argued that internal supervision could provide more challenge to the coach than external coaching does:

> "There are nine of us who qualified together originally. We're very mature and have been together for three years so we're able to go much deeper, much quicker. We can challenge each other directly and robustly because we've been together so long. We trust each other a lot and will experiment more because it feels safe. The external supervision felt a bit 'soft'."

Another saw one benefit of her being an internal supervisor as being that she understands the system, the internal politics, and the functional specialisms (quite complicated in her medical world). She is also very familiar with what is going on within the organisation: for example, if a particular department is carrying vacancies or coping with high sickness absence and therefore under a lot of pressure.

Long (2012) has articulated some additional benefits:

- Training some of your internal coaches to be supervisors recognises their contribution: it represents encouragement and support to them by the organisation.
- Along with getting internal coaches qualified to independent professional standards, building supervision skills sends out the message to the business that internal coaches are actively concerned in developing the quality of their coaching.
- If lead coaches train as supervisors, they will be able to spot trends and themes and assess whether the coaching is addressing the sorts of issues that underlay the purpose for which the pool was set up.
- Developing internal coaches' supervision skills will enhance the quality of their coaching practice by broadening the range of lenses that they use and enabling them to work more effectively with process and ambiguity.
- A lead coach trained as a supervisor can play a stewardship role in a way that an external supervisor could not.

So would all your coaches be suitable to train as supervisors? Moyes (2009) asks the question: "Do good coaches automatically become good supervisors?" (p. 168). Drawing on therapeutic literature on the role transition from practitioner to supervisor she notes that any assumption that a competent counsellor will necessarily be equally effective as a supervisor is "dubious" and cites Borders (1992) who concluded that: "a pivotal skill in this role transition is the cognitive shift from thinking like a counsellor to thinking like a supervisor." As lead coach you would therefore need to make a judgement as to which of your coaches was most likely to be able to make this cognitive shift; who shows readiness for being trained to use a supervision framework competently and who has the skills to combine the roles of educator, supporter, and quality assurer (i.e., the three aspects of supervision).

Challenges in using internal supervisors

The three key concerns expressed within the coach supervision world about the use of internal supervisors are:

a. that they are hooked into the organisational culture and the same systemic dynamics as their supervisees, which may make it more difficult for them to challenge assumptions, or even to see the need to challenge them, because they share them
b. that their relationships with coaching colleagues may make it less easy for those colleagues to give them honest feedback about the quality of their supervision
c. that there is an inherent conflict that needs to be managed by the internal supervisor between the needs of the coaches and their clients and those of the organisation. This can be delicate, particularly where the supervisor is also the lead coach with managerial responsibilities for assuring the quality of the internal coaching pool.

Thomson (2011) says some interesting things relevant to the last point in his writings about a non-directive approach to supervision that draws on C. Rogers' (1961) work on a client-centred approach (majoring, amongst other things, on providing an environment of unconditional positive regard and non-judgemental acceptance). He highlights the inherent conflict between the supervisor's role in enhancing a coach's learning in a non-directive, client-centred, unconditional, non-judgemental way while at the same time "holding a responsibility to ensure the quality of a coach's work and to monitor the coach's compliance with a relevant code of practice", arguing that "their acceptance necessarily becomes judgemental and their positive regard becomes conditional" (p. 107).

None of these points outweighs the benefits enumerated above but it is important that lead coaches should be aware of them so that they can manage the risks.

How frequent should supervision be?

The most important thing is that supervision is regular and achieves the best possible balance between the coaches' needs and the resources available. Several lead coaches said that they were changing supervision from being a privilege for the coaches to a condition of practising. This should promote better attendance and could help those coaches having difficulty in convincing their bosses of its importance. Butwell (2006) reported that coaches were: "nervous about spending too much time on something that, though they saw it as a 'necessity', might be seen by their line manager as a 'luxury'" (p. 51).

All the professional bodies recommend regular supervision. The ICF and APECS make no specific recommendation about frequency but other bodies do.

EMCC: one hour to every thirty-five hours of coaching (minimum quarterly)

AC: one hour to every fifteen sessions (minimum of one hour per month)

BPS: minimum of one hour per month

CIPD: one hour to every twenty-five hours of coaching for experienced coaches or one hour to every twenty hours coaching for trainee or newly qualified coaches. The gap between sessions should be no longer than six weeks.

Rather than aiming at a particular ratio, most lead coaches look at what the appropriate interval between sessions should be, irrespective of how many client relationships the coaches actually have. Some supervisors felt strongly that supervision should take place monthly, particularly where the coaches were quite inexperienced, on the grounds of a) keeping the momentum up and b) keeping the coaches learning. The phrase was also used that "supervision needs to map the development of the pool": where the coaches are still inexperienced or do not have many clients, supervision tends to be more developmental and skills practice oriented. If resources only permit meeting every two months or quarterly, supervisors often encourage members of a supervision group to co-coach each other between sessions. Some lead coaches felt that having time for reflection on one's practice at least every two months was probably the ideal but it did not necessarily have to be full-on supervision (as in: discussion with a trained supervisor).

However, many organisations, if they offer supervision by a qualified supervisor at all, only provide it on a quarterly or twice-yearly basis, often in conjunction with the some CPD. One of the reasons is that there is a limit to how much off-the-job time the coaches can make available. Many supervisors would question whether that level of frequency really constitutes "supervision" at all. One of Butwell's (2006) conclusions from closely studying the workings of one internal supervision group was that quarterly meetings provided insufficient opportunity for a real focus on client cases.

There can be an issue around accessibility of supervisory support between sessions, particularly if they are infrequent. Fortunately, coach supervisors tend to be conscientious and to take seriously their duty of care towards their supervisees, and I have heard of innumerable cases where this conscientiousness has led external supervisors to offer unpaid *ad hoc* help, by telephone, where coaches have ethical dilemmas to resolve quickly. However, this is taking advantage of their goodwill and, ideally, organisations should negotiate a call-off contract for "emergency" telephone consultations of this kind. Nearly all the internal supervisors said that they were one hundred per cent available for *ad hoc* supervisions. They regarded this as very much part of their role.

One point that a number of lead coaches made was that while their budgets did not stretch to providing supervision more often than, say, quarterly, they encouraged their coaches to use other ways of reflecting on and developing their practice, including CPD. These are looked at later on in this chapter.

Issues in supervising internal coaches

Supervisors with experience of supervising both internal and external coaches noted issues that seem to come up more from internal coaches:

- They get a more "issue-based agenda": that is, the clients present with day-to-day work issues that they want to sort out in the coaching sessions. The coaches can feel a) that they are being forced into the role of mentors or b) that they are helping the client with issues that are properly the responsibility of their line managers
- They more often bring ethical issues around confidentiality and role conflicts
- They more often have a problem with the boundary between coaching and counselling: for example, a client who is depressed or keeps crying while refusing to get help from professional sources. An external coach would normally be pretty clear about that boundary but an internal coach who is part of the same system, and may find the culture pretty stressful themselves, may be seduced into thinking that it is "normal" and part of their coaching role to help the client through it
- They find that their clients are not always "fully engaged": that is, they do not follow up on the actions they committed to. Their perception is that because the coaching is not charged for, the client does not take it seriously. This may sometimes be about how the service is

promoted internally. If there is no senior flag waver it can be easy for the service to be eroded and for the client to allow the day job to take precedence

- Internal coaches seem to get "bounced" much more—clients cancel a lot. The coaches have to rely on their personal influencing skills and being firm. But when someone reschedules, the coach may have a sense of relief that they have some time released for the day job and that relief may be transmitted to the client and then things can begin to drift. It is really important that the coaches contract clearly around cancellations and for the organisation to make it clear in guidance too

- Coaches often have anxieties around the three-way meetings involving the line manager at the beginning and halfway points because of:
  - difficulties in organising it—pure logistics, particularly if the client and their line manager work on different sites
  - nervousness about handling the conversation—the supervisor sometimes has to help them to rehearse
  - finding it hard to be assertive about the necessity for the three-way meeting—answering the question: "What's the point?". This suggests that the guidance needs to be clearer about the purpose
  - worries about having credibility with the client's line manager—particularly if they are junior to them

- Because they are unlikely to have more than three coaching clients at any one time, and may well have only one or two, internal coaches will have fewer client issues to bring so the focus may be more on skills development and the supervision will have more of a CPD feel about it. Partly as a consequence of having fewer "flying hours" they may also have more issues around lack of confidence or feeling deskilled

- They may bring frustrations about their organisation with them and be holding emotions from their clients that have reinforced their own feelings, by virtue of being part of the same system. It can be a challenge to the supervisor how much to allow the internal coaches to offload their own frustrations about their organisation. As one said: "You don't want them to bitch and moan throughout the session. On the other hand, they are carrying the frustrations of their clients and if this parallel process is not surfaced then it can get in the way."

Procuring supervision

Humphrey and Sheppard (2012) examined what "good" supervision looks like (see table below). Irrespective of whether you decide to go for internal or external supervision, the supervisor will need to balance the needs of the coaches, their clients, and the organisation. The importance of understanding the system dynamics involved in coaching means that ideally they should have a level of psychological understanding that requires in-depth, coach supervision training. Many of the institutions that train coaches now also offer training in coach supervision.

What does "good" supervision look like?

"Good" personal experience	"Good" supervisor	"Good" process
Reflect more deeply	Is independent and challenging	Switch supervisor every few years
Develop skills	Has qualified with a recognised organisation	Attend both group and individual supervision
Develop practice	Is doing training in line with the market	Coaching organisation provides supervision for its coaches
Feel "held" and supported	Has a different framework to the coach and/or the previous supervisor	Provider runs coaching circles
See patterns in my thinking and coaching	Engages in supervision on their supervision	
Increase my awareness of projection and transference		

Reproduced from *Coaching at Work, 1 7*: 6 (Autumn 2012), p. 49, "Supervised behaviour" by Sam Humphrey and Louise Sheppard.

Models of supervision: There are many different theories drawn from a variety of fields that can inform supervisory practice: Gestalt, positive psychology, systemic, psychodynamic, cognitive/behavioural, and neuro-linguistic programming (NLP) are examples of the approaches underlying the practice of many supervisors. One of the most popular models currently used in coaching supervision is Bath Consultancy Group's Seven-eyed Process Model (Hawkins & N. Smith, 2006)—which has been adapted from a therapeutic model of supervision to meet the needs of coaches. Many coaches have started the journey towards "psychological-mindedness" during their coach training and the use of these models guides them further along the track. There is still a debate about how much psychological experience and knowledge coaches and coach supervisors need. Some would say that coaching for performance improvement and behaviour change does not require psychological input. However, many others would argue that operating in such territory is bound to throw up emotional and psychological issues for clients and coaches and that psychological understanding will result in an earlier recognition that such issues may be getting in the way of progress. Speaking personally, as someone with no background in psychology before I trained as a coach, I have found the insights and new approaches gained through many years of being supervised by a former gestalt therapist (who also had experience of working as a coach and of training coaches), plus undertaking CPD in a variety of psychological approaches to coaching, absolutely invaluable for working with clients. But others may take a different view and regard supervision as more of a consultative process.

The Coaching Supervision Academy takes its trainee coach supervisors through the "Full Spectrum Model" which is, in effect, a map rather than a model. Conceptual tools covered include:

- Hawkins & Smith's seven-eyed model
- Karpman Drama triangle
- Coaching psychology—gestalt, transactional analysis, and transpersonal
- Relational psychology
- Organisational psychology
- Working with image and metaphor
- Arts-based enquiry
- Advanced dialogue process.

Finding supervisors and procuring their services: Many organisations that decide to recruit external supervisors find that they can source supervision from the consultancy or training establishment that trained their coaches. However, others believe that it is important to bring in different perspectives—through both the supervision and CPD that they arrange—so consciously procure from a different source. It is important to check out that: a) a supervisor is well trained and qualified; b) they can provide references of satisfied client organisations to whom you can speak; and c) they supervise in the way that suits you. There are a number of organisations that hold a register of supervisors who have been properly trained. They include the Association of Coaching Supervisors, the Coaching Supervision Academy, and the Association for Professional Executive Coaching and Supervision. In 2013 the EMCC launched their European Supervision Quality Award (ESQA)—an independent accreditation awarded to providers of supervisor training. They are also working on an individual accreditation scheme for supervisors. Also in 2013, the Association for Coaching launched their Coaching Supervisor Accreditation designed for individual supervisors.

As lead coach you need to think about what you want from your supervisors and to have a really good contracting conversation with them. It would be unwise to hire a supervisor simply on the basis of someone's recommendation that they are "good", only to find out down the track that while they may be very insightful when working with coaches on client issues, they do not really cover all the bases (i.e., normative, formative, and restorative). Many organisations purchasing coaching services do care about the "normative" aspect of supervision as they are concerned to protect the client and minimise the risk to the organisation of unethical or unprofessional practice. However, how many of them would ask the supervisor how they would actually deal with a situation where one of their supervisees comes across, over a period, as on the margins of competence or even unethical? Or ask them what methodology they would use to extract from the coaches systemic themes to feed back? There has been comparatively little research into coaching supervision and many purchasers may not currently have a clear picture of what they are buying.

The EMCC provides guidance on some criteria to use when choosing a supervisor. They were developed to help external coaches find a supervisor but are nonetheless relevant. The criteria include that:

- they have experience as a coach
- they have experience of being supervised
- they have experience as a supervisor (not necessarily of coaches)

- they evidence a theoretical framework for their own practice and you find this relevant to your own work
- they evidence theoretical framework(s) relating to supervision
- they have an understanding of the context of coaching (as practised by supervisee)
- they are aware of the impact of values, beliefs, assumptions (of supervisor and of coach in their own practice)
- they are respectful of diversity in its many forms and alert to its potential benefits and pitfalls
- they demonstrate a capacity for self regulation (as will need to foster this in supervisee)
- they show commitment to CPD for themselves and others. (EMCC, 2013)

Supervision for the supervisors

It is good practice for supervisors to be supervised on their supervision practice. Where a supervisor is external it is up to them to arrange this, though it would be sensible to check out with them what their arrangements are during the contracting conversation. If you have decided to train your own internal supervisors, then the responsibility for providing supervisory support for them is yours. However, in many organisations—who may only be able to offer supervision to their coaches two or three times a year—resourcing this is a step too far. Some internal supervisors whom I interviewed were paying for their own external supervision. However, virtually all of them also coached in their organisation, so a common practice was to use their supervisor to supervise them on both their coaching and supervision practice and they consciously allocated different parts of the session to each.

Alternative approaches to supervision with a fully trained supervisor

Butwell (2006) and Pinder (2010) are both advocates for the presence of a trained supervisor as role model—someone who has "been there, seen it, done it"—especially for inexperienced coaches and this is considered best practice in the profession. However, if funds will not stretch to that then there are other routes that you could pursue to ensure that your coaches have opportunities to reflect on their practice and develop their skills. Many of the "alternatives" in this section have significant benefits in their own right.

Co-supervision/peer supervision

One approach is for coaches to supervise each other in pairs or, more commonly, groups. Most coaches who were using this approach said that if it is to work well then the coaches in the group need to be: a) fairly experienced; b) properly trained in how to use a specific model of supervision; and c) comfortable with having their practice discussed by others. Training in co-supervision, such as the two-day course run by the Coaching Supervision Academy, offers learning about basic group dynamics: for example, noticing who is leading the group (even though it has no designated leader); how to give someone feedback in front of others; how to re-contract in the moment, and so forth. Such programmes may offer live demonstrations, practice in triads and training in accessing one's "internal supervisor" (i.e., getting in touch with one's cognitive, intuitive, and somatic responses). Co-supervision groups have to work out how they are going to deal with confidentiality issues and articulate that. In terms of holding each other to account, they examine ways of challenging each other in a learning environment and how to invite someone into better, or more ethical, practice without shaming them. Advocates say that as long as a given structure is followed it can work very well. Without that "it can wobble". A temptation to be avoided, as in coaching, is giving advice.

Peer supervision for supervisors: Peer supervision can be particularly valuable for supervising internal supervisors' practice because the participants already have the skills. The NHS in England and Wales has a network of internal supervisors and in some regions they meet quarterly for co-supervision. Others use an external supervisor. One interviewee mentioned that she was part of a supervision network made up of supervisors who trained together but work in a variety of different organisations. They act as a support group for each other.

Action learning supervision

Action learning was founded by Reg Revans (1982) in the 1930s. He noticed that his colleagues could help each others' learning even if they were from different parts of the organisation with diverse issues to resolve. The simple act of articulating their problems, asking each other direct questions, and sharing experience was valuable even without any directly relevant expertise.

Running an action learning set is a structured process, run by a facilitator, usually involving:

1. Check-in—set members have a few minutes to report any significant developments since they last met (job move; wedding; new baby)
2. Decision as to running order and how much "airtime" each set member will have
3. Articulation by the first "presenter" of their issue, without interruption, ideally specifying the nature of the contribution that they want from the other set members
4. Questioning of the presenter by other members, with the aim of helping the presenter to clarify and come to a deeper understanding of the issue and their options for resolving it. Set members are discouraged by the facilitator from giving advice, telling stories of how they have dealt with similar issues (although occasionally a presenter may specifically ask for such input), or passing judgement. Open questions are actively encouraged and sometimes the facilitator might ask a member to phrase a question in a more open way
5. Help by the members to the presenter to decide what action should be taken
6. Reflection by all set members on what happened and what questions were particularly helpful. Childs, M. Woods, Willcock, and Man (2011) suggest that questions they could ask themselves could include whether they "helped the presenter to:

   - clarify the situation, the options or the way forward
   - achieve a deeper insight
   - consider new ideas or options
   - identify/release hidden emotions that are blocking the process."

7. The next presenter takes their turn.

Generally a quarter of an hour or so is allocated at the end of the session to reflect on what went well, what less well, and how the learning could be even better next time. Since the membership of a set stays constant, members build strong relationships and feel able to hold each other to account. The emphasis is on learning and the absence of judgement.

Action learning as an approach is peculiarly well-suited to coach supervision because the kinds of questions that set members are encouraged to ask the "presenter" are coaching style questions, so the process itself is a mechanism for developing coaching skills. In an action learning set being used for this purpose, the issues being brought to the set will clearly relate to the coaches' experiences with their clients but, as with co-supervision, there is no trained supervisor present (though there is an action learning set facilitator—at least for the first few sessions while the structure is being established) so the set members need themselves to have an eye to the "upholding standards" aspect of what is a supervisory activity. It is also cheap—any trained action learning set facilitator could run it effectively without needing to be a coach.

Childs, M. Woods, Willcock, and Man (2011) suggest the following benefits of supervisory action learning sets:

- Low cost—while you start with a facilitator they can become self-managed groups
- They provide an antidote to the isolation that internal coaches can experience
- Even inexperienced coaches feel empowered as they learn that they have perspectives that are helpful to others
- The sets provide an opportunity for the coaches to take risks in a safe environment, experiment, and try out different approaches and behaviours
- All members are actively involved and engaged
- The process is self-sustaining—group members can continue to meet even if funding dries up.

Action learning sets and peer supervision groups both build the idea of developing "an internal supervisor on your shoulder" and, as Childs, M. Woods, Willcock, and Man put it, "honour the fundamental belief of all coaching—that the coachee already has the skills and answers to his or her most important questions" (p. 35).

It is common for groups of this kind to draw up some ground rules in the opening session. Moyes (2009) provides an example of what one group drew up as the rules for their "working alliance":

- *What does success look like?* We are all open, we can be ourselves, relaxed, excited, supportive atmosphere, becoming more challenging as time goes by, not blaming or condemnatory, everyone feeling valued. Everyone participates, we all learn and develop

- *"What I fear happening in supervision is ..."* It doesn't deliver value—it falls apart, gets boring, not challenging or informative enough, jargon gets in the way
- *How do we evaluate?* Fairly formally after three or four sessions; informally in the last five minutes of each session to review how the meeting has gone. Our criteria are:

  – Have we tried new things with clients—have we increased our confidence to do so?
  – "unsticking" stuck cases;
  – Increased professional development;
  – Managing anxieties about "doing it right". (p. 72)

Other methods of support

What other forms of quasi-supervisory support might you offer your coaches? Organisations are pretty creative in what they provide.

Mentoring: A fairly common approach is to provide new coaches with a mentor. While not trained supervisors, the mentors are other internal coaches in the business who understand what it is like and can offer support and, if necessary, advice so that there is a slightly supervisory aspect but they are more easily available and they are free. Of course, the lead coach (often not a trained supervisor) is also there to provide an ear.

Co-coaching: Another approach is the idea of a "coaching buddy"—usually someone who was trained in the same cohort so the coaches already know each other and have had an opportunity to bond. These buddy arrangements can be more or less formal. The value is that they offer an opportunity for coaching practice to develop skills in both coaching and providing feedback and challenge. Some buddies arrange regular co-coaching sessions. Others take a more *ad hoc* approach.

Coaching circles: A variant on the buddy approach is the idea of the "coaching circle" involving three coaches, with A coaching B, B coaching C, and C coaching A. Depending on the geography, interactions could involve bilateral telephone coaching sessions or they could all meet up as a triad and observe each other's coaching and give feedback.

Reflective learning: One aspect of "classic" supervision with a trained supervisor is guided reflective learning but an inexpensive method of achieving the same aim is for your coaches to reflect on their own experience by keeping a journal. It is good practice to write a reflection after every coaching session and, in addition, to reflect at intervals more generally on your thoughts and feelings, aspirations and worries, as a way of exploring what is going on in your work. It all contributes to the learning cycle of action, reflection, new understanding, and new practice.

One model for doing this in some depth is the reflective coaching practitioner model (Campone, 2011). She points out that reflective practice:

> differs from simply "thinking about what happened" insofar as it is characterised by intention, purpose and structure … The purpose of reflective practice is to facilitate one's own learning from experience. (p. 15)

D. Woods (2011) carried out a small-scale study with some coaches and similarly noted that, in their post session reflections, coaches: "typically log gaps in their practice or ideas about practice improvements" (p. 266). However, the following case study is an example of where a coach has reviewed her work against a set of coaching competences and recognises both what she does well and what she does less well.

Case study 9.1: Extract from a learning diary

Contextual background

The material below is partly recorded from notes taken during a coaching session—the last of four sessions. In reviewing her notes, the coach noticed:

Competencies frequently demonstrated	*Competencies (not) frequently demonstrated*
She frequently demonstrated the following competences: • Establishing the coaching agreement • Active listening • Managing accountability and progress • Powerful questioning	She also noticed the following competences were less evident in this coaching session: • Building the relationship • Developing trust and intimacy

Post-coaching reflections and learning

On reflection, I recognise my coaching had become stale over recent weeks and I was bored by the typical pattern of my coaching, that is, listen; reflect back; work the issue towards achieving goals. I notice these elements are areas where I have received very positive feedback from coaches and peers (acute ability to listen; ability to connect issues/threads and offer insights; and use of my cognitive skills to manage accountability towards achieving a practical task). My coaching seemed to lack depth and connection, however, and I felt jaded by the *sameness* of it.

I realise my coaching had hit a plateau and I was searching for ways of moving through this and developing my coaching skills. Through supervision, I found focusing on emotions (my own and the coachee's) helpful, which led to bolder interventions on my part and a greater use of self as an instrument of change for the client as part of my expanded everyday practice.

Woods, D. (2011). "Coaches' use of reflective journals for learning". Reproduced with permission.

To become an expert reflective practitioner takes practice. Most coach training encourages trainee coaches to reflect on their experiences and what they are learning from them. If you are thinking that it could be a useful continuing tool for your coaches, you could consider discussing with the trainer what model of reflective learning might best suit their needs.

Continuous Professional Development (CPD)

Megginson and Whitaker (2004) define CPD as a process "in which individuals can take control of their own learning and development by engaging in an on-going developmental process of reflection, goal setting and action."

What are the benefits?

There are many reasons why you should ensure that your coaches have access to CPD:

- It is best practice and those of your coaches who wish to become members of professional bodies must be able to demonstrate their commitment to CPD as part of their registration. For example, the Association for Coaching requires members to undertake a minimum of thirty hours of CPD in the theory and practice of coaching per annum.

- It is a way of ensuring that your coaches continuously improve, that the quality of what they deliver remains high, and that they extend their portfolio of approaches over time. Since internal coaches do much less coaching than externals, they need regular input of CPD and supervision to keep their skills levels up.
- Ideally coaches should model learning behaviour and demonstrate that continuous learning matters ("practise what we preach").
- Delivering CPD as a joint learning experience helps to build your coaching community of practice.

You could argue that all the types of supervision and quasi-supervisory support outlined earlier in this chapter are forms of CPD but this section looks at other kinds of support you might offer your coaches that could contribute to their professional development.

The Chartered Institute of Personnel and Development (CIPD) (representing trainers and HR professionals) sets out five key principles for CPD:

1. Professional development is a continuous process that applies throughout a practitioner's working life.
2. Individuals are responsible for controlling and managing their own development.
3. Individuals should decide for themselves their learning needs and how to fulfil them.
4. Learning targets should be clearly articulated and should reflect the needs of employers and clients as well as the practitioner's individual goals.
5. Learning is most effective when it is acknowledged as an integral part of work rather than an additional burden.

It can be seen from this that a key principle is self-directed learning. Ideally your coaches will emerge from their training with a learning and development plan, and it is up to you to encourage them to keep it up-to-date and to use it as the basis for an annual or six-monthly conversation with you about their progress and development needs.

However, as lead coach you will also have a sense of what the whole pool needs on the basis of what you are hearing from the supervisor(s), the coaches themselves, and your steering group. Also, there may be particular approaches that you would like to expose your coaches to or skills you would like them to practise, so there will always be a balance to strike between the needs of individuals and the requirements that the business has of the coaching pool as a whole. For example, you may decide that it would be useful to train your coaches to give managers feedback on a 360 instrument used by your organisation or to offer selected coaches training in a development tool like MBTI or FIRO(B).

On top of what you lay on, there is nothing to stop your coaches from attending evening CPD events run by coaching professional bodies and training organisations, to follow up particular interests, as they are commonly open to non-members too. An issue, however, might be whether your organisation would be prepared to reimburse the cost. The EMCC offers corporate membership that includes access to some free CPD for internal coaches.

What are the options?

Skills practice

As already mentioned, internal coaches can feel a little isolated once they finish their training so it helps to arrange some CPD events to keep them feeling connected and enhance their skills. An inexpensive way of doing this is to have regular lunchtime sessions when coaches can come along and practise coaching each other in triads (coach, client, and observer). They will have become used to this process during their training and it offers them an opportunity to practise contracting, coaching, and giving and receiving feedback—particularly helpful if they do not yet have any clients. In ninety minutes you can fit in twenty minutes of one person coaching another followed by ten minutes of feedback from observer and client and discussion, then the same for the other two in turn.

One of the member benefits offered by the Association for Coaching is their co-coaching groups that are organised on a regional basis in the evenings. You simply show up, are invited to join a triad, and get coaching. There is usually a small charge for refreshments but the opportunity for new coaches to practise, in a supportive learning environment, is invaluable.

Introducing new approaches and techniques

Many organisations try to run at least three sessions a year introducing their coaches to something new. Examples of topics would be the use of clean language, introduction to NLP, scaling, use of metaphor, a systems approach, or Nancy Kline's thinking environment. Commonly a workshop will include the introduction of a theory, model, or approach and then allow time for the coaches to practise using it. Provision need not be expensive. Consultancies would normally charge for running a workshop but often, if someone has written a book on a subject, they are prepared to come and talk about it for a very small fee. Many organisations discuss the provision of CPD with their coaching training provider.

Whole day events

It is sometimes easier for internal coaches to block out a whole day in their diaries for supervision and CPD and there seem to be an increasing number of organisations who are taking the approach of organising a whole day event twice-yearly for: CPD in the morning, networking as a community of coaches over the lunch break, and then running supervision groups—or using some methodology for sharing experience—in the afternoon. These are sometimes styled as a "conference" and can include a presentation by a senior coaching champion (ideally the CEO or someone else at Board level) to show appreciation for what the coaches are doing and to talk about the organisation's strategic priorities and how the coaching effort is helping to support them. Some organisations time these events to coincide with the end of a training programme for a new cohort of coaches so that they can attend and even be awarded some kind of certificate.

Your community of coaches should ideally include the external coaches who work in the organisation too, as there can be great value in including them in such events and promoting the sharing of experience between the external and internal coaches.

Resources on the intranet

While all coaches need to practise, many coaches also have a preference for reading about coaching. It can be useful to establish a library of coaching books and journals and also to put electronic resources onto the intranet in a space devoted to the internal coaches. If you have invested in a sophisticated coach management system, there is likely to be an area especially reserved for resources. These can take the form of articles, Powerpoint presentations, descriptions of new tools or techniques, questionnaires (e.g., the short, non-proprietary version of Honey & Mumford's Learning Styles questionnaire), tools to help reflection, or short videos of coaching sessions. A number of coaches said that they found helpful, and also contributed to, reviews of books—both classics and more recently published books. There were also references to some useful coaching demonstrations on YouTube. One coach said that her organisation had a shared drive for the coaching community where anybody could put articles or book reviews or a report on some workshop they had been to or new tool they had used. It was very popular with the coaches.

Summary

Coaching supervision and continuing professional development are essential for coaches. They are key to ensuring that the standards and integrity of the internal coaching service are maintained, risks are managed, and the coaches continue to grow. Supervision also provides one route for systemic themes arising from the many coaching conversations to be fed back into the organisation. Despite these benefits, many organisations that have invested heavily in training their internal coaching resource fail to ensure that their coaches receive regular supervision and CPD.

As coaching supervision becomes more firmly established and the need for continuous professional development recognised, organisations are starting to explore how it can be delivered rather than ask why their coaches need it. This chapter has looked at ways of providing it to suit different budgets. Not only do these processes increase the coaches' capability and give added value but they play a key role in the development of coaching within the organisation.

QUESTIONS TO REFLECT ON

Factor to consider	What are the implications for the organisation?
Purpose of supervision Creating an understanding of the crucial role of supervision as a means of: • Upholding coaching standards • Developing coaches' skills, understanding and ability to reflect on their practice • Providing a place for them to offload emotions taken on from clients	• What do we need to do to gain organisational support for the funding of supervision? • How can we engage our coaches in the process of supervision? • What are the implications of introducing supervision in terms of: – time demands on coaches? – how the coaches contract with clients? – handling competence issues ? • Will we take advantage of the opportunity offered to harvest organisational learning?
Group supervision *vs.* one-to-one supervision What approach to supervision will best suit our organisational needs? What are the implications for confidentiality?	• If we run group supervision how will we deal with confidentiality issues if coaches have a personal or professional relationship with other group members' clients? • Have we been explicit in the contracting between coaches and clients around the levels of disclosure when a coach discusses a client issue during supervision? Do we need clients to sign a release form? • What frequency of supervision will work best for our organisation? • How can we ensure that coaches who have a minimal coaching load get value from supervision?

(Continued)

QUESTIONS TO REFLECT ON   (*Continued*)

Factor to consider	What are the implications for the organisation?
Internal *vs.* external supervision There are advantages and disadvantages to using internal supervisors. What would work best in our organisation?	• What are the factors that are relevant for our organisation when assessing the pros and cons of internal *vs.* external supervisors? • Will it be more cost effective for us to train and use internal supervisors? • What do we need in place to ensure that we can deal effectively with any need for "emergency supervision" in relation to an ethical dilemma that needs immediate resolution? • What are our expectations for supervision of our supervisors?
Issues in supervising internal coaches How can we ensure our supervision targets the type of issues that internal coaches are likely to experience?	• What do we need to do to ensure our supervisors appreciate how the challenges for internal and external coaches are different and that they can meet those needs?
Procuring supervision What are we looking for in a supervisor? How will we find someone who is suitable for our organisation?	• Are we clear on our criteria for a supervisor? • What selection and assessment process do we need to put in place to identify an individual who will meet our needs?

(*Continued*)

QUESTIONS TO REFLECT ON   (*Continued*)

Factor to consider	What are the implications for the organisation?
Alternative approaches What resources do we have in our organisation or wish to create that would be viable alternatives to one-to-one or group supervision?	• Are there any L&D initiatives that are already in place such as action learning sets, or mentoring that we could adapt as alternatives to supervision with a fully trained supervisor? • What could we include in the coach training to give our coaches a model for reflecting on their practice? • Could co–coaching, coaching circles, or peer supervision give our internal coaches sufficient support as an alternative to supervision?
Continuous professional development (CPD) What commitment do we want to make as an organisation to supporting CPD for coaches?	• Will we ask our coaches to have personal development plans to discuss? • Should we encourage our coaches to take responsibility for their own CPD? • Can we afford to resource expert speakers? If not, what are our options for providing CPD at low or no cost to the business? • What are the options for sharing CPD with other organisations that have internal coaches?

CHAPTER TEN

Evaluation

One of the great mistakes is to judge policies and programs by their intentions rather than their results

—Milton Friedman

What this chapter is about

Your internal coaches are doing a great job. Why would you not want to demonstrate that to them, to your sponsors, and to the rest of the business? This chapter looks at evaluation, finding a suitable way of measuring what you and they are achieving and how this adds value to the business. What are you going to measure? Who are you going to ask? How will you collect the information? Will it be quantitative or qualitative? You will ideally need some metrics but without some sense of the clients' experience, the data will be the poorer: success stories do bring a spreadsheet to life.

This chapter explores:

- What evaluation is and the key reasons for evaluating your coaching scheme
- What to evaluate and how to do it

239

- How Kirkpatrick's four levels of training evaluation can be applied to coaching
- Approaches to gathering data focusing on a) the client, b) feedback from colleagues, and c) data gathered at an organisational level
- The evaluation of the coaching service
- The challenges of demonstrating return on investment (ROI) from an internal coaching service.

What is evaluation?

Let us distinguish at the outset between monitoring and evaluation. Most lead coaches monitor, in the sense of keeping track of how many live coaching relationships there are. If you have invested in coach management software, this sort of information will be available to you at the click of a mouse. This is about the activity. However, evaluation is about the outcomes: analysing the impact of those coaching relationships on the individual client and more widely on the team or business. There is a wide variety of practice at present, from virtually no evaluation at all to very sophisticated multi-stage evaluation processes, sometimes using external consultancy expertise.

However starved of resources a lead coach might be, it must at least be possible to ask every client at the end of an assignment (plus every client who drops out before the end of the expected number of coaching sessions) to rate the coaching as:

UNHELPFUL	*A waste of time*
POOR	*Of little value*
NEUTRAL	*Interesting but unclear yet if valuable*
FAIR	*I got some value from it*
EXCELLENT	*Very valuable use of my time*

One very busy lead coach said that she felt the absolute minimum data to collect was:

Inputs (measuring activity and coach utilisation)

- How many coaches were active
- How many clients each coach had

- How many hours each coach devoted per client, or in total
- Whether any coaches had any spare capacity.

Outputs (capturing the impact)

- A post coaching questionnaire for the client to complete, including:
  - some yes/no answers e.g., "Was coaching a good use of your time?" or "Would you recommend coaching to a colleague?"
  - some kind of "satisfaction index" such as: "How successful was the coaching in helping you to meet your goals?" Very successful, quite successful, etc.

Answers to such questions provide valuable data (if ninety-seven per cent say that they would recommend coaching to a colleague then you already have a very helpful statistic to go into any promotional material about the internal coaching scheme) that can help you to check out how your coaching scheme is doing. But evaluation can provide a lot more than that.

If you plan to evaluate your coaching scheme—and you really should—do think about it right at the outset because you need to tell your coaches how you are going to do it and they need to tell their clients, in their contracting conversations, about what will be expected of them by way of input. If your coaches are going to be involved in information gathering, you will need to alert them to that and also perhaps offer guidance about the best way of making goals SMART, with measurable outcomes (if that is what you want). If you decide to use a questionnaire, it would be helpful to show it to coaches and clients at the beginning and explain the process to them.

It may also be necessary to establish some kind of baseline. For example, if the coaching is to support more women to reach senior positions, then you will need a sense of how many there are now, and at what levels, in order to evaluate further down the track if the coaching has made a positive impact. Or if you are aiming to support a culture change away from a macho style, then the number of harassment cases may be a measure you are interested in. Or do you want to see if leadership coaching for managers in your talent pool leads to more home-grown senior managers and directors than in previous years? These are all examples where you would need to establish your baseline.

At the moment, by no means all organisations evaluate the impact of their coaching service. You may have started off small, with two or three internal coaches, and feel that a brief check-in with your coaches and their clients from time to time to check that there are no problems is sufficient. One organisation in Snape's (2012) research said: "we made a decision not to get too involved in measuring effectiveness because it is so difficult to do—we prefer to spend the money on making our coaches better" (p. 36).

A number of lead coaches said that they were so busy delivering coaching and managing the service that making time for formal evaluation was unrealistic. They knew that the coaching was valuable from anecdotal feedback received from the coaches, clients, and clients' line managers and that was good enough for them. Usually they had a supportive senior champion and they trusted to the professionalism of the coaches to make good use of the time that they spent with their clients—they did not feel the need for quantitative data to tell them what they "already knew". A case study by Pilbeam, Anderson, Hope, and Campbell (2013) gives some support for this approach, raising the concern that "focusing too much on measuring the results of internal coaching may result in losing the essence of learning". They point out that a difficulty for organisations is "achieving a balance between being able to articulate what the purpose of the role of an internal coach is, being able to measure the impact of the role on the bottom line, and not losing the quality and value of the coaching relationship." Rather than tying oneself in knots trying to measure the connection between the coaching and observable results their findings suggest that "the coachee receives value … and the challenge is to *trust* that this translates into enhanced performance" (p. 190, my emphasis).

However, there are major drawbacks to undertaking no evaluation. Say your coaching champion leaves the organisation or the financial climate demands deep cuts in expenditure. Suddenly you may be required to demonstrate the value of what your coaching service provides to someone who may have no experience of coaching and be unaware of what it can do. Can you answer the question: "What value has your internal coaching scheme been delivering?" For sustainability reasons, if no other, it is good practice to monitor your coaching service from the outset and gather some basic metrics even if your current sponsor does not ask for it. However, there are actually many other good reasons for evaluating what you are doing—which we shall come to—including feeding back to the coaches themselves the value that they are adding. I hope to demonstrate that some level of evaluation is essential. It need not be complicated or expensive, although it clearly involves some expenditure of thought and time.

One tip volunteered was to capture and track every single cost from day one, and from year to year, associated with the venture. These could include: set-up costs (e.g., building, buying, or leasing a coach management system); any training you source; supervision and CPD; refreshments for coaching events; salary of the lead coach; and so forth. Those items will probably come out of different budgets but make sure you are tracking them all because even if no-one asks for that data in the early stages, it could be useful to have at your finger tips at some point in the future, particularly if a future sponsor wants you to attempt a return on investment calculation.

Why evaluate?

Research undertaken by the CIPD (2010) found that only thirty-six per cent of the participants in their study were evaluating their coaching. They sent a strong message, saying that for sustained investment organisations must evaluate. The most basic reason for evaluating is that it is the only way that you can be sure that your coaches, and the overall coaching service, are doing a good job. You probably have a strong belief in the efficacy of coaching and you no doubt hear anecdotes from coaching clients or their managers that reinforce that belief but that is not the same as solid evidence. It is best practice to evaluate any learning and development intervention and a recent report from the Chartered Management Institute (McBain et al., 2012) found that higher performing organisations evaluate their leadership development provision to a greater degree than poorer performing ones.

If you have a steering group, they would normally expect a regular report covering a variety of metrics, with a summary of both the quantity and quality of activity on at least an annual basis. However, demonstrating value to a sponsor or steering group is only one reason for evaluating the coaching service. Having looked at examples of how organisations have gone about evaluating their coaching, Carter, Wolfe, and Kerrin (2005) identified three basic categories of evaluation: organisations were seeking to prove something, improve something, or learn something.

Proving something: Most of the lead coaches who told me about their approach to evaluation were seeking to prove something:

- They wanted evidence that the coaching pool was fulfilling the purpose for which it was set up
- They wanted to demonstrate to sponsors, funders, or their steering group that the organisation's money was being spent to good effect
- They wanted data to show whether the internal coaching service was providing equal or better value for money than the previous strategy of sourcing coaching externally.

Sometimes providing the proof that a coaching intervention has been useful may not require much of an investment in time at all. In the case study below, monitoring the numbers of people leaving the firm was almost all that was required.

Case Study 10.1: Linking evaluation to strategic purpose

In 2008 a medium sized law firm based in the City of London realised that it was steadily haemorrhaging good young lawyers to larger firms offering them more money. Individual partners had conducted informal exit interviews with those who left but there was no process for aggregating that information. However, when the managing partner started asking partners what had come out of their exit interviews it quickly became clear that there was a common message: while most of them were increasing their salaries by leaving, that was not the main driver. The key issue was that two to three years post qualification they began to feel seriously undervalued. They were working very long hours but were still way off partnership; they could not see where their careers were going; they received little if any feedback and they had no sense of how they were doing. The managing partner had experienced coaching himself and proposed a twin pronged strategy: a) to introduce an "associate partner" designation to give them something more immediate to aim for and b) to identify three people in the L&D department to train as internal coaches. These coaches were to conduct career development interviews with every lawyer in the one to eight years post qualification group, to talk through with them their aspirations, worries, and challenges and help them to draw up a development plan with specific actions to take forward.

The purpose was clear: to improve retention rates. While a formal mentoring scheme was not introduced, the coaches encouraged participants to think through whom they might like to be mentored by and to approach those partners informally. The coaches reported that the lawyers felt that being allocated coaches gave them a very positive message about how they were valued by the firm and that their futures within it were secure. Retention rates were monitored monthly and very quickly the figures confirmed what everyone already knew: the defections had dried up.

In this example, the numbers spoke for themselves but there was some qualitative, anecdotal data in there too about the value of the coaching: the clients reported feeling more valued and also empowered to take some control over their careers by approaching partners to mentor them. Evaluation may often be seeking to collect qualitative data of this kind.

Improving or learning something: Evaluation can also be about finding out what is working well and what less well so that you can use that learning to improve a) what the internal coaching service is delivering or b) the effectiveness of the organisation.

Some "learning" reasons for evaluation cited by lead coaches:

- They wanted to know how effective the clients were finding the coaching so that they could develop/improve the offer.
- They wanted to know how good their coaches were and if there were any additional training or need for "refreshers" for the coaches being identified.
- They wanted to build up a picture of what issues were coming up in the coaching conversations in case there were some common themes that might benefit from a concerted effort/special initiative across the organisation.

An evaluation undertaken within the NHS used a pre-coaching questionnaire to ask clients about the benefits they expected and what topics they intended to focus on. This data was not only used to compare with the results of a post-coaching questionnaire about whether the benefits actually materialised but it also provided useful aggregated data on what sorts of issues people wanted to work on. This data provided some insight into systemic issues and was used to improve (or make more focused) leadership development interventions (Mortlock & Carter, 2012).

It is easy to see that if you find that a significant volume of the coaching goals proposed by your managers are around, say, dealing with long hours, burn-out, poor work–life balance and stress, then there is a systemic issue that needs attention.

Case Study 10.2: Using evaluation to inform business strategy

One international NGO, operating in fragile states around the world, found that their coaches were regularly reporting that their clients, who were often working away from their families for long periods of time, seemed to be hovering on the borderline between stress and real anxiety. It was so much part of the culture to "grin and bear it" that clients felt that it would be taken as a sign of weakness if they asked for professional help. The lead coach included this evaluation finding in a report to the head of HR. As a result, a pilot project was set up introducing a small, peripatetic counselling team in one region of the world in conjunction with a message from the CEO to say how important it was that staff paid attention to their health and well-being. The very positive feedback from the pilot resulted in the introduction of counselling teams in every region.

What will you evaluate?

If you have a strategy that clearly articulates the purpose of the coaching then you may already have some defined success measures and they will be your starting point. Are you seeking, by coaching women who have returned to work after maternity leave, to raise retention levels? Are you coaching managers from ethnic minorities in your talent pool for promotion to increase their representation at senior levels? Are you focusing on improving managers' ability to performance manage by coaching them in holding difficult conversations? Also, who needs the data and why? Are you seeking to persuade someone of something? The reason for the evaluation will dictate what kind of information you decide to gather and in what form.

I have been very struck by the degree to which some lead coaches have, in effect, told their sponsors or steering committee what they are going to evaluate, while others have completely moulded their evaluation approach to suit their sponsor. For example, one lead coach from a professional services organisation said that what information he collected depended on "how much the sponsor liked data". His first sponsor wanted to hear anecdotes: what the partners were saying about the coaches; perceptions of the credibility of the coaches; and some quotations from coaching clients of what they had gained from the coaching. That was good enough for him. His successor, however, wanted a spreadsheet with numbers of clients seen; numbers of clients achieving their coaching goals; numbers of clients getting through promotion boards; retention figures ... It was horses for courses.

The structured approach is to develop success measures at the outset and evaluate against them—but this will be easier to do for some kinds of outcomes than others. In real life, the purpose may also change over time, so lead coaches need to be alert to that and adapt their measures accordingly. A mixture of hard metrics plus more qualitative information such as quotations, testimonials, or case studies to bring them to life tends to work well for most people.

Kirkpatrick's four levels of evaluation

Coaching is all about facilitating learning for the client and the most widely used model to evaluate learning interventions is Kirkpatrick (1994) and his concept of the four different levels:

- Reaction
- Learning
- Behaviour
- Results.

Kirkpatrick's model was developed to evaluate training rather than coaching, which raises some issues discussed below, but it is nonetheless a useful model, so I am translating it into coaching terms.

Level one: Reaction

This level measures what the client's response is to the coaching. What did they think and feel about it? How valuable did they find it? How did they feel about the way the coaching was delivered? Did they think their coach was effective? Did they achieve their objectives? What worked well and what less well for them? Did it accommodate their personal learning style?

Level two: Learning

This level measures what the individual has learned. The learning could be an increase or change in the client's knowledge, skills, capability, levels of awareness, or attitudes. While the sort of learning that takes place in a coaching session is less easy to measure objectively than, say, demonstrating through a "before and after" test whether someone has mastered a new computer programme, some organisations do administer a before and after questionnaire asking the client to score themselves against a number of items. They could include such things as:

- The quality of my working relationships
- My ability to manage organisational change
- My ability to manage my time
- My ability to cope with stress
- My ability to manage politically complex situations
- My levels of self-awareness
- My levels of self confidence
- My resilience at work.

Changes in the scores can be used to demonstrate learning. More commonly though, clients are simply asked what they have learned.

Level three: Behaviour

This level measures the extent to which the clients apply what they have learned so that their behaviour visibly shifts. If there are no changes in behaviour this does not mean that no learning has taken place. It could mean that the individual has chosen not to apply it or the context has made it difficult for them to apply it. A "before and after" 360 feedback report is used in some leadership development programmes to try to capture such changes. The "after" 360 questionnaire is often administered three to six months after the coaching has finished. In many coaching programmes, feedback from the line manager provides evidence for behaviour change.

Level four: Results

This level examines the impact that the coaching of a particular individual has had on the organisation (or the unit/division could be used rather than the whole organisation). This is the most complex level to evaluate because of the need to show a causal link between a) the coaching and the impact a client is having and b) the client and any effect on the organisation. This level is often approached at an aggregated level, for example: what impact on the business have a cohort of people who were all being coached had?

Limitations of Kirkpatrick: Applying Kirkpatrick's model to coaching may feel like a stretch to some. Coaching is different from training: it does not have generic outcomes, unlike a course addressing a specific topic. Training courses have formal aims, objectives, and outcomes providing a common basis for an evaluation of what the trainees have learned, whereas coaching clients can sometimes find it hard, even with a diligent coach, to articulate and define measurable success measures. Plus, it is common in coaching for the goals to change: the issue that a client presents with frequently turns out not to be the crux of what needs to be worked on. Or there may not have been a goals-based approach to the coaching anyway. Also, each coaching relationship will be unique whereas, even though they will experience it differently, every trainee on a training course will have been exposed to the same material. Carter, Wolfe, and Kerrin's (2005) research with UK employers highlighted other differences, such as: the way that the timing of the evaluation (i.e., whether immediately after the final session or some months later) could affect the information gathered on the effectiveness of the coaching; the fact that the success measures might not be agreed upon until the process has begun making it difficult to measure pre- and post- the coaching intervention; and the fact that the confidential nature of coaching meant that evaluation information would be less readily accessible. However, even accepting these limitations, the model is still a helpful one.

Gathering data

To gather data that addresses Kirkpatrick's four levels there are three broad approaches:

1. Focusing on gathering information from the coaching client
2. Widening the scope of those who provide feedback
3. Collecting data at a divisional or organisational level.

Focusing on the client

Feedback from participants is the most common approach to evaluation by employers (CIPD, 2004). Most organisations collect information about a coaching client's experience by asking them to complete a questionnaire at the end of the assignment. This can sometimes be a problem, as completing the questionnaire can slip to the bottom of the client's priorities once the coaching is finished. Some lead coaches address this by either interviewing the client at the end of the coaching programme—taking them through a series of questions—or asking the coach to do so in the final session and then feed the answers back into the system. However, there are drawbacks to asking the coach to do this because clients often find it hard to be a) objective or b) completely honest when they are in the presence of the coach, particularly when there may be emotion around the fact that it is the final session. In a successful coaching assignment the coach and client will have built a close relationship and it is natural for the client to want to be complimentary. They may find it easier to be objective if talking to the coach lead.

If you use a questionnaire that includes questions about the effectiveness of the coach, the client may again feel protective of the coach or may be concerned about hurting their feelings. Or they may simply not want to say anything critical if the coach will know that they have done so. To deal with this issue, it can be helpful to point out in the preamble that the questions are partly being asked in the cause of learning—so that the programme can be improved and the coaches can develop. An alternative is to say that any comments about the coach will be confidential. This lack of transparency may not sit well with the spirit of learning and open feedback but may be more comfortable for the client.

Questionnaires seeking to capture Kirkpatrick's Levels One and Two information (the client's reaction and what they think they have learned) are particularly common but it only takes a few more questions to capture data about behaviours (Level Three), contribution to the organisation (Level Four) and some feedback about the efficacy of the coaching. The following sorts of questions can do the job:

1. What were your goals?
2. What did you learn during the coaching?
3. What are you doing differently as a result?

4. What are the key benefits that you have gained? (For example, do you have any greater understanding/awareness of how you come across to people? Are you doing or thinking or approaching anything differently from how you did before?)

5. What benefits has the organisation gained? (e.g., is there anything in terms of improvement in effectiveness, delivery of challenging targets that you can attribute to coaching)

6. How has the coaching contributed to the broader work of your team or the organisation?

7. What aspects of the coach's approach did you find particularly helpful?

8. What could have made the coaching work better for you?

The questionnaire could also give prompts for the client to think about, such as:

- Did the coach talk too much/too little?
- Did the coach support you too much/too little?
- Did the coach challenge you too much/too little?
- Was the coach too directive/not directive enough?
- Was the coach too structured/not structured enough?
- Would you have preferred a more practical approach?
- Would you have preferred a more theoretical approach?
- Did you feel there was enough psychological/behavioural input?

If you have the time and energy you could analyse all the goals listed by all the coaching clients and draw out categories or themes; or you could ask the clients to score the extent to which they felt they met their goals. Most questions can be either a yes/no or have a scale attached such as Strongly agree, Slightly agree, Neither agree nor disagree, Slightly disagree, Strongly disagree. At Appendix One is an example of an evaluation form that collects a considerable amount of data in quite a simple way.

A more demanding approach that yields more data is to ask the client, at the beginning of the coaching, to do a lot of thinking and complete a form that covers such things, as:

- These are my coaching goals
- This is how they will link to my business objectives

- These are my success measures
- This is how my changes in behaviour will be measured
- These are the business benefits
- These are my personal development benefits.

At the end of the coaching assignment the client can then self-score against their pre-coaching criteria and those scores can be fed into the system to provide data that can be aggregated. To get even more of a fix on the impact of the coaching, you can ask questions such as "What percentage of the change would you attribute to the coaching?"

However, even with this level of sophistication, clearly there are limitations to a process confined to the client scoring what impact the coaching has had on them. Not only is it hard for the client to be objective about some things, but they may be natural optimists (or pessimists) or feel an obligation to demonstrate that they benefited from the organisation's investment in them and this will produce a bias.

This may be the moment too to raise the issue of goals. Goal setting is still *de rigueur* in many organisations and the approach does lend itself to an evaluative approach—which is why they are mentioned a lot in this chapter. However, over the last five years or more, questions are increasingly being raised about the efficacy of using goals. Megginson (2008) writes rather poignantly of the chief executive of an NHS trust saying to his coach in his first coaching session: "I don't have to set targets in these meetings, do I? It will be such a boon just to look at what is happening at work and have some time to think about it. Is that okay?" (p. 2). In the increasingly demanding environment of most organisations, the coaching sessions may be the only time when clients can get away from targets and goals and be able to reflect on what they are doing. So there can be no assumption that every coaching assignment will be goals oriented and it would be a pity if a desire to evaluate were to be translated into the necessity for a goal driven approach (unless the goal were broadly drawn in terms of "taking time to reflect").

Timing: A further wrinkle concerns the timing of any post-coaching evaluation. There is a school of thought that says that the full value of coaching may not become apparent for some months. If there has been an attitude shift it may take a while to settle and for the full impact to materialise. There is also a reverse argument around sustainability. Some organisations ask the client to complete a questionnaire immediately after the coaching programme and then again six to nine months later to capture whether the change has been maintained or if the client has relapsed into old ways.

Widening the scope of those who provide feedback

Widening the scope to include feedback from third parties—in particular the client's line manager—provides another layer to any evaluation. The questions above, about goals, linked to business objectives, success measures, behaviour changes, and business benefits could ideally be discussed and agreed with the client's line manager in the initial three-way meeting (allowing for the fact that the client may well also want to work on some more personal issues that are not articulated on the form). This then provides the basis for feedback at the end of the coaching from the client's line manager and a joint scoring at another three-way meeting of the client's progress. Another, less time-consuming, approach is simply to send the closing questionnaire to both the client and the line manager. You will then have two different sets of scores rather than agreed scores, which could be interesting in itself—though it means that a useful opportunity for direct feedback from the line manager to the client may have been lost.

Involving third parties is particularly helpful for measuring perceptions of changes in behaviour (Kirkpatrick Level Three). In this context, do not forget the coach. Even if the coach works in a different part of the organisation and never sees the client actually performing in a work setting, they may well have observed differences in the course of an assignment, particularly if one of the goals has been around personal impact. Seeing a shy client approach for a final session making strong eye contact, smiling confidently, and shaking hands firmly has been one of my happiest coaching moments!

The following case study shows the value of including third party input when evaluating behaviour change. It was carried out by a researcher using sophisticated statistical techniques but the principle holds good for less complex evaluations. Two interesting outcomes were that a) the sponsors gave lower scores to the perceived behaviour changes than the participants did (thus underlining the usefulness of third-party input) and b) involving sponsors in this particular evaluation resulted in increased engagement in the coaching process by the clients.

Case Study 10.3: Third-party input to evaluation

A pilot coaching programme was set up in twenty-four local councils across the North West and Eastern region of England to determine whether coaching might contribute to improvements in strategic thinking, and to corporate leadership, among senior HR professionals. A comprehensive approach to evaluation included an end of programme impact questionnaire for participants, their coaches, and their organisation sponsors (typically the CEO) that sought information relating to the perceived and actual impact of the coaching along three key dimensions:

- Personal effectiveness
- HR function leadership
- Strategic thinking and corporate leadership.

They used a Likert scale questionnaire to score behavioural changes and the results included:

- Along all impact dimensions, and for all items, "positive responses were found for all the evaluation groups." So there was agreement that changes in behaviour had taken place.
- Participants consistently rated the extent of change much higher than their sponsors did—on fifteen of the nineteen assessment items. Sponsors did rate the impact of the coaching positively along all of the items, but to a lesser extent than the participants.
- Participants whose sponsors took the trouble to complete the evaluation were more engaged in the process than those whose sponsors did not. The implication for coaching being that "we can be confident that engagement on all sides, not merely from participant and coach, is vital to the overall success of the programme."

This case study is a shortened version of one that appears in Carter, Wolfe, and Kerrin (2005), by kind permission of the authors.

360-degree feedback: Another way of involving colleagues is using a 360 feedback instrument. I have personal experience of coaching participants on a leadership development programme in which the client and their colleagues (line manager, peers, and staff) completed a 360 feedback questionnaire both before and after the programme. The results of the pre-programme 360 feedback played an important role in helping the clients to identify what issues to work on and the post-programme 360 gave them a fix on how much progress they had made. In a programme lasting nearly a year inevitably there were changes in personnel—the client sometimes moved roles or a significant proportion of their "raters" did—so that the results were not always comparing like with like. Also, the client's goals often included issues not wholly addressed in the items covered by the questionnaire. However, the clients did find that it made a very useful input to their development and it is a good way of bringing additional voices into the coaching room. There is a potential issue around confidentiality if 360 feedback ratings are to be used as one component of evaluating the success of a particular coaching relationship though. Most clients would be happy if the scores were used as part of an exercise to aggregate scores across the coaching service but less so if their scores were traceable to them.

Another approach used is where the coach undertakes a qualitative 360 feedback exercise by talking to half a dozen colleagues of the client focusing, before and after the coaching, on specific areas requested by the client. They could always ask the interviewees to score the client out of ten against different attributes in order to introduce a comparative and quantitative element, if required.

Data collected at organisational level

Information gathered at an organisational or sub organisational level can play a number of roles in evaluation. It can sometimes be used to shed light on the impact that coaching may have made on an individual. For example, the Southern Railway case study in Chapter Six found a strong positive correlation between the leaders who had been coached and employee engagement scores. Or if the entire leadership cadre receives coaching, then more effective leadership can show up in the leadership scores in an organisational climate survey. You might reasonably ask: "But how do you know that increased scores can be attributed to the coaching?" Organisations tend to be more relaxed about assuming causal links than an academic researcher might be. One lead coach told me, "It's generally agreed that any changes in how leaders are viewed, if they have received coaching, can be partly attributed to the coaching they've received."

Carter and Peterson (2010) suggest using metrics that your organisation already gathers. What regular surveys are conducted and what statistics are habitually collected? You can be quite creative about using these metrics. Can they be adapted for your purposes or could they be broken down to a level that could be useful to you? Metrics that may be available and can be helpful include:

- Increased employee retention
- Increased productivity
- Higher morale
- Lower sickness absence
- Promotion rates for women and ethnic minority staff
- Reduced waste
- Increased sales
- Higher quality ratings
- Increased customer satisfaction
- Fewer staff complaints
- Higher performance markings.

An alternative is to conduct a specific piece of research to test out whether the coaching has had an impact at organisational level. For example, if your coaching programme has been targeting an organisational problem around poor performance appraisal meetings by senior managers (by improving the attention that the managers give to the reports, coaching them in holding difficult conversations, and helping them to be better at giving developmental feedback to their direct reports) then you could a) do some research into the quality of the paperwork produced before and after the coaching and/or b) monitor the number of appeals made by staff disagreeing with their performance reports (if such a process exists in your organisation). If your organisation conducts a regular staff survey, an alternative approach with this same example could be to add new questions or use a "pulse survey" to check things out. Why not include a question about staff's views of the quality of appraisal meetings across the organisation and see if scores rise after the coaching? Or specifically target one part of the organisation for the coaching and see if scores rise relatively in that part? Tools such as "Survey Monkey" can be very simple to set up and quick to use and can be a cheap and effective way of determining whether coaching in a particular part of the organisation is having an impact.

Evaluating the coaching service

Any of the evaluation methods described above can contribute to how you evaluate your overall coaching service. You may decide to do separate evaluations targeting different coaching programmes, if you have a variety, but organisations find having a standard assessment process for every coaching assignment can be useful and helps to compare like with like.

Many lead coaches carry out a regular (quarterly, annual) audit on the service and feed the results into a report for the sponsor/steering group. Such reports often include information such as:

• The number of clients seen
• The number of active coaches
• The total number of hours of coaching delivered
• A breakdown of different levels and functions
• The range of feedback scores from the clients
• Scores against achievement of goals.

Something mentioned by both Carter (2013) and Yedreshteyn (2008) is the importance, when evaluating the overall service, of accessing the feedback from clients who drop out of the process. Post-coaching questionnaires are often only filled in by clients who complete all the sessions—so the voices of those who dropped out can be unintentionally excluded.

Another approach to evaluating the effectiveness of a coaching service, particularly if it is focusing on one area, can be to undertake a comparison between the performance of a group of clients who have received coaching and another group who have not. The case study below is a specific example, using two control groups.

Case Study 10.4: Using control groups

In June 2003 the head of training and recruitment at a major UK financial services provider decided to experiment with supplementing training programmes with one-to-one post-training coaching sessions to see if it helped participants to transfer the learning into the workplace. For a small-scale pilot evaluation, they selected a "selling skills" training course as the input activity and the performance of the sales force as their output measure. The sales performance of twenty-four financial planning managers was followed over a six-month period and, for each manager, sales figures from the three months prior to the training were compared with the three months after it. Twelve managers attended the course: six of these were assigned a coach for three months following the course; the other six were not. The remaining twelve managers acted as a "control group". The results showed that for the control group, sales grew by four per cent. For the training-only group they grew by eight per cent. For the group that received training plus coaching, sales increased by twenty-seven per cent.

These evaluation results led the company both to value their training programme and to appreciate the value of follow-up activity to embed the learning. They used the findings as evidence that there might be benefits of post-training coaching for other groups or contexts. Incidentally, this case study reveals some of the differences between academic and practitioner research. The organisation concluded that there was no need to conduct a return on investment calculation since it was clear that the increase in sales significantly exceeded the cost of the training and coaching. Nor did they feel the need to prove a causal link between the sales increase and the training/coaching. The fact that they had comparative results from the control group was proof enough for them.

This case study is a shortened version of one that appears in Carter, Wolfe, and Kerrin (2005), by kind permission of the authors.

Return on investment (ROI)

Some organisations have made an attempt to calculate the return on investment (ROI) of their coaching effort and consider it to be a logical extension to Kirkpatrick's model. The standard method for calculating ROI involves subtracting the costs of coaching from the estimated value of the outcomes of coaching and then expressing this as a percentage of the costs. Jo Holliday, ROI evaluation specialist at abdi ltd., points out that a negative return is common in the first year of rolling out programmes, as evaluation measures are based on the first year after the programme, with no time for benefits to mitigate initial outlay (Soulsby, 2012).

While in principle calculating ROI sounds like a useful activity, the difficulty in doing so stems from the heroic assumptions that have to be made to put a monetary value on the benefits of coaching. If someone gains confidence and gets the promotion they deserve—what is the monetary value to the organisation? If someone starts delegating better and works ten-hour days rather than twelve-hour days, thus seeing more of her husband and children, feeling less stressed and shouting less at her staff (who are feeling happier too and more fulfilled because their work is more stretching thus developing them for the next level)—what value? And what if that more effective delegation results in some of her staff being busier and more stressed themselves so that some of them decide to leave? What value then?

One of the issues is making that causal link between the impact of coaching on an individual, any changes in attitude or behaviour by that individual, and how that translates into results for the business. Sarah Jones, Group Head of Leadership Development at Standard Chartered (quoted in Hawkins & Schwenk, 2006) clearly had no such doubts when she commented: "We are keen to ensure that employees receive individual attention and development. This results in higher staff engagement and we see the results in stronger business performance and lower employee turnover" (p. 18). But it can be difficult to establish precise business benefits that can be directly attributed to the work of an individual client or to prove the extent to which that client's work has been improved by the coaching they have received. Where the client manages others (as most recipients of coaching do) to deliver organisational priorities, the causal chain between coaching and financial outcomes becomes even more difficult to establish. There are difficulties on the other side of the equation too. While the direct costs can usually be calculated reasonably accurately, the indirect costs, such as the opportunity cost of the coach spending time coaching rather than delivering on the day job (and do you add in time taken to prepare and reflect after?), tend not to be taken into account. So there is considerable uncertainty associated with both the cost and benefit figures.

A further dimension arises when internal coaches work in the public sector, where it is even more difficult to ascribe a monetary value to delivering a strategic priority. What if a senior civil servant in the diplomatic service is being coached around her relationship-building and negotiation skills in the run-up to a high level negotiation which results in a successful diplomatic alliance being formed with long term political benefits. The civil servant may ascribe thirty per cent of the result to the impact on her of the coaching, but thirty per cent of what?

However, the fact that something is difficult does not mean that there is no point in trying to do it. The way that you collect your data, like asking the coaching clients to form precise impact objectives, will make it easier. But this is far away from what many coaches would perceive their role to be!

A less complex approach that a number of organisations have tried, rather than attempt a full ROI calculation, is to work out a notional figure for the cost per internal coaching session, with the objective of comparing it with the cost per session charged by external coaches. Some years ago, the BBC worked out that their internal coaching sessions cost £50 per hour (Macann, 2012b), having taken into account two full-time staff managing the coaching programme, the costs of in-house training, CPD, and accreditation costs (they did not include opportunity costs). The internal coaching service had delivered, at that time, 600 programmes of ten hours of coaching. Then they took the lowest fee charged on the external coach list, multiplied it by 600 programmes of ten hours, and reported the sizeable difference back to the organisation. It was an eye-catching way of demonstrating value. If you decide to do something similar, remember that there are also central costs involved in the assessment, selection, administration, invoicing, and so forth of external coaches that could be taken into account too—not just their fees.

Carter (2013) reported that she has undertaken notional cost exercises with a number of organisations and has asked lead coaches to work out a figure for the cost per coaching engagement. She has found that very different figures can be produced for the same coaching programme: it all depends whom you ask and what they perceive as a cost. In one case, two regional lead coaches from the same organisation included supervision and CPD costs but one also included the opportunity cost of staff time (using average salary costs for a "typical coach" and a "typical client"). Both approaches may be appropriate but it makes sense to consider carefully what to include and apply it consistently within the same organisation or programme. Otherwise any comparisons you try to make are meaningless.

A different approach from looking for a financial return on investment is to measure some other variety of return and both Grant (2012) and Hicks, Carter, and Sinclair (2012) have looked at well-being and staff engagement as alternative measures. Grant argues that ROI is an unreliable measure of coaching outcomes and that we do coaching a disservice by overly focusing on the financial outcomes of coaching. He suggests focusing on well-being and engagement on the grounds that "organisations function better with mentally healthy employees who are engaged in their work activities." Hicks, Carter, and Sinclair cite a meta-analysis of Gallup studies by Harter, Schmidt, & Keyes (1999) that showed that the:

> presence of positive workplace perceptions and feelings are associated with higher business-unit customer loyalty, higher profitability, higher productivity and lower rates of turnover. (p. 3)

Their own research revealed that coaching had a positive impact on both the way that the coaching clients worked and their feelings towards work and, specifically, that:

> coaching increased overall well-being scores both at work and in general by improving coachees' ability to feel relaxed, to feel useful and to think clearly. At work, the coaching also helped coachees to improve their ability to deal with problems well and to feel closer to other people. (p. 31)

You could therefore consider using well-being and engagement as alternative measures. There are a number of well-validated instruments suggested by Grant (2012) that can be used to assess well-being and employee engagement—most are free but you should get permission to use them. They include:

Well-being:

- Warwick-Edinburgh Mental Well-being Scale (Tennant et al., 2007)
- Positive and Negative Affect Scale (PANAS) (Watson, Clark, & Tellegan, 1988)
- Depression, Anxiety, and Stress Scales (Lovibond & Lovibond, 1995)

Staff engagement:

- IES Employee Engagement Scale (Robinson, Perryman, & Hayday, 2004)
- 12-item Gallup Q12 (Harter, Schmidt, & Keyes, 2003)
- Utrecht Work Engagement Scale (Schaufeli, Bakker, & Salanova, 2006).

Some of you might be thinking "and where would I find the time and resource to use instruments such as these and analyse the results?" I have included them because I am conscious that while some of you will be fighting a battle against all the odds to keep coaching alive in your organisation using minimal resources, others will have considerable resources at your disposal and might see some benefit in trying a new approach such as this and then publicising your results to help other organisations using internal coaches to evaluate the effectiveness of their coaching service. One approach that several lead coaches have used is to approach a university offering a coaching Masters to see if one of their Masters students might be interested in conducting an evaluation for you for their research project.

Summary

Coaching is becoming embedded in organisations despite cuts in learning and development budgets. We talked about the fact that CIPD research suggests that while the use of coaching is steadily increasing, organisations are missing the opportunity to evaluate so failing to capture its value. As a successful internal coaching resource requires ongoing investment, being able to demonstrate that coaching has lasting value is essential.

You have read about a number of ways to collect data, evaluate the process, and provide feedback on your internal coaching programme. This can help you decide what the specific needs are for your organisation. Being able to articulate the tangible benefits and value that your internal coaching contributes to those in the business who determine organisational priorities and control budgets can be key to the sustainability of the internal coaching programme.

QUESTIONS TO REFLECT ON

Factor to consider	What are the implications for the organisation?
Why evaluate? What are the key reasons why we need to evaluate coaching in our organisation?	• Are we clear about the purpose of evaluating the internal coaching offer? What do we want to demonstrate? Whom do we want to demonstrate it to?

(Continued)

QUESTIONS TO REFLECT ON   (*Continued*)

Factor to consider	*What are the implications for the organisation?*
• What do we need to prove? • What do we want to improve? • What would we like to learn?	• What is the role of our steering group in evaluation? Can we use members to help engage directors in supporting data collection and cascading learning from our evaluations?

What will you evaluate?
How does our strategic purpose inform what we need to evaluate?
	• What data do we need to collect in terms of:
	  – inputs: measuring activity and coach utilisation?
	  – outcomes: capturing the impact?
	• What needs to be covered in guidance and for coaches, clients, and line managers to explain their role in providing feedback for evaluation?
	• Which approach to evaluation would work best in our organisation:
	  – consulting key players on what they want or
	  – deciding what makes most sense and presenting them with it?
	• What are the reporting requirements for other key projects and initiatives within L&D? What statistics are they providing? Can we follow the same processes?
	• How should we present the data? Is our organisation more responsive to metrics or a more qualitative approach (e.g., case studies or testimonials)?

(Continued)

QUESTIONS TO REFLECT ON   (*Continued*)

Factor to consider	*What are the implications for the organisation?*
Kirkpatrick's four levels of evaluation Do we want to evaluate at all four Kirkpatrick levels? • Level 1: Reaction • Level 2: Learning • Level 3: Behaviour • Level 4: Results	• What are the implications for data collection at each level? • What levels are other L&D interventions evaluated at in our organisation? • What would we need to have in place at the start of coaching relationships to ensure we can measure learning and behavioural change? • How realistic is it for us to be able to demonstrate level 4? • Do we want to plan for rigorous evaluation from the outset or take one step at a time?

Approaches to gathering data: Focusing on the client
How do we collect honest and accurate feedback from recipients of our coaching service?
	• What methods shall we use to get feedback from clients:
	  – post coaching questionnaire?
	  – interview with lead coach?
	  – oral feedback via their coach?
	• What do we need to consider in terms of:
	  – maintaining client confidentiality?
	  – encouraging clients to give honest feedback in situations where they like their coach but did not get a lot of value from the coaching relationship?
	• If designing a questionnaire:

(*Continued*)

QUESTIONS TO REFLECT ON   *(Continued)*

Factor to consider	*What are the implications for the organisation?*
	– what questions could we add to capture data about behaviours (Level 3) and contribution to the organisation (Level 4)?
	– would a pre and post coaching questionnaire add value?
	• When do we want clients to complete post-coaching evaluation? How can we balance the need to give clients time with the decreased likelihood of getting questionnaires returned as time passes?
Approaches to gathering data: Feedback from colleagues Would including feedback from third parties add value to the evaluation?	• Could we use three way meetings with the client's line manager at the start and end of the coaching programme as the basis for evaluating progress?
	• Could we use 360 processes that are already being used in the organisation to feed into our evaluations?
Approaches to gathering data: Data at organisational level How can we use information gathered at an organisational or sub-organisational level to inform our evaluation?	• Does our organisation regularly gather any metrics that could be useful in evaluating the coaching service? Could we use any existing surveys or add a few questions to, for example, an annual staff engagement survey?

(Continued)

QUESTIONS TO REFLECT ON   (*Continued*)

Factor to consider	*What are the implications for the organisation?*
	• Could we conduct or commission a specific piece of research to test out whether the coaching has had an impact at organisational level?
Evaluating the coaching service How do we evaluate the overall coaching service?	• If we have a variety of coaching programmes should we evaluate these separately?

	• Looking at how progress on other initiatives is fed back into the business:
	  – how often should we audit the service and
	  – what information should we include?

	• When evaluating the overall service how should we collect information from clients who drop out during the coaching process so do not complete the post coaching evaluation?
	• Can we undertake a comparison between the performance of a group of clients who have received coaching and another group who have not?
Return on investment Does our organisation require us to demonstrate the return on investment (ROI) of the coaching scheme?	• Does calculating ROI make sense for our scheme?

(*Continued*)

QUESTIONS TO REFLECT ON   *(Continued)*

Factor to consider	*What are the implications for the organisation?*
	• How would we estimate the cost of coaching? Would we include the opportunity cost of the coach's time? If relevant budgets are held by different departments, to whom would we speak to obtain accurate figures?
	• How would we estimate the value of coaching outcomes? Whom would we need to engage in a discussion to get the business perspective?
	• What factors would we take into account if we wished to estimate the cost of delivering one hour of internal coaching to a client?
	• What alternatives to financial ROI might we consider? Could we link our evaluation to key organisational objectives, for example, increasing staff engagement or improving wellbeing?
	• How could we resource the evaluation cheaply? Could we find a coaching Masters student to conduct it for us as part of their research project?

The future for internal coaching?

The trend for organisations to develop an internal coaching resource is clearly no flash in the pan—the Ridler Report 2013 showed that seventy-nine per cent of participating organisations expected to see an increase in internal coaching over the next three years. That is a phenomenal figure and suggests that the future is bright for internal coaching. I expect to see it become increasingly professionalised over the next ten years, in the sense of more resource being invested in a) the training and accreditation of the coaches and b) ways of continually developing them and keeping their skills fresh. I also wonder if the internal coach role will develop from being an activity undertaken on top of the day job to being an acknowledged, valued, and recognised part of some individuals' work roles; and also if there will gradually come to be more full-time internal coaches working within organisations. Another development that I expect to see in the future is more and more organisations publicising and lauding what their internal coaches are achieving. Currently it is often only the clients and their line managers who know that the coaches are there, working beneath the surface, but I can see that this is likely to change as they become more embedded. I am very much looking forward to witnessing this!

APPENDIX

EXAMPLE OF AN EVALUATION QUESTIONNAIRE

Your name

Grade

Part of the Business

Sponsor (who endorsed the request for coaching)

Coach name

Type of coaching received

How well did the coaching address your initial goals and objectives, as agreed in your contract?	• Not at all • Slightly • Moderately • Significantly • Completely
How well did the coaching meet your personal needs and expectations?	• Not at all • Slightly • Moderately • Significantly • Completely

(Continued)

EXAMPLE OF AN EVALUATION QUESTIONNAIRE   (*Continued*)

Was the coaching successful based on the measures of success discussed in your contract?	• Not at all • Slightly • Moderately • Significantly • Completely
Was this coaching a valuable investment of your time?	• Not at all • Slightly • Moderately • Significantly • Completely
What were the benefits for you? (tick all that apply)	• Developing a specific skill • Behaviour change • Job satisfaction • Confidence • Clarity • Focus • Safe place • Time to reflect • Other, please give details
Did this coaching benefit the business?	• Not at all • Slightly • Moderately • Significantly • Completely
In what way do you think the business benefited?	
What evidence have you got for this business benefit? (tick all that apply)	• Feedback from director/senior manager • Feedback from line manager • Feedback from team • Feedback from client • Higher performance rating • Higher sales results • Promotion • Other, please give details

(*Continued*)

EXAMPLE OF AN EVALUATION QUESTIONNAIRE   (*Continued*)

How will you embed what you have learnt?	
How well did your coach's style and approach suit you and your coaching needs?	• Not at all • Slightly • Moderately • Significantly • Completely
What did you value most about working with your coach?	
What one thing would you have liked more or different from your coach?	
Did you have a three-way conversation with your line manager?	• Yes • No
If so, what did you value most about involving your line manager?	
What one thing would you have liked more or different from your line manager?	
Would you recommend coaching to others?	• Yes • No • Maybe
Are you happy for this information to be shared with your coach?	• Yes • No
Any additional comments?	

REFERENCES

Allan, J., Passmore, J., & Mortimer, L. (2011). Coaching ethics: Developing a model to enhance coaching practice. In: J. Passmore (Ed.), *Supervision in Coaching: Supervision, Ethics and Continuous Professional Development* (pp. 161–172). London: Kogan Page.

Association for Coaching Good Practice Guide (June 2012). Downloaded from www.associationforcoaching.com/pages/about/code-ethics-good-practice on 3 July 2013.

Borders, D. (1992). Learning to think like a supervisor. *The Clinical Supervisor, 10*(2): 135–148.

Butwell, J. (2006). Group Supervision for coaches: is it worthwhile? A study of the process in a major professional organisation. *International Journal of Evidence Based Coaching and Mentoring, 4*: 43–53.

Campone, F. (2011). The reflective coaching practitioner model. In: J. Passmore (Ed.), *Supervision in Coaching: Supervision, Ethics and Continuous Professional Development* (pp. 11–29). London: Kogan Page.

Carroll, M. (2006). Key issues in coaching psychology supervision. *The Coaching Psychologist, 2*: 4–8.

Carroll, M., & Shaw, E. (2013). *Ethical Maturity in the Helping Professions: Making Difficult Life and Work Decisions.* London: Jessica Kingsley Publishers.

Carter, A. (2005). *Providing Coaching Internally: A Literature Review.* HR Network Paper MP43. Brighton: Institute of Employment Studies.

Carter, A. (2009). Your Best Bet. *Coaching at Work, 4(6)*: 44–47.

Carter, A. (2013). Conversation with the author on 29 January 2013.

Carter, A., & Peterson, D. (2010). Evaluating coaching programmes. In: J. Passmore (Ed.), *Excellence in Coaching: The Industry Guide 2nd Edition* (pp. 228–239). London: Kogan Page.

Carter, A., Wolfe, H., & Kerrin, M. (2005). Employers and coaching evaluation. *International Journal of Coaching in Organizations, 3(4)*: 63–72.

Childs, R., Woods, M., Willcock, D., & Man, A. (2011). Action learning supervision for coaches. In: J. Passmore (Ed.), *Supervision in Coaching: Supervision, Ethics and Continuous Professional Development* (pp. 31–43). London: Kogan Page.

Churchard, C., & Warren, C. (2013). HR: the damning verdict. *People Management, January 2013*: 10–11.

CIPD. (2004). *A Guide to Coaching and Buying Coaching Services.* London: CIPD.

CIPD. (2008). *Learning and Development Survey Report.* London: CIPD. Available to download from www.cipd.co.uk/onlineinfodocuments/survey

CIPD. (2009). *Learning and Development Survey Report,* London: CIPD. Available to download from www.cipd.co.uk/onlineinfodocuments/survey

CIPD. (2010). Real-world coaching evaluation: A guide for practitioners (CIPD). www.cipd.co.uk/binaries/5350_Real_World_Coaching_guide.pdf (downloaded 14 June 2013)

Clarkson, P. (1997). *The Bystander: An End to Innocence in Human Relationships.* London: Whurr Pubications.

Duff, M., & Passmore, J. (2010). Coaching ethics: a decision-making model. *International Coaching Psychology Review, 5*: 140–151.

EMCC Guidelines on Supervision: Interim Statement. Downloaded on 17 June 2013 from www.emccouncil.org/src/ultimo/models/Download/7.pdf

Feldman, D. C., & Lankau, M. (2005). Executive coaching: A review and agenda for future research. *Journal of Management, 31*: 829–848.

Figlar, M., Adams, M., & Hornyak, L. (2007). Strengthening the leadership pipeline through internal human resources-based executive coaching: A white paper, *12th Annual Global Forum for Action Learning.* Retrieved •27/06/13 from www.InquiryInstitute.com

Fletcher, A., & Macann, E. (2011). Balancing act. *Coaching at Work 6(1)*: 30–33.

Frisch, M. (2001). The emerging role of the internal coach. *Consulting Psychology Journal: Practice and Research, 53*: 240–250.

Frisch, M. (2005). Extending the reach of executive coaching: The internal coach. *Human Resource Planning, 28*: 23.

Grant, A. M. (2012). ROI is a poor measure of coaching success: towards a more holistic approach using a well-being and engagement framework. *Coaching: An International Journal of Theory, Research and Practice,* 5: 74–85.

Haden, S. (2013). *It's Not About The Coach: Getting the Most from Coaching in Business, Life and Sport.* Winchester, UK: Business Books.

Hall, D. T., Otazo, K. L., & Hollenbeck, G. P. (1999). Behind closed doors: what really happens in executive coaching. *Organisational dynamics,* 27(3): 39–53.

Harter, J. K., Schmidt, F. L., & Keyes, C. L. M. (2003). Well-being in the workplace and its relationship to business outcomes: A review of the Gallup studies. In: C. L. M. Keyes & J. Haidt (Eds.), *Flourishing: Positive Psychology and the Life Well-lived* (pp. 205–224). Washington DC: American Psychological Association.

Hawkins, P. (2011). Building emotional, ethical and cognitive capacity in coaches—a developmental model of supervision. In: J. Passmore. (Ed.), *Supervision in Coaching: Supervision, Ethics and Continuous Professional Development* (pp. 285–307). London: Kogan Page.

Hawkins, P. (2012). *Creating a Coaching Culture.* Maidenhead: Open University Press.

Hawkins, P., & Schwenk, G. (2006). *Coaching Supervision: Maximising the Potential of Coaching.* London: CIPD.

Hawkins, P., & Smith, N. (2006). *Coaching, Mentoring and Organizational Consultancy: Supervision and Development.* Maidenhead: Open University Press/McGraw-Hill.

Hicks, B., Carter, A., & Sinclair, A. (2012). *Impact of Coaching: An empirical longitudinal study into coachee well-being, engagement and job satisfaction following a coaching programme at work.* IES Research Network Research Report, Institute for Employment Studies.

Humphrey, S., & Sheppard, L. (2012). Supervised behaviour. *Coaching at Work,* 7(6): 48–50.

Hunt, J., & Weintraub, J. (2006). *Coaching on the Inside: The Internal Coach.* Taken from www.babsoninsight.com

International Coach Federation. (2012). *2012 ICF Global Coaching Study Executive Summary.* Downloaded on 05/04/13 from www.coachfederation.org/includes/media/docs/2012ICFGlobalCoachingStudy-ExecutiveSummary.pdf

Jarvis, J., Lane, D., & Fillery-Travis, A. (2006). *The Case for Coaching: Making Evidence Based Decisions.* London: CIPD.

Kadushin, A. (1992). What's wrong, what's right with social work supervision. *The Clinical Supervisor,* 10(1): 3–19.

Kaupman, S. (1968). Fairy tales and script drama analysis (selected articles). *Transactional Analysis Bulletin,* 7: 39–43.

Kirkpatrick, D. L. (1994). *Evaluating Training Programs: The Four Levels*. San Francisco, CA: Berrett-Koehler.

Kitchener, K. S. (2000). Foundations of ethical practice, research, and teaching in psychology. *Counseling Psychologist, 12*: 43–55.

Lambert, A. (2008). *What's New in Coaching & Mentoring? An Update*. Corporate Research Forum: October 2008.

Leedham, M. (2005). The coaching scorecard: a holistic approach to evaluating the benefits of business coaching. *International Journal of Evidence Based Coaching and Mentoring, 3*(2): 30–44.

Levenson, A.R., McDermott, M., & Clarke. S. (2004). What coaching can do for your organization ... and what it can't. *Centre for Effective Organizations, Marshall School of Business, CEO Publication*, G-04–20 (472). Retrieved from http://ceo.usc.edu/working_paper/what_coaching_can_do_for_your.html on 27/06/13

Linehan, L. (2011). Unpublished presentation made to Ashridge Coaching Special Interest Group. 10 May 2011.

Long, K. (2012). Building internal supervision capability in organisations. *The OCM Coach and Mentor Journal, 12*: 2–6.

Lovibond, S. H., & Lovibond, P. F. (1995). *Manual for the Depression Anxiety Stress Scales*. Sydney: Psychology Foundation of Australia.

Macann, E. (2012a). Reflected glory. *Coaching at Work, 7*(2): 15–17.

Macann, E. (2012b). Conversation with the author on 6 December 2012.

Maccoby, M. (2009). The dangers of dependence on coaches. *Harvard Business Review*, Special issue: "Transforming Leaders", Section title: "What can coaches do for you?".

Mackintosh, A. (2003). Why the internal company coach has to be strong! *The Coaching and Mentoring Network Resource Centre*. Downloaded from www.coachingnetwork.org.uk/resourcecentre/articles/ViewArticle.asp?artId=37 on 28/06/13

Maxwell, A. (2011). Supervising the internal coach. In: T. Bachkirova, P. Jackson & D. Clutterbuck. (Eds.), *Coaching & Mentoring Supervision* (pp. 183–195). Maidenhead: Open University Press/McGraw-Hill.

Maxwell, A. (2013). Conversation with the author on 5 February 2013.

McBain, R., Ghobadian, A., Switzer, J., Wilton, P., Woodman, P., & Pearson, G. (2012). *The Business Benefits of Management and Leadership Development*, CMI/Penna (free to download from CMI website—www.managers.org.uk)

Megginson, D. (2008). Is goal setting the only way to coach? *In View, The journal from the NHS Institute for senior leaders*. A Special Supplement, April 2008.

Megginson, D., & Whitaker, V. (2004). *Continuing Professional Development*. CIPD: London.

Mortlock, S., & Carter, A. (2012). Quality assured. *Coaching at Work, 7*(6): 34–37.

Moyes, B. (2009). Literature review of coaching supervision. *International Coaching Psychology Review, 4*: 160–171.

Mukherjee, S. (2012). Does coaching transform coaches? A case study of internal coaching. *International Journal of Evidence Based Coaching and Mentoring, 10*: 76–87.

Myers Briggs, I. (2000). *Introduction to Type.* Oxford: OPP.

Nash, R. J. (2002). *Real World Ethics: Frameworks for Educators and Human Service Professionals* (2nd ed.). New York, NY: Teachers College Press.

Patterson, E. (2011). Presence in coaching supervision. In: J. Passmore (Ed.), *Supervision in Coaching: Supervision, Ethics and Continuous Professional Development* (pp. 117–137). London: Kogan Page.

Peltier, B. (2001). *The Psychology of Executive Coaching: Theory and Application.* New York: Brunner-Routledge.

Pilbeam, S., Anderson, V., Hope, S., & Campbell, A. (2013). Coaching for employee and organisational performance: A strategic intervention. In: D. Hall, S. Pilbeam & M. Corbridge (Eds.), *Contemporary Themes in Strategic People Management: A Case-Based Approach* (pp. 182–196). Basingstoke, UK: Palgrave Macmillan.

Pinder, K. (2010). Experiences of supervision. *The International Journal of Mentoring and Coaching, VIII*(*I*): 124–129.

Proctor, B. (1986). Supervision: A co-operative exercise in accountability. In: A. Marken & M. Payne (Eds.), *Enabling and Ensuring: Supervision in Practice.* National Youth Bureau and Council for Education and Training in Youth and Community Work, Leicester.

Rawls, J. (1971). *A theory of justice.* Cambridge, MA: Harvard University Press.

Revans, R. W. (1982). *The Origin and Growth of Action Learning.* Brickley, UK: Chartwell-Bratt.

Ridler & Co. (2008). *A Survey of Trends in Buying Executive Coaching.* London: Ridler & Co. Limited.

Ridler & Co. (2013). *Trends in the Use of Executive Coaching.* London: Ridler & Co. Limited.

Robinson, D., Perryman, S., & Hayday, S. (2004). *The Drivers of Employee Engagement.* IES Report 408. Brighton: Institute for Employment Studies.

Rock, D., & Donde, R. (2008). Driving organisational change with internal coaching programmes: Part one. *Industrial and Commercial Training, 40*: 10–18.

Rogers, C. (1961). *On Becoming a Person.* Boston, MA: Houghton Mifflin.

Rogers, J. (2013). *Manager as Coach: the New Way to Get Results.* Maidenhead: McGraw-Hill.

Rogers, K. M. (2011). Legal considerations in coaching. In: J. Passmore (Ed.), *Supervision in Coaching: Supervision, Ethics and Continuous Professional Development* (pp. 175–189). London: Kogan Page.

Schaufeli, W. B., Bakker, A. B., & Salanova, M. (2006). The measurement of work engagement with a short questionnaire: A cross-national study. *Educational and Psychological Measurement, 66*: 701–716.

Smith, K. (2011). The rise & rise of internal coaching. *The Listener, 14*: 15–18. Downloaded from www.kensmithcoaching.co.uk on 28/06/13.

Snape, S. (2012). *An Evaluation of Internal Coaching in the UK*. Unpublished Masters dissertation. Henley Business School, University of Reading.

Soulsby, R. (2012). Interventions must increase credibility through evidence-based results. *Coaching at Work, 7*(6): 8.

St John-Brooks, K. (2010). What are the ethical challenges involved in being an internal coach? *International Journal of Mentoring and Coaching, VIII*(1): 50–66.

Steare, R. (2009). *Ethicability (n): How to Decide What's Right and Find the Courage to Do It*. Great Britain: Roger Steere Consulting Limited.

Stern, L. R. (2004). Executive coaching: a working definition. *Consulting Psychology Journal: Practice and Research, 56*: 154–162.

Stokes, P. (2007). *The Skilled Coachee*. Paper delivered at 14th EMCC Conference in Stockholm, 2007.

Tamkin, P., Hirsh, W., & Tyers, C. (2003). *Chore to Champion: The Making of Better People Managers*. IES Report No. 389.

Tehrani, N. (2010). Compassion fatigue: experiences in occupational health, human resources, counselling and police. *Occupational Medicine, 60*: 133–138.

Tennant, R., Hiller, L., Fishwick, R., Platt. S., Joseph, S., Weich, S., & Stewart-Brown, S. (2007). The Warwick-Edinburgh Mental Well-being Scale (WEMWBS): Development and UK validation. *Health and Quality of Life Outcomes, 5*: 63.

Thomson, B. (2011). Non-directive supervision of coaching. In: J. Passmore (Ed.), *Supervision in Coaching: Supervision, Ethics and Continuous Professional Development* (pp. 99–116). London: Kogan Page.

Townsend, C. (2011). Ethical frameworks in coaching. In: J. Passmore (Ed.), *Supervision in Coaching: Supervision, Ethics and Continuous Professional Development* (pp. 141–159). London: Kogan Page.

Turner, E. (2012). Confidentiality and CPD opportunities top internal coaches' wishlists. *Coaching at Work, 7*(4): 8.

Varkonyi-Sepp, J. (2013). Report: Special Group in Coaching Psychology 8th Annual Conference. *International Coaching Psychology Review, 8*(1): 104–108.

Wasylyshyn, K. (2003). Executive coaching: An outcome study. *Consulting Psychology Journal: Practice & Research, 55*: 94–106.

Watson, D., Clark, L. A., & Tellegen, A. (1988). Development and validation of brief measures of positive and negative affect: The PANAS scales. *Journal of Personality & Social Psychology, 54*: 1063–1070.

Whitmore, J. (2002). *Coaching for Performance: Growing People, Performance and Purpose*. London: Nicholas Brealey.

Williams, P., & Anderson, S. (2006). *Law & Ethics in Coaching*. New Jersey: Wiley.

Wilson, C., & McMahon, G. (2006). What's the difference? *Training Journal*, September 2006: 54–57.

Woods, D. (2011). Coaches' use of reflective journals for learning. In: J. Passmore (Ed.), *Supervision in Coaching: Supervision, Ethics and Continuous Professional development* (pp. 265–284). London: Kogan Page.

Wrynne, C. (2011). *How Might the Experience of Internal Coaching Differ From the Experience of External Coaching?* Unpublished Masters dissertation. London Southbank University.

Yedreshteyn, S. (2008). A qualitative investigation of the implementation of an internal executive coaching program in a global corporation, grounded in organizational psychology theory. *Dissertation Abstracts International, 69*(7): 4471B.

INDEX

PROFESSIONAL COACHING SERIES

This series brings together leading exponents and researchers in the coaching field to provide a definitive set of core texts important to the development of the profession. It aims to meet two needs—a professional series that provides the core texts that are theoretically and experimentally grounded, and a practice series covering forms of coaching based in evidence. Together they provide a complementary framework to introduce, promote and enhance the development of the coaching profession.

"A very pragmatic and balanced view looking at the complex world of managing an internal coaching pool. There is a lot of food for thought contained in this book, with practical points to ponder and some very thought-provoking questions. A very useful 'toolkit' for those of us who manage internal coaching within large organisations."

—Leigh Naylor, Leadership and Talent Consultant, British Airways PLC

"This book strikes that fine balance, providing thorough insight and plenty of stimulation and challenges, whilst also being concise. Invaluable for anyone setting up an internal coaching scheme or thinking about becoming an internal coach."

—James Hutton, Head of Talent and Development, News UK

"A thoughtful and thorough exposé of the reality of coaching inside organisations. The counsel of coaches and sponsors of coaching is all here: start-up tips, checklists, case studies, lessons learned,

295

and, above all, a celebration of achieving great things through perseverance and business focus."

—Trevor Elkin, Leadership Development,
Home Office Capability and Change Team

"This book is an invaluable guide for all internal coaches and organisers of internal coaching services. It brings to life what it is to be an internal coach—with all its rewards, pitfalls, and complexities—and provides a veritable feast of examples of how organisations all over the world are approaching the challenge of setting up, supporting, and harnessing the power of internal coaching. Essential reading."

—John Leary-Joyce, CEO of the Academy of Executive Coaching
and Chairman of EMCC UK

"*Internal Coaching* is essential reading for any lead coaches and supervisors looking to protect and build on their organisation's investment in coaching, engage and support internal coaches, and assure ethical and accountable practice. I'm sure many will wish they had had this resource when they first embarked on their journey with coaching."

—Katherine Long, Director of Development
and Supervision, OCM

"Highly practical, engaging, and long overdue. This book is an important contribution to a growing area of coaching. The combination of experience, research, practice, and theory present in this book make it a must for organisations and practitioners thinking about, or currently running, internal coaching programmes. While targeted towards internal coaching, the wide variety of case examples, insightful commentary, and a willingness to approach difficult issues makes this book an important resource for all coaches."

—Dr. Michael Cavanagh, Coaching Psychology Unit,
University of Sydney

"This book will become the Bible for organisations wishing to harness the power of coaching. Wisely deployed, the right blend of external and internal coaching can transform an organisation. As a passionate advocate of internal coaching, I welcome Katharine's practical yet erudite perspectives on the ethical and operational issues. Katharine has insightfully identified the critical factors that will determine the ultimate success or failure of any internal coaching programme."

—Head of Financial Times Executive Coaching and
CEO of The Coaching Space, a Pearson company

"Finally, a book dedicated to the internal coach. Finally, a handbook for coaches that puts ethics before everything else. It gives me great pleasure to recommend this accessible and inspirational book for everyone engaged in helping conversations inside organisations."

—Erik de Haan, Director of Centre for Coaching, Ashridge,
and Professor of Organisation Development and Coaching,
VU University, Amsterdam

Printed in the United States
by Baker & Taylor Publisher Services